THE BUSINESS
PODCASTING
BIBLE

Wherever My Market Is...
I Am

PAUL COLLIGAN &
ALEX MANDOSSIAN

THE BUSINESS PODCASTING BIBLE

ISBN: 1-933596-37-6 (Paperback)

Published by:

Heritage House *publishing*
An Imprint of Morgan James Publishing, LLC

Habitat
for Humanity®
Peninsula
Building Partner

Heritage House Publishing, Inc.
An Imprint of Morgan James Publishing, LLC
10 Hayford Court
Novato, CA 94949
Phone: (415) 382-1212
Fax: (415) 382-1222

Cover and Interior Design by:
Tony Laidig
www.thecoverexpert.com
tony@thecoverexpert.com

Table of Contents

 # About the Authors

ALEX MANDOSSIAN

Alex Mandossian, co-host of the popular Marketing Online Live Podcast (http://www.MarketingOnlineLive.com) is considered one of the top 10 freelance direct marketers in America today.

Since 1991, Alex Mandossian has generated over $233 million in sales and profits for his clients and partners via "electronic marketing" media such as TV Infomercials, online catalogs, 24-hour recorded messages, voice/fax broadcasting, Teleseminars, Webinars, Podcasts and Internet Marketing.

Alex has personally consulted Dale Carnegie Training, NYU, 1ShoppingCart Corp., Mutuals.com, Pinnacle Care, Strategic Coach, Trim Spa and many others. He has hosted teleseminars with many of the world's top thought leaders such as Mark Victor Hansen, Jack Canfield, Stephen Covey, Les Brown, David Allen, Vic Conant, Brian Tracy, David Bach, Harvey Mackay, Robert Cialdini, Harv Eker, Bobbi De Porter, Michael Masterson, Joe Vitale, Gay and Katie Hendricks, Bob Proctor, and many others.

He is the CEO of Heritage House Publishing, Inc. – a boutique electronic marketing and publishing company that "repurposes" written and spoken educational content for worldwide distribution. He is also the founder of the Electronic Marketing Institute.

Alex has trained over 8,300 teleseminar students since 2002 and claims that practically any entrepreneur can transform their annual income into a weekly income once they apply his principle-centered electronic marketing strategies.

He lives in the San Francisco Bay Area with his wife, Aimee and two children, Gabriel and Breanna and enjoys over 90 "Free Days" each year.

Alex's blog can be found online at http://www.AlexMandossian.com

PAUL COLLIGAN

Paul Colligan is co-host of the Marketing Online Live Podcast (http://www.MarketingOnlineLive.com) and owner of several popular Internet properties that include The My Podcast Center Podcast Directory, Automate Sales, Podcast Tools, and Premium Podcasting.

His Passion: the Business of Podcasting.

Paul produces a number of Business Podcasts that include (but are not limited to) Marketing Online Live, Podcast Tools Weekly Update, Paul's Profitable Podcasting Podcast, and Big Seminar Live.

Paul has played a key role in the launch of dozens of financially successful Web sites and Internet marketing strategies that have seen tens of millions of visitors and millions of dollars in revenue. Previous projects have included work with Peak Potentials, InternetMCI, the Oregon Multimedia Alliance, Rubicon International, Microsoft, the Electronics Boutique, and Pearson Education.

He is also a popular speaker on Internet technology topics and frequently speaks online, on the air, and before audiences about his passions. He has presented at events around the world that include Podcast Expo, The Business Podcasting Summit, Internet World, Linux World, Commission Junction University, Big Seminar, the X-10 Seminar, and Microsoft Tech-Ed.

Paul lives in Portland, Oregon with his wife, Heidi and daughters Lindsey and Paige and enjoys hiking, theater, music, fine dining, and travel.

Paul's blog can be found online at http://www.PaulColligan.com

The Authors Would Like To Thank ...

In no particular order, other than saving *the best for last*.

Don Katz for pushing the power of the digital spoken word long before it was popular.

Steve Jobs for making us want to strap a hard drive to our hip and stick pieces of plastic in our ears.

Adam Curry and Dave Winer for their roles in starting this revolution.

Mike Stewart for preventing the fear of microphones, USB cables, audio software and digital hybrids.

Tim Bourquin for saying, since the beginning, that you can monetize this stuff.

Todd Cochrane, Michael Geoghegan and Dan Klass for being gutsy enough to write the first round of books.

Ricky Gervais and Leo Laporte for making Podcasting (and Podcasters) "cool."

Doug Kaye for demonstrating the power of great repurposed content sent down the Podcast channel.

Robert Scoble for teaching us the power of a "Naked Conversation."

Chris Pirillo for daring to ask for 6 figures.

Rob Walch for giving us the 411 on our Podcasting heroes.

Marketing Online Live listener Andrew Smith for suggesting the title for this book.

Marketing Online Live listener Dan Safkow for being gutsy enough to launch a business from an idea mentioned on our show.

Our thousands of other listeners at Marketing Online Live for continuing the conversation and inspiring us to continue to produce the show we love so much.

T. Harv Eker, Armand Morin and Mark Victor Hansen for giving us great additional content to Podcast.

David Hancock and the Team at Morgan James Publishing for making this book look great, and for getting this book into the hands of thousands.

Larry Genkin and the Team at Larstan for helping us start this project.

Our Case Study Participants for giving us content that proves that this is much bigger than just this book.

Gutenberg for introducing the original, affordable portable media device.

Alexander Graham Bell for inventing the original place shifting device.

Tivo for making time shifting so much fun.

PortlandPodcasting.org for putting a face on the technology.

The Support Teams at Heritage House and Colligan.com for making it possible for us to do this.

Everyone we didn't mention here for understanding that we'll mention you at the Website the second we realize we forgot.

And ... our wives for being the best friends we've ever had. We owe you more than we can possibly deliver in this lifetime. Thanks for being our *real* secret weapons.

 THE AUTHORS WOULD LIKE TO THANK...   ix

THE BUSINESS **PODCASTING BIBLE**

What They're Saying...

ALEX MANDOSSIAN

"I want to talk to you about my great friend, Alex Mandossian. Here's one of the most effective, hard-working, clear thinking, originating guys on the planet. He has plowed my soul, helping me with all the mega universities I do. I've been doing Mega Speaking University and Mega Book University (how to make every book a best-seller), and Mega Marketing University.

"I am massively impressed with the clean, crisp solidness of his original thinking and if you want somebody that can get the results you want, when you want, because you want, with effortless ease, the height of Maslow's hierarchy, he is your man.

"He is a master's master, and a very fine friend, and he delivers the goods that he promises to deliver on time, without fail, and without complaint. I deeply appreciate his goodness, he greatness, and his grandness, and his generosity of heart and spirit, and brilliance of mind."

Mark Victor Hansen
Co-author and creator
Chicken Soup for the Soul
One Minute Millionaire

"I have never been more impressed by a marketing consultant, a virtual GURU, in knowing what needs to be done to reach precisely the clients that we need to connect with, and create a profound and emotionally based relationship with them. Our clients now really are clients for life, through Alex's principles.

"We have been able to give them what they need vs trying to make them "fit" into our concept of what it is we thought they might want. Huge difference! We've been able to apply some of Alex's concepts on consumption, so now they are using not only our service, but our products more efficiently than ever before.

"And I have just begun to apply Alex's concepts and methodologies. I am so impressed, and more importantly, I know this year alone we will pocket an additional $100,000 plus in profits, and again, it's only after, what, six weeks of applying his principles."

Joel Bauer
President/CEO, Bauer and Associates

"Alex Mandossian is a marketing genius – but more important, he's a teacher. He's been there. He's done it. And he knows how to teach it. Anyone can create an audio Podcast. But there is nobody on God's green earth more qualified to teach you how to make money from your Podcast.

"Listen to Alex, and grow rich."

Rick Raddatz
CEO, Xiosoft.com
http://www.xiosoft.com

"I just want to say that Alex Mandossian gets my highest endorsement when it comes to teaching people pretty much anything about marketing.

"I've never been steered wrong by Alex; I think he is an extraordinarily bright guy, and he really understands the business, inside out. I think his teaching style provides clarity and enormous amounts of content.

"He has the most prepared methods of teaching from the stage, from teleseminars, from almost anyone that you would ever want to run across."

Joe Polish
President, Piranha Marketing

PAUL COLLIGAN

"I rely on Paul Colligan every day to learn what works and what doesn't when turning my Podcasts into real dollars. Paul is truly an expert in Podcasting and no one knows more about how to make money from this new medium.

"Before you say one word into a microphone, hear what Paul has to say!"

Tim Bourquin
http://www.PodcastExpo.com
http://www.PodcastBrothers.com

"As a new CEO in the Podcasting space, I have found Paul Colligan to be an invaluable advisor. His pragmatism, experience, and raw marketing savvy have pushed me to make Podango a far more viable company than it would be otherwise."

Lee Gibbons
CEO, Podango.com
http://www.Podango.com

"Let's face it; the purpose of business is to make money. Most people in Podcasting will not even attempt to answer that question. Paul Colligan not only answers it, he invents it. Do yourself a favor; read the Bible."

Declan Dunn
http://www.DunnDirectGroup.com
The FunMoneyGood Life Style Network

"Paul Colligan truly gets the power of Podcasting, especially when it comes to using it for business and making money. He is a valuable source of information on profitable Podcasting for anyone smart enough to listen."

Jason Van Orden
Author, Promoting Your Podcast
http://www.PromotingYourPodcast.com

BOTH

"When opportunity knocks there are few people who can open the doors to success as quickly as Paul Colligan and Alex Mandossian. Their years of successful online marketing experience give them a unique ability to distinguish between what really works and what is merely a passing fad. The Podcasting phenomenon is knocking on the door and you can feel confident knowing that Paul and Alex are there to welcome you in."

Alan Stewart
www.themarketerspodcast.com

LISTENER REVIEWS
of MarketingOnlineLive.com at Podcasts.Yahoo.Com

"Awesome show. One cannot ever get enough information on how to market online. And it's so cool to have two of the top online marketers telling it like it is. You will not find more accurate information anywhere else."

"Listen to the whole episode each time. It isn't always the topic itself that matters, but the insightful comments that get mixed in that prove these guys know what they are talking about and can help me understand how to make money off Podcasting or just my web site in general."

"This was one of the 1st Podcasts I signed up to when I 1st found out about Podcasting as I am in marketing. It is without a doubt my most favourite Podcast. These 2 guys are not only very entertaining but very thought provoking. I love it!"

"Paul is always a fun and energetic host and Alex Mandossian always gives excellent information and encourages strategic thinking to get ahead. Get a head of your competitors today! Listen to these guys."

"Alex and Paul don't just look at a situation... they look through it to see the future and the incredible possibilities. Brilliant! Thanks!"

Introduction

Information is amazingly powerful and profitable, when marketed and distributed correctly. My publishing franchise for *Chicken Soup for the Soul* alone has sold more than 100+ million books. We have over 100 licensed products on the market today. I know a lot about information publishing and the true value of content, in all forms and have dedicated my life to explaining it to others. Believe me friends, when I tell you, that information doesn't want to be free: It wants the marketing and distribution required to give it value in a marketplace that wants to embrace it.

In July of this year I stood on stage in front of hundreds and hundreds of authors at my yearly Mega Book Marketing University Event. The amazing thing was that I wasn't holding a book, I was holding an MP3 player with my name and logo on it. The product for sale wasn't the player, but the content sold within—the player was the razor and the content was the blade. Digital media has changed the way I sell my information, and I know it will have the same effect on you. I sold a tremendous amount of product that day, and not a single tree was killed in the process.

Podcasting is but a few years old is already changing the marketplace. I know that you feel the power of this medium or you never would have picked up this book. I'd like to add to this dialogue with the simple suggestion that what we say is far more important than how it is consumed. Great content without distribution is pointless and the distribution opportunities provided by the Podcast channel and medium are worth a thorough exploration by anyone intending in staying in business.

I'll be launching my own Podcast later this year under the guidance of Alex and Paul and the truths contained in this book. Friends, I hope you'll consume it with roaring enthusiasm that I know you'll take on *The Business Podcasting Bible*. I'm thrilled to know that I can be wherever my audience is, and I know you want the same.

Mark Victor Hansen
http://www.MarkVictorHansen.com

FOREWORD

"The sole purpose of a business is to create a customer."
— Peter Drucker

"Innovation distinguishes between a leader and a follower."
— Steve Jobs

We begin our book on Podcasting by juxtaposing quotes from two exceptional but different business thinkers. Peter Drucker, the "classical" communicator, reminds us of the timeless purpose of business: to create customers and make money. Steve Jobs, the prophet of the new digital economy, conveys today's overriding importance of innovation. Today's economy melds the philosophies of both thinkers, because now any business must exhibit innovation to attract paying customers.

Podcasting is a disruptive technology that is revolutionizing business communication. As such, it is a proven innovation that creates customers. Johannes Gutenberg's Bible is an instructive analogy, because when it appeared in the 15th century, it revolutionized communications and society. Previous to the printing press, "the elite" in the Middle Ages controlled mass communication, which essentially entailed the Bible and the pulpit. As soon as the printing press came into play, ordinary citizens – not just the rich and powerful – could gain access to the Bible by simply ponying up the necessary money. As the printing press became more advanced, the Bible became cheaper and more accessible.

Print is an understood technology, even in the poorest of nations. As print became more prevalent, the elite no longer exercised sole control over it. That was the first step of print's disruptive effect. Secondly, print literally passed into the hands of the masses. Instead of being squirreled away in special libraries and protected by monks, anybody could grab a book and – as the old joke goes – bring it with them to the bathroom.

Because it went from the elite into the hands of the masses, anyone with a Bible could start a church. People had vital data in the palms of their hands: they could read what they wanted, when they wanted. To get information, they no longer were forced to attend a Mass in which selected data is presented and interpreted for them. They could come to their own conclusions, based on what they read. This freedom of information was a catalyst for the Reformation and the Renaissance that transformed all of Europe.

We derive parallels from other historical sources, not just the Gutenberg Bible. Something important happened when the Jews began to pass along the Torah and scriptures through scroll, as opposed to an oral tradition controlled by a political and cultural oligarchy. Messages were no longer malleable through the oral tradition; an objective, accessible and portable record existed. People no longer needed to be in the physical presence of a priest or a rabbi to derive the benefit of their words. They could be in their own home and read scripture before going to bed, or after getting up in the morning, or anytime at all.

A TREASURE TROVE OF MAPS

For all of these reasons, surveys of historians often cite Gutenberg as the most influential person in history. He exercised the most reach and the greatest mass appeal, because he not only provided a map to a treasure chest full of wealth and riches – in this case communication – but his map led to a treasure chest full of *other* treasure maps. Revelation was no longer a hierarchical, top-down process. He empowered other people to communicate their own truth.

By creating portable communications, Gutenberg generated the first "time shift" in society. The Bible was the most influential book at the time, a good reason to print it.

Striking parallels exist between Podcasts and the historical trends described above. Podcasts encompass the same qualities, except the medium is digital, the sheer speed of which accelerates change. Disruptive technologies are powerful because they're initially uninvited guests. They first appear like an irritating wart or a pimple, because they're outside of the comfort zone. Comfort zones rob people. They rob people of love, marriage, friendships, business deals, wealth, and riches. A comfort zone is a silent thief.

Disruptive technology has appeared in many forms, whether it's the Palm Pilot, the Macintosh, the PC, or the punch card system. They start out as disruptive and then end up becoming adopted (and embraced) by society.

Technology disruption is a good thing; it's a healthy revolution. Sometimes revolutions are bloody; sometimes they're not. Revolutionizing communication means portability and the capability to time shift, defined by convenience and most importantly speed. The faster people have access to information, the better – even if they're physically nowhere near the origin.

During the Napoleonic Wars, an investor named Nathaniel Rothschild could discern timely battlefield information through the use of homing pigeons. He learned how the conflict was faring and made a killing in the European stock market. Similarly, CNN has changed the face of news, because through its ubiquitous 24-hour immediacy, it puts viewers into the trenches and a result, is shaping the actual result of wars. If you remember, CNN got its hand slapped during the first Gulf War for revealing strategic areas to the world (and thus to the enemy).

Accelerating the speed of communication hastens change, but it also opens doors to opportunities. Putting information into the palm of anyone's hand makes communication faster and better, with less human effort. This transformation helps people find not pre-packaged truth, but a personalized truth that's right for them, because the process is permission based.

Clinton Christian's "The Innovator's Dilemma" was the first book to coin the phrase, "disruptive technology." The title of Part One of his book is "Why Great Companies Can Fail." We'll suggest (and examine) the concept that disruptive technologies cause great companies to fail. Podcasting isn't just a hot new fad that somebody might want to grab onto to keep up with what the kids are doing. Christian writes of how the hard disk drive industry radically changed business.

It is the belief of your authors that Podcasting represents a transformation of similar magnitude.

THE POWER OF TIME SHIFTING

It's important to realize Podcasting's greater power, in contrast to other communication vehicles. Let's start with traditional media, which is consumed at a location and time that's chosen by those who control the material. The movie theater presents the new Harry Potter movie at midnight exactly; the evening news starts at six o'clock; CNN Headline News begins at the top and bottom of every hour.

Podcasting, on the other hand, is a time-shifting phenomenon. Plenty of time shifted technologies already exist: books on tape, the newspaper, etc. However, Podcasting represents the first time that traditional audio and visual media have been time shifted.

Podcasts also derive their power from portability. Again, portable media concepts have existed before, but Podcasts convey even greater portability, in light of the fact that viewers must be in their living rooms to consume television news or in their cars at the right time to hear the traffic report. Immediacy is another advantage. In a movie theater, the audience must wait for the movie to begin. When watching a newscast, they must wait for the news anchor to sign on. With Podcasts, the moment of participation is flexible.

And the flexibility is power – for both the consumer and the producer.

What's more, no transmitters or towers are needed. Pioneering Podcasters cried, in effect: "We don't need no stinking transmitters!"

That's absolutely true. Traditional media requires significant infrastructure. Newspapers and magazines require printing presses. Broadcast media requires towers, generators and licenses. For more closed media, film canisters get transported in trucks. When a new CD is released, shipments must get from warehouses to stores. With Podcasting, transmitters, towers and middlemen are eliminated.

Constraining time formats are eliminated as well. Typically in Hollywood, only an independent renegade, or a recognized "genius" with industry clout, can make a movie longer than two and a half hours. In television, sitcoms must last 30 minutes and dramas an hour, including commercials. By studio decree, the classic Warner Brothers' "Looney Tunes" cartoons had to be exactly six minutes long, no more, no less. News segments are usually a maximum of two minutes long, sometimes one. Everything is conveniently packaged into a format or a time constraint, to work with the un-time shifted, un-immediate, un-portable products generated by media conglomerates today.

With Podcasting, these formatting and time constraints are eliminated. (To be sure, there is no format constraint to a Podcast program. However, 20-30 minutes in length seems to be the generally "consumable" amount of time.) Regulatory constraints have been eliminated as well, from getting permission to put up "stinkin' transmitters" to the licensing of information. Just a few years ago, to transmit audio or video content over the Internet you needed to purchase or license a host of trademarked software packages. Now, an open-source web server is all that's needed.

All of which brings us to our next point: Podcasting is extremely cheap. Hundreds and hundreds of gigs of Podcast content can be easily delivered for less than $20 a month, with no licensing or additional hardware fees. In fact, one Web host called TenBuckTerabyte.com offers a terabyte of data for $9.95 a month. This makes Podcasting one of the most cost efficient mediums out there.

Whether or not the Podcast is tracked, it's entirely permission based. The power is with the listener. In an untracked Podcast, you don't know who the listeners are. You know very little about them, but even more importantly, you don't know what portions they're listening to, you don't know when they listen, you don't know what they've downloaded and archived. Despite their good intentions, you don't know when or whether they intend to listen. Even for tracked Podcasts, using technology such as PremiumPodcasting.com or the Wordcast.Audible.com system, once they've been downloaded, they're still permission based. The listeners hit the play button when they want to (and you'll probably never know if they ever did).

If a Podcaster plays a lot of music and plays different elements that a listener isn't interested in, the listener can simply fast forward past them, because Podcasting isn't an all-or-nothing medium. Podcasting doesn't labor under linear constraints. You can click the scroll wheel in your iPod and play the content out of order. You can jump through segments that don't interest you, whether they entail music, news, jokes, or whatever. There's even an option to actually take Podcasts and remix them, similar to the way producers remix music.

GREATER INTIMACY

Podcasting is an extremely intimate marketing medium. Television is viewed across the room; a newspaper is read at the kitchen table while the kids are running around; a radio is played in a car full of passengers. They're a mass listening exercise. Most mediums are disjointed because the presenter is in charge of the time, the location, the medium, and the method. However, receiving information becomes a much more intimate experience when the person is in charge of when and how they listen. This important theme of intimacy will be explored throughout this book.

In this context, intimacy often means one-on-one communication. One person is typically listening to a Podcast; it's not even two people listening to a newscast that's on the television. A Podcast listener can be in a New York City subway; on a bus in Tennessee; in an airplane flying over California; in front of their home office computer; or maybe at a seminar where the speaker is boring them to tears. Whatever the situation, a Podcast is a one-on-one medium and permission based.

In her first book, "The Popcorn Report," Faith Popcorn introduced the now famous concept of "cocooning," whereby individuals withdraw into their own personalized media. Podcasting is a cocooning communication medium. Listening to a Podcast, you can feel as if you're in a cocoon, even if surrounded by 50 people in a subway car.

Along with intimacy, the beauty of a Podcast is that it encompasses many types of content. It's not just news, education or entertainment. A Podcast can combine all of those niches. It can constitute "infotainment" in its best and highest application. Many of the best Podcasts today do just that.

Podcasts push "1's and 0's" through another form of media that's extremely inexpensive and intimate. The purpose of a commercial is to fund media operations. In the early days of television, networks generated revenue for specific broadcasts through single sponsors, making those sponsors uninvited, but necessary, guests. Broadcasts often exist to hold viewers long enough to view commercials, and pay for the operation. A Podcast requires none of this, and it never will[1]. In our view, Podcasts are sufficiently "monetizable" based on the inherent value of the content, versus the traditional sponsorship model. Moreover, expensive infrastructure doesn't need to be subsidized, so profits can be seen with considerably less intrusion. They're extremely cost effective, so anyone can be a Barbara Walters or a Larry King. A Podcast entrepreneur can become a William Paley, create a network, and grow rich.

Podcasting's immediacy and portability is powerful. Listeners can hold the Podcast in the palm of their hand; it's an existing platform, an umbilical cord that can be plugged into the digital economy, akin to the jack in the back of Keanu Reeve's head in "The Matrix." Listeners can feed themselves information and continue on their merry way. They receive news, education and entertainment simultaneously.

Podcasting represents nothing less than the emergence of a one-on-one (and extremely intimate) economy of inexpensive media communication,

---

1. While it is true that many Podcasts are ad or sponsor supported, it is the belief of your authors that this, although sometimes necessary, limits the effectiveness of the Podcast medium. The introduction of an uninvited sponsor "ruins" the intimacy the medium offers. As you'll see throughout this book, we support other options of Podcast monetization that embrace the medium's strength for the best profit options.

THE THREE A'S

Podcasts accomplish what we call the "Three A's": activate, amplify and accelerate.

Podcasts *activate* someone to have a one-on-one dialogue, not a monologue, as with a newscast. It can be a Socratic dialogue that's amplified by delivering great content and fulfilling expectation[2]. You can tell listeners what they will get; give it to them, and then tell them what they've just got – without commercial interruption or useless "ear candy." The intimacy of the dialogue will activate the conversation.

Podcasting is a communication modality by which intimacy derives from voice. For example, written words can't convey the simple beauty and power of silence. Lack of sound can *amplify* feeling; perhaps it's uneasiness, or a sense of "I wonder what he's going to say next" or "I wonder if he forgot what he was going to say next." Whatever it is, you can't do that (as well) with the written word.

The nature of the Podcast can also *amplify* the message. An "urgent" update made by cell phone and pushed down the Podcast channel minutes later carries a sense of urgency a press release or newsletter never will. The right presentation of your content, in such an intimate setting, has powerful implications.

Podcasters can *accelerate* the learning process, by teaching listeners how to learn and by exhorting them to provide feedback (there are few learning accelerators like the communication of what you just heard).

Obviously, not every Podcast is disruptive in nature. Many people use Podcasting to serve their existing market (or employees) and supplement what already exists, a situation that constitutes a good model for any Business Podcaster. A Podcast that supplements existing content is faster and more efficient than any alternative, whether it's a teleseminar, broadcast, or mailing. It's certainly more powerful. Expecting an entire sales force to be involved with an 8:00 a.m., Monday morning teleseminar is

---

2. Obviously a recorded Podcast can't provide interactivity but supplemental technologies such as user comments by email, voice or Web can facilitate true dialogue.

pure insanity. However, it's reasonable to expect that same sales force to carry a $30 flash-based MP3 Player that they can plug in and listen to anytime, in case they missed the Podcast. This sort of communication option isn't just obtainable; every company should embrace it immediately.

In this scenario, intimacy also confers an advantage. The sales force member who missed the teleseminar, but jumps into his car and listens to the Podcast on the way to the next sale, is now interacting with the boss instead of with Howard Stern. That sales member will have a considerably better relationship with his job and his boss, at least subconsciously. If you're not using Podcasting as a disruptive technology, you can still use it to make existing methods and content faster, more efficient, more powerful, and more memorable.

In June of 2006, National Semiconductor received a considerable amount of press (and the topic for an entire Episode of Marketing Online Live) for purchasing a 30gig iPod for every employee to facilitate this very kind of communication.

BUSINESS AT THE SPEED OF SOUND

Business at the speed of sound is a more powerful modality for learning than through written words, because sound must be absorbed passively through the ears when reading is impossible. You still can multitask while listening to a Podcast. Video is powerful too, but it's active. You must pay attention. You can't watch a video Podcast while you drive, but you can listen to an audio Podcast while you're driving.

You can plug into a Podcast, whenever and wherever you want, completely at your convenience. It's a heck of a lot more convenient than touting around a half dozen CDs in your car that fall all over the place, into every crevice, and scratch beyond repair in the process. With Podcasts, all you need is a USB plug, a media player, and a little bit of free time. This represents a "New Economy" of learning and entertainment that we and our children will feast on. Unlike our parents or grandparents, we now have the entire world in the palm of their hands.

It's all very exciting, but you still must be careful in planning a Podcasting strategy. The adoption of Podcasting is rapid, but it's still early in the game. Taking your organization and moving its communication into an entirely Podcasting mode is not the best strategy. Initially, Podcasting should not be a replacement for existing marketing and promotional efforts. It should be a complement and serve as an adjunct. In this book, we will discuss when it makes sense to take what exists and kill it for a Podcasting strategy, but in the beginning you need to take a look at what you have and how it can be supplemented and complemented by Podcasting.

There are two types of technologies. First, there are those that replace existing ones. The CD replaced the LP; the DVD replaced the videocassette, etc. Then there are complementary technologies that make existing markets bigger. Those in stage-bound theater once worried that when movies came into being, nobody would come and see plays anymore. That didn't happen; more people attend the theater than ever. When television was introduced, movie moguls fretted that people would watch television and no longer go to the movies. That didn't happen. When home video arrived, Hollywood was afraid that people would stop attending movies in droves and only watch at home. Home video didn't kill movie theaters at all; the movie experience is bigger and better.

Today, the introduction of DVD and home theater systems is indeed eating into movie theater attendance, but Hollywood isn't focusing on the part of the pie taken away by DVD sales. It's focusing on how movies can generate DVD sales (reportedly near 50%). DVDs supplement, but do not supplant, the movie-going experience.

Podcasting is both a replacement and complementary technology. "The Business Podcasting Bible" will pinpoint the communication elements that Podcasting replaces and those elements it can make better.

THE BUSINESS PODCASTING BIBLE

The goal of this book is to help each business user, entrepreneur, developer, and big thinker better understand which elements of the business can be enhanced through a Podcasting strategy. Our vision is to teach people that Podcasting provides an intimate and hopeful way to communicate *within* a business – and a faster, cheaper way to monetize *outside* a business.

Podcasting pushes 1's and 0's though the 'Net and utilizes one media player, instead of involving a huge pile of physical CDs, DVDs and cassette tapes. As with Gutenberg's Bible, no intermediaries with vested interests stand in the way. There is no hierarchy, no interpreter and no scribe. There's only a sender, a medium and a receiver. The receiver decides whether or not the sender should keep sending. That's the transcendent strength of Podcasting: all extraneous elements are stripped away and you're left with value. Without value, there is no Podcast, because it's permission based. The receiver will not tune in if there is no perceived value.

Keep in mind, a sender sending doesn't always translate into a receiver receiving. Someone could Podcast the greatest content in the entire world and never get listeners. Part of any Podcasting strategy is to make sure that you're listened to. The strategy isn't just about Podcasting – it's Podcasting in such a way that forges a dialogue. As the disruptive book "The Cluetrain Manifesto" makes clear, markets are now conversations, conducted in a human voice. The mere existence of a Podcast does not promise success. You must pursue an overall strategy that ensures the consumption of your valuable content – and the conversation that will come from it.

This book will show you how to create this strategy, step-by-step. You must determine which existing elements of your business will be enhanced by a Podcasting strategy; which elements should be replaced; and what new elements a Podcast strategy can bring to the forefront.

You'll notice that this book is roughly structured according to the "Five Ws (and One H)" rules of print media, derived from the inverted pyramid: why, how, what, who, where, when. We'll also discuss the road from here – how Podcasting will evolve and the changes it will facilitate in coming years. One thing already is certain: there will be a shakeout in Podcasting and many of the Podcasting entertainers of today will no longer exist, because value will be the sole determining factor as to which Podcasts survive and which don't.

In the spirit of Steve Jobs, every reader of this book must ask: "Will I be a leader or a follower in my industry?" To put it another way, if you're not the lead dog, the scenery never changes.

THEBUSINESSPODCASTINGBIBLE.COM

The danger of any book about technology is the inevitability of change.

Although we have designed this book to be as timeless as possible, we can guarantee that things will change on a regular basis. New technologies and paradigms will be introduced after this book is published that will be as important as what you'll read in these pages.

With your purchase of The Business Podcasting Bible comes lifetime access to our private Website:

(located at http://www.TheBusinessPodcastingBible.com).

The site will include Premium Podcast content, information updates, additional case studies, technology alerts, errata, and the follow-up content on the case studies at the end of this book. Be advised that within a few months, the content contained at the private member site will be as important as the content contained here.

Registration is free. Register today at

http://www.TheBusinessPodcastingBible.com/register.

YOUTHEMEDIA.COM

When one modality of communication makes another obsolete, you must wonder, what is the next level? What will replace Podcasting? At this point, we can't fathom one. It seems to us that the only better way of communicating is telepathy.

Regardless of what changes, or what comes next, there is little chance that the middleman will return and that the disruption brought by Podcasting will disappear.

When we present in front of audiences, we always end by asking a simple question that sums things up considerably, *"Who the Media?"*

The response is now, *"You the Media!"*

Where we can't help but respond with, *"And so are you."*

We start with chapter 1 – *Why Launch a Business Podcast?*

THE BUSINESS PODCASTING **BIBLE**

CHAPTER ONE

"The unexamined life is not worth living."

—Socrates

It's what we learn after we know it all that really counts.

—John Wooden

In chapter 1 we ask the most important question "Why Launch a Business Podcast?" The answer to that simple question is understood by few and implemented by even fewer – and that's why we start with it. You need to know the "why" before anything else.

As this industry grows, the technology will change and the terminology will evolve. In just a few years, we will look at early Podcasting tomes (and consume early recordings) and wonder how we ever survived in the "early days."

And that is because so many people launch a Podcast (business or otherwise) without asking the question *"Why?"*

WHY LAUNCH A BUSINESS PODCAST?

These are exciting and uncertain times. The entire notion of Business Podcasts is barely examined as a tremendous amount of time, money and effort is spent in their launch.

And, yes, we're "not there yet."

The Podcasting landscape is not as well defined as many would like to claim it is. Podcasters with different ideas (and different goals) keep saying, "One day we're going to do this or that," but they are *not* doing it. In addition, the infrastructure isn't even necessarily built to do the very things they claim are "coming" (or *hope to see one day*).

The same phenomenon occurred with the Internet during the initial gold rush of '95. Lots of people launched websites very quickly and (many) hoped "one day" to monetize them, to make sense of them, to bring them into their business fold. Just a decade later, we're watching history repeat itself with Podcasts.

But this time, we have (recent) history to learn from.

Fortunately, you can avoid a great deal of that grief with the assistance of this chapter and the rest of *The Business Podcasting Bible*.

The aim-ready-fire approach that prevailed during the often messy genesis of the Podcasting industry is no longer necessary. You can launch your Podcast with a thorough and complete understanding of *why* you are launching your Podcast. That is what this chapter is about.

Some will launch a Podcast without understanding *why* for the same reason they want to see themselves on television (or be heard on the radio). *They want to have a voice / they want to be heard.* They want the media to cast out their message even if they have no idea what that "message" is. The "promise" of Podcasting is that anyone can potentially become a Larry King (or a David Letterman). You might be playing to an audience of one, but *you can have your own show* – and that is very attractive to many

If your reason for picking up *The Business Podcasting Bible* is a vanity play that enables you to find your own voice in this new media, this is not the best book for you. If you want to develop a Business Podcasting strategy that boosts your bottom line, keep reading.

Think of Podcasting as a powerful new communications channel instead of a flashy new technology. Now that you have a faster, better, more instant, more permission based way to communicate with another human being—do you have a voice? What is your topic or objective? In the words of W. Edwards Deming, "Every system and everything needs an aim." What is the aim of your Podcast?

"What is my message?" is the single-most important question for an individual or company who wants to Business Podcast. If you don't know the answer to that question, this book isn't for you.

If you have a message, this book will enable you to strengthen it (and broadcast it in powerful ways previously impossible). Author Marcus Buckingham in *First, Break All the Rules* talks about strengthening your strengths versus strengthening your weaknesses as one of the core principals of any good business. If you already have a message that is working, Podcasting opens another channel of communication that's fast, user friendly, and permission based. And, very profitable, if done "right."

In short, you launch a Business Podcast to get your message to your audience, exploiting a powerfully new medium, the *Podcast*.

THE FACE OF PODCASTING WILL CONTINUE TO CHANGE

The danger of producing a book like this is that by publication, many technologies and Podcasts discussed will have evolved into something bigger and better. *The only constant in this industry is change.*

What if you "have no voice?"

A recent publication of *Business Week* mentioned a teenager who is using Podcast to teach French. Imagine a young kid Podcasting with a $50 Sony EMC S80 microphone and entering the foyer of national publications beside the man who invented management, Peter F. Drucker.

That is the power of Podcasting.

Many passionate, articulate people will be using Podcasts as a medium to find their voice and clarify their position. Some have already launched a Podcast without a business strategy in mind and are finding it incredibly difficult to backtrack. Bringing everything in this book along on the ride will accelerate their process. Once they find a voice (and a purpose), and understand how to leverage this channel, they can enable monetization.

Author Stephen Covey talks about "finding your voice" as *The Eighth Habit* following his *Seven Habits of Highly Effective People.* If you haven't yet found your voice, your authors recommend this book highly

Podcasting can be an excellent medium of discovery and a great place to begin. The cost is low and even a simple vision can catch fire. We only suggest that you launch with the goal of *finding your voice,* then develop the business strategy once this is accomplished.

Remember the days when marketing experts said a commercial could never be longer than two minutes? Along came the infomercial and proved that something 15 times that long could be incredibly effective. Television (the channel) has always provided an amazing connection with a potential customer, the media of the commercial continues to evolve.

The same is true with Podcasting.

A recent issue of *Business Week* asked, "Can Podcasting do business?". More and more of these articles are popping up with questions about the viability of Business Podcasting. With a constant of change, we have to answer this question *outside of the technology,* but *inside of what the technology allows us to do.* Even more important than innovations in technology, the business opportunity is the real power behind Podcasting. Even in its embryonic state, Podcasting is brimming over with potential.

We are seeing Podcasts today that run 20 to 30 minutes, but that could change. The specific *content* of the Podcast will ultimately match the message with the market and drive monetization.

Podcasting will continue to organically evolve into the way people would most like to receive media communications – *what they want, when they want, and where they want it.*

WHAT ARE THE BENEFITS OF BUSINESS PODCASTING?

1. Maximizes business intimacy

Podcasting is intimate.

An invitation is always more intimate than an interruption. Podcasts are not interruption marketing—a piece of spam, a commercial email piece, a banner on a website, or a commercial during your favorite television show. Podcast listeners actually *invite* you into their ear or their car. When they hit *play*, something magical happens. They have invited you in, and the dialog begins in a way that is simply unprecedented marketing intimacy.

But Podcasting is also a "push" technology, where the business can push the content directly to the consumer instead of, like in traditional media, hoping that the consumer "pulls" the content towards them (by remembering to turn on a specific channel at a specific time). *Messages just arrive*; they don't have to be retrieved. With a Podcast, consumers interactively give you *permission* to come into their world, to "push" your content in their direction. The value of this permission can not be overstated.

The warning: *you can be extinguished for life at a consumer's fingertips with a click of a mouse*. Podcast intimacy is as real as the customer, who now, for the first time ever, is completely in charge of the marketing dialogue.

Podcast invitations are made by the market, not the creator of the message. Choices that drive the decision to say yes or no are made by sifting through introductions, recommendations, favorites lists, titles, domain names, descriptions, or online directories. The choice for such intimacy comes from a number of sources.

Side note: It is important to point out that creating captivating ways of encouraging listeners to select a specific Podcast is one of the next frontiers. Within the past five years, Internet marketing has honed a variety of teasers designed to convert a lead coming to a website into a customer, client, or patient depending on the business. It is the prediction of your authors that Podcast marketing success is more likely to be measured in the longevity of the intimate relationship between broadcaster and listener.

Intimacy in marketing and business falls on a continuum. Billboards are extremely low on the intimacy scale. The most effective messages are complete in eight words or less. "Got milk?" can be read as you are driving 60 or even 65 mph down the road. Add the visual of a celebrity sporting a milk-stained lip, and you have a one-time message that provokes awareness. Just flashing a phrase within the context of speed and frequency does not create intimacy.

Frequency is critical to the thermometer of intimacy. Think about it. Everyone's best friend was once a stranger. Accelerating the frequency of exposure was probably one of the key factors that turned that stranger into a friend, and ultimately into a best friend. You can become best friends in a month if you speak every single day, or you can do the same thing with a single heartfelt letter. This is the same result that many marketers try for in a campaign of marketing frequency. The first time you saw the "Got milk?" campaign, you snickered a little bit. On viewing 2,643, you might think twice about what you drink at dinner that night.

For many people, emails are actually higher on the ladder of intimacy than a physical letter because of the speed whereby they can be delivered. Most people take the time to read postcards because they are quickly consumed and unique in nature, placing them on a higher intimacy level than a physical letter. Because of this fact (your postal worker can read the same postcard), intimacy can't be defined as "closeness" or the privacy of the message. Technology has done something to dialogue: *Intimacy has become defined by our ability to accelerate and strengthen the relationship.*

Applying this new definition to business relationships leaves drive-by billboards at the bottom of the intimacy thermometer (although a great model for the power of frequency). Direct mail letters are next, followed by postcards, faxes, and then email. Faxes step up the level of intimacy because they arrive *inside* your home or office (instead of being brought in by the consumer), and emails go one step further by being delivered inside your (personal) computer. That's why most people consider junk faxes and emails more annoying than junk mail: the intrusion is more intimate and can happen every single day, forcing us to constantly decide what we are going to read.

Now consider the phenomenon of instant messenger. The immediacy of the message and the back-and-forth speed makes this form of communication more intimate than email and far faster than "snail mail" letters. It is also very personal as these messages, too, are delivered on our "personal computers." We tend to give our IM address only to a smaller circle than those who have our email address because of this intimacy and potential for interruption.

Podcasting brings the intimacy thermometer to yet a higher level. Surpassing the intimacy of even IM, a Podcast introduces intimate mechanized communication with the subtle nuances of tone and inflection. Even in writing the very intimate words "I love you," IM offers few font or style choices without adding a smiley face or some other emoticon. When someone can actually *hear* the richness of your intonation or speed of delivery, the message takes on an entirely different feeling. Whispering "I love you" is not something you can do in an email or IM. It is something that requires audio. Audio is intimate. Audio plugged into your ears is extremely intimate. This is a good part of why Podcasting is so powerful.

Why do we mute the TV during a commercial? Even if you leave the room for a quick snack, you can still *hear* the commercial. Whether you are multitasking or not, you know the sound will reach your ears. Audio is intimate, and sometimes you just aren't in the mood to listen.

Obviously, one-on-one phone conversations are much more intimate than any Podcast because we can respond in a back-and-forth dialog. One-on-one is probably the most intimate form of communication, but Podcasting comes closer than any other (one to many) communication vehicle we have today. With its permission based nature, Podcasting falls in line with email and instant messaging on the intimacy continuum. Despite looking or sounding like them, Podcasts are far more intimate than radio or television.

Regular Podcasts enable the power of frequency that a billboard provides, are intimately permission based, leverage the powerful modalities of senses (visual, auditory, haemostatic, and others), and add a physical presence, or touch, to the business dialogue.

Frequency is important. Listening to three Podcasts in a row creates a higher level of intimacy with the content provider than hearing a Podcast once and then unsubscribing. However, be careful: too much frequency (and forced intimacy) makes you a stalker of sorts. We have already seen (and experienced) the effect of autoresponders, email marketers, and other communicators who seem like the guy parked outside some woman's door at 5:30 AM saying, "Hey, I just wanted to take you to school." With so much frequency already in the system, and so much intimacy at play, *Podcasters have to find a delicate balance.*

If your website (or Podcast) is annoying, visits (and listens) drop in frequency. Just like spamming the search engines will reveal that Google is no longer sending traffic your way, a reputation for being long-winded will prevent many new listeners from giving you a try. Even if your subscribers are downloading your Podcast, are they listening to it? The brash, in-your-face junk mail approach and push marketing only invites frustration and disgust.

Intimacy invites dialog.

Our Marketing Online Live Show (http://www.marketingonlinelive.com) draws, at our request, a tremendous amount of email from listeners who share valuable personal things about their life, i.e. how long their commute is to work, their occupation, and where the Podcast helps them. Instead of relying on stats and numbers that can paint a distorted picture, a Podcaster can use this *intimate dialog* to match the message to the market. Unless you embrace the intimacy that is so unique to Podcasting, you'll miss out on the dialog it enables.

Podcasting is likely to shatter any existing definitions in the interplay to intimacy and marketing by bringing *location and convenience* into the foyer of communication. Beyond frequency and dialog, *where* are you listening to this? You're listening in the car, in the subway, in the bus, in your bedroom, in the restroom, at work, in front of your computer, on a bike— or on your John Deere mower. You can listen just about anywhere. Podcasting drives a new post into the ground that says, "This is marketing intimacy." It's never been discussed before in any context; and thanks to Podcasting, we have a definition.

Consumption of information and how it is used are other concepts that have yet to be explored by big business. It is our topic in chapter 2. A Podcast can be consumed anywhere. The aftermath of a couple's argument might have the guy or gal accelerating from the house, listening to a reprieve in the car. That's pretty darn intimate. Today's embryonic conversations about marketing intimacy may well mature into an intimacy quota with a measurable scale that embraces multiple factors. Developing the context and formulating a clean, graphically illustrated scale would enrich our grasp of marketing intimacy and break the back of former definitions.

2. Accelerates communications

Podcasts are a fast communication medium.

The Marketing Online Live Podcast is usually recorded in the morning and posted online 10 minutes after the recording is finalized. Without fail, at least one response email pops up before the computer is shut down for the day. These intimate conversations with our customer base are perfect examples of the acceleration of communications.

Adam Curry, famous for the Daily Source Code, talks about the flood of emails he receives if his show is 30 to 45 minutes late, "Hey, I'm waiting to catch the bus and I need to download your show so I can listen to it on the way into work."

This book will take some time to reach the shelves[1]. Not so with our Podcast messages. Different media provide different benefits. People decide the speed of consumption with Podcasts, but the Internet accelerates their decision-making process (and demands). *Am I going to raise the volume of this teleseminar or turn the channel? Am I in or out? Will I listen to this whole thing?* Using this permission base makes is easy to know whether or not your audiences likes you—clearly and quickly with minimal effort. And listeners who like and trust you are more willing to buy something from you.

---

1. It took almost a year for this book to reach the shelves after the concept was received.

Back in the '80s, Lee Iacocca convinced the federal government to lend him money for commercials that pushed Chryslers and new product forms like the minivan. If one man can turn around the image and fortunes of one of the world's largest corporations, an individual with a message and a voice can definitely create a name or even a sensation in Podcasting.

Dialog should not be limited to response. It can be, and is often best described as someone actively listening and choosing to respond (in action or in word) later. We can all relate to clicking through 99 TV channels with a remote and deciding, "Nothing is on." With Podcasting, tens of thousands of channels may have "nothing on", but the active Podcaster listener will have something in their queue "worth listening to" and will actively respond accordingly. There is no "down time" for the Podcast listener. Communication has been accelerated.

The iPod came into the world as entertainment media. Without a constant flow of originality, the acceleration of entertainment can easily lead to boredom. Ask anyone with an iPod with 10,000 songs and "nothing to listen to."

On the other hand, look at the success of ageless self-help books like *Think and Grow Rich* or *How to Make Friends and Influence People*. What if the authors had been able to accelerate that popular spin into education and information through Podcasting?

Monetization will become much easier when information, news, and education fully awaken to the benefits of Podcasting.

3. Boost bottom lines

The "right" Podcasts can immediately produce revenue.

Effective marketing communication results in sales, plain and simple. Something is very wrong with your marketing strategies when you have a personal, fast, intimate, marketing media and fail to utilize that to boost your bottom line. Podcasts enable multiple, effective, personal marketing messages to be consumed by your audience at the location and time of their choosing.

Attempting to extend your brand through Podcasts with some vague motif or theme is *not* effective marketing communications. Aimless exercises in brand awareness are not the same as multiple, effective personal intimate messages. The goal is direct response Podcasting.

The impact of general advertising can only be evaluated over time, but Podcasters have the advantage of immediate responses in the form of dialog, feedback, and sales. Many people confuse the bottom line with the "top line" of sales growth. Even if your Podcast is not monetizable—even if you don't use it to make money—you can still use it to boost your bottom line. You can fatten or widen your bottom line by utilizing Podcasting as a stick strategy for retaining and serving customers, clients, or patients.

Sometimes boosting the bottom line results in top line growth. Perhaps more importantly, Podcasts make it possible to immediately fatten the bottom line by saving money and increasing disposable income. Marketers need to take a long, hard look at any strategies and activities that could be effectively replaced by Podcasts. For example: Instead of paying for traditional stick strategies like a follow-up postcard or a 24-hour recorded message, direct those consumers to a website through a customer Podcast. Chapter Two goes into greater detail about existing Podcast direct-response mechanisms and possibilities for the future.

4. Time and place shifts information content.

Podcasts put the customer in control – a place they haven't traditionally been, but a place they now won't leave without a fight.

No matter how well planned or well executed your message may be in real time, your listeners will never be the entirety of your desired audience. Accepting the impossibility of catching everyone in a single time and place, our business strategies tend to maximize whatever audience we can grab at any given moment: What cities make it easy, affordable, and attractive to attend a major event? What weekends have no competing events? What strategies will draw the most people into the room—perhaps to their television set or car radio?

The Podcasting business is no longer trapped by these constraints. All of these issues potentially melt away with a Podcast. Thanks to the time (and place) shifting of information content, people can listen when, where, and how they please. Little wonder that TIVO stirred an international hunger for time shifted content and the freedom it brings[2]. Few forces can rival the validation power of television in permission based marketing and entertainment. The Podcast is only one of many places this revolution is appearing.

Most traditional marketing strategies have to rely on a couple of shots or opportunities. Consider "Black Friday" in the retail environment—the one day of the year during the holiday season when your store can go into the black if enough people walk through the door. Heart-attack levels of stress go into making sure those multi-colored ads are stuffed into the right papers on the exact day that shoppers will pick them up and read them. If you miss, you die.

Not so when a Podcast is the medium. Some people will grab the message instantly. Others may find it several weeks later or even a year from now. The energy, manpower, and fear that we pour into "making it all happen at once" can now be redirected into improving the message and the response to the message.

The most powerful element of time and place shifting is the surprising fact that the same freedom the consumer receives from a Podcast can also be had by the content producer. The emphasis can move from getting the message out on time to getting the message out right.

The beauty of time shifting goes back to accomplishment. Renowned productivity experts like David Allen and Barbara Hemphill, author of *Paper Tiger*, talk frequently about segmenting *what* you have to do from *where* you do it: Concentrate only on computer activities when you are tethered to the computer. Don't waste time and energy thinking about

---

2. At publication, the most recent release of the Tivo Desktop Software made it possible for users to easily transfer their recorded television shows to their video iPods, Playstation Portable Game Players, or Treo Cell Phones. Place shift is quickly becoming as important to the consumer as is time shifting.

Internet activities while you are driving your car or sitting in an airplane without connectivity. The concept is simple but profound in diminishing the sense of overwhelm. How does that relate to Podcasting? A Podcast can be consumed anytime and anywhere (when it makes the most sense to the consumer – not the producer). Whether the field is education, entertainment, training—video or audio—that Podcast could potentially appear in every single context of a David Allen "to do" list.

The place where we consume information holds a certain power, and time and place shifting usually increases that power. An obvious example of an exception would be material that is waiting to be viewed on TIVO when the world at large already knows the critical outcome—like the winner of a reality TV show. TIVO and Podcasting offer time-shifting capabilities, but Podcasts tend to be more specific and personal to the listener. While a Podcast might include the date and time as a point of reference, the focus is often on content and material development (and for marketers, the response mechanism). Being able to consume content anywhere, anytime, lends itself to convenience and permission based communication. Freeing the framework of consumption opens the door for a growing audience who can be built in new and exciting ways. An awareness of the non-moment in time, nature, or the very time-shift element is vital to developing a Podcast monetization strategy.

Time-shifting is destined to take more and more center stage in the consumption of mutable information and principal-centered teachings. Marketing Online Live often uses a timely news piece as the sizzle or hook to introduce the principal centeredness of a conversation beneath it. This format is not only valid and viable but may set the future standard for business education Podcasting.

Television, radio, and the concept of the monoculture have *dictated an artificial need for immediacy*. "Sweeps weeks" and season finales are the epitome of generating as much hype as possible at a specific time and place to draw the maximum number of viewers to the screen at the critical moment.

Good and/or powerful content is ageless. Most people would find that the authors of their all-time favorite books are dead—not writers who have emerged within the past year or two. The monoculture paradigm has dictated a dumping down of content with artificial time restraints and limitations that Podcasting can eliminate.

The *personality of the Podcast* captures attention in the same way that any personality draws attention. What we see initially draws us to another person, like the first touch. Every Podcast should have that "first touch." Every first-time listener is just a single Podcast away from unsubscribing, held by the glue of personality—not by the news stories – or the immediacy of the monoculture. Too many of today's shows provide personality devoid of character. Content that applies a timeless approach to principal-centered teachings give relevance to what is happening in the life of the consumer.

Planned obsolescence is a once-powerful marketing strategy that is quickly losing strength. A new toothbrush has a computer that indicates when to throw it away and buy a new one. While Steve Jobs seems to still practice planned obsolescence with the constant upgrading of the iPod platform, others such as Bill Gates have found the bigger/better/faster next version of Windows has little play on the consumer if there is nothing in it for "them." You'll be seeing less of this technique over the coming years as the bond between time and message is quickly being dissolved – thanks in part largely to time and place shifted media.

Planned obsolescence is part of modern business that many people deem as a necessity. Certainly, some Podcasts like the Kansas City Weather Podcast are disposable (there's really only one day it makes sense to listen). In our opinion, the opportunity to create something ageless is infinitely more exciting, potentially more powerful, and fully embraces the opportunities made available by time and place shifting.

5. Places the power of the Internet in your hands

Your audience can take your Podcast with them. Wherever your audience is, you have the power to be. This isn't just a subtitle for our book, it is the profound reality that should change the way you communicate today.

No one questions the power of the Internet, but that power is still limited by its application. Many people were not fans of Internet radio because it required sitting in front of a computer – a tethering to a $2,000 piece of equipment that is providing the same service as a $9 portable radio.

Internet radio and the computer are not the radio experience. Radio experiences happen in the car or with a portable player or the home stereo—and are most often associated with *movement*. Remaining "plugged in" is the number one problem with the Internet. Anyone who flies frequently can walk down the airplane aisle and see six-figure employees using their $5,000 laptops to play solitaire. They are unplugged from the corporate network so they can't surf or even email. They don't know what else to do.

The time and place shifting nature of Podcasting introduces a tremendous freedom of consumption. A phenomenal number of people deal with the confinement of being plugged into the Internet by printing pages and taking them somewhere else to read – *they want to take the Internet with them*. Consultants will often find the entirety of their websites already printed out, stapled, and sitting on the desk of a new serious customer. People are used to this modality of consumption and Podcast is no different. The "Internet radio" is now in a portable player that looks a lot like your old Walkman®. The iPod that transmits to your FM receiver on your stereo may not be the highest of fidelity but it represents a familiar paradigm. The person who goes to 98.7 for a news update can just as easily go to 98.4 for a Podcast. The Internet is the channel; the portable media player is the player. The Internet is now portable. The freedom from plugging into a connection introduces infinite possibilities.

According to the U.S. Census Bureau, Americans spend more than 100 hours commuting to work every year with drive times averaging 24.3 minutes. Millions of people are alone in their cars for nearly 30 minutes twice a day with nothing to do. Flying on an airplane, working out at the gym, walking the dog in the park, cooking in the kitchen—at night when you can't sleep—a Podcast places the power of the Internet in the palm of your hand. It's portable and self-sufficient. One of the most exciting technologies on display at the first annual Podcast & Portable Media Expo was a silly little $15 adapter that recharges an iPod with a 9 Volt battery. No longer limited to about two hours of iPod power on a trans-Atlantic flight, you can now bring your video iPod, the training DVDs you burned to it, and a pack of 9 Volt batteries.

We have just witnessed the resurrection of dead time. We have matched it with the power of the Internet. Communications will never be the same.

The power of the Internet, the medium, and virtually unlimited content is now portable. The Podcast has cut the "umbilical cord" required by the Internet, whether that connection is wireless or a USB port. Consumers can enjoy an entirely new level of freedom in the way they gain information, from entertainment to education. Portability enhances that new level to the point that we will be looking for batteries to continue the communication versus picking out a good book for a long airplane ride. People will be making pre-flight plans based on their desired Podcasts and how many 9 Volt batteries they are going to need before their plane touches down in Singapore.

Anyone who wants to remain productive is no longer stuck with playing solitaire in dead time because they are disconnected to the rest of humanity. Sometimes it might be necessary to listen to a Podcast prior to a meeting or conference call with key executives. The field is open, including intranets and Podcasts within companies and corporations. Sam Walton used to prepare a message to his Wal-Mart employees every Saturday morning, using big-screen video to simulcast to every store. Today, employees could listen to such a message during the dead time of their daily commute or at daybreak while they walk the dog. Cutting the Internet umbilical cord, adding unlimited convenience, and retaining full information value are the advantages that are sending the power of Podcast to the forefront.

The Podcast itself doesn't offer two-way communication like the email messages that Blackberry™ users can send. It is not a medium of "chat" like text messaging on phones or instant messaging on the desktop. Podcasts offer time shifted content that is monetizable—content that is available in any situation, in any context, virtually anywhere in the world;

dead time or live time, *it doesn't matter*. The method of choice of consumption of information is portable, not requiring a direct connection to the Internet (something the other technologies mention do require), and in the hands and ears of the listener. Command is no longer owned by the broadcaster. There is no longer a fixed and time and place for the broadcast.

That's why Podcasting can be defined simply as *the power of the Internet in the palm of your hand.*

THE BUSINESS PODCAST

The hyper-growth of technology and Internet has left a growing and continual wake of fancy, flashy, technological bells and whistles that have all been heralded as "the next best thing – *until something better comes along*. This constant barrage of technologies has left many business users understandably numb and unwilling to change technologies on a daily/weekly/monthy basis.

Podcasting should not be included in this grouping. It is not "the new thing" but a change in the use of some technologies that has profound impact on business as we know it today.

Perhaps the best way to explain the power of this technology is to compare it to the history of email: at one point, as most of our readers will recall email used a different system within nearly every company or

iPod versus Blackberry

The iPod is complete fidelity and a total media experience. With a capacity that is sure to quickly outstrip today's larger 60GB models, the iPod offers everything you might possibly need with a friendly interface quality assurance that you already know and trust.

Another popular business tool is the "Blackberry" email device – often referred to as a "crackberry" because of the addictive nature of the Internet in the palm of your hand.

One of the major drawbacks with the Blackberry is the inability to retrieve data out of cell range—including airplane (or foreign) travel. Communication train wrecks can happen, since the sender has no way of knowing whether or not you are "within range" to receive the message. It is a technology of hope and good timing. Having the ability to do something and suddenly losing it is infinitely more frustrating than never having the ability at all. The Blackberry experience is powerful and portable but unpredictable, where the iPod is portable and totally predictable.

While the Blackberry offers email capability, the keyboard is only conducive to the briefest of notations: see you at 5P meeting. The Blackberry was never designed to transmit dialogs in their entirety. The experience does not duplicate sitting in front of a computer with a copy of Outlook running. Podcast *does* offer the entirety of the medium. An executive can board a plane and answer five brief questions in a few minutes using a Blackberry, but she might spend the next five hours catching up on Podcast media material on her iPod.

online service provider. CompuServe users couldn't email their internal Lotus Notes system and an AOL user had no chance of communicating with someone attached to the now-defunct Prodigy service. Whereas email was a "great idea" – it wasn't functional enough in the real world to be part of any realistic communication strategy. When email standardized on the protocols we know today, it changed from a great technology to a powerful business application. The same is true of Podcasting.

MP3 (compressed audio) and XML (a format for computer-processed data), the technical foundations of Podcasting, have been around for some time. Some would be surprised to know that portable media players are more than a decade old[3]. It is the integration of all of these technologies and the open nature that mean so much more to the business process. With the introduction of Podcasting, a single media file; produced once, can be consumed on an Apple iPod on a plane to Australia, burned to a CD, listened to on the way to work, sent to a $30 Wal-Mart Portable Media Player or streamed to your cell phone using one of the many Podcast to phone services. Just like nobody worries about the receipt mechanism for email anymore, the technology for Podcast consumption doesn't matter – the opportunity does.

---

3. The original portable media player, developed by Audible, is currently behind glass at the Smithsonian institution. The technology of Podcasting is, by no means, "new."

Many of the terms and technologies—and specifically the brand names that appear in this version of *The Business Podcasting Bible*—may vanish in five years. It is quite possible that some companies mentioned in this book (or the case studies at the end) will be out of business when you read this. However, the Podcast breakthrough of time shifted, place shifted, intimate, portable media consumed on demand by the end user has already changed the face of media as we have known it. The opportunity for businesses to embrace this technology in their communication strategy can not be encouraged enough.

Podcast technology goes far beyond offering a new level of intimacy and dialog, or catching eyeballs and getting people to pay attention. From a base of proven technologies, the Podcast extenuates what is already "out there" in the realm of audio communication by lifting the limitations of time and space. It enables business in a way that business has never before been enabled. No longer just an entertainment vehicle, Podcasts must be viewed and almost inventoried as a valuable strategic asset.

Like most other educational products—particularly with time-shifting and portability features that bring the power of the Internet into your hands or in your dashboard—the duration of a typical Podcast will largely be determined by average commute times of 20 to 30 minutes. Nightingale-Conant creates personal development tapes and CDs that run about 20 minutes per side, an ideal length for a daily commute. That's why the company has been the world's leader in personal development since 1960 with a customer base of more than two million: People appreciate the convenience of dead-time learning in their cars. A Business Podcaster should not undervalue this reality.

In the early 1900s, advertisers of soap and shampoo actually motivated Americans to bathe more often. Advertising created behavior, and behavior is another factor in determining Podcast length. The sweet spot seems to be 20 minutes, since it remains the lowest common denominator and most functional time shifted duration for any area of dead-time consumption[4]. Those who have a 10-minute commute or even less are not

---

4. It is also the length of time of a traditional sitcom minus commercials. It is a time segment many are programmed to consume.

likely to use that dead time for education or business updates as there simply isn't enough time to digest important information. The principal-centered approach that Nightingale-Conant used four decades ago still holds true: the behavior of the consumer directly influences format.

Podcasting offers a world of benefits beyond that of recorded portable media like educational tapes and or books on CD-ROM. In fact, we have been working with Nightingale-Conant's number one marketing program on ideas for repackaging their products as *fully automated Podcasts*. They would not only be immediately and easily accessible online, they would be delivered to you in the background.

Since the birth of the Internet, people have placed media files online and said, "Grab these at your leisure," which is akin to the VCR frustration that many of us remember. Sure, a VCR will tape virtually any show—but most of us have a stack of untouched blank tapes just gathering dust. *Who really learned how to program their VCR anyway?* Once Tivo entered the picture and made the "taping" of an entire season of shows possible at the click of a single button, or subscription request, the benefit of "taping" shows was suddenly realized again.

Portable media player Podcasts represent a step beyond traditional online automation or pushed content. *You can listen to content after your computer is shut down – after you have been disconnected from the Internet.* As soon as your portable media player is undocked, something new is available that is completely different than any recorded media. Instead of surfing between the AM stations in your car to find an interesting dialog, you can review the Podcast menu of your iPod and see new Podcasts by X, Y, and Z. The newer high-quality video iPods can contain about 300 hours of video, not to mention the same amount of audio. Rather than grabbing some training program on the way out the door, the entire library is now at your fingertips. The consumer is empowered to consume when they want, where they want, and what they want to consume as they have taken not just the content, but the library with them.

In addition, wireless delivery (no longer attached to a computer) is coming into the forefront very quickly. Audible, Inc.'s, Audible Air program is delivering Podcast content to wireless phones today. A number of programs for the Windows Mobile platform allow for wireless "Podcatching." In short, Podcasts no longer require connectivity to a computer; they can be picked up through a phone data network or a local WIFI hot spot. A desktop-based automated system allows you to listen to the Podcast you want at the place and time of your choosing— without waiting for the stream.

Unlike Internet radio that offered poor audio quality and often choked 15 minutes into the program, Podcasting (and the market penetration of broadband internet connectivity) makes it possible for even a desktop-based person with a set of headphones to enjoy high-fidelity audio. The days of waiting for stream or trying to listen over the hiccups and tatty sound quality are over. Podcast also allows the media to be pushed and not pulled, a key advantage over recorded and portable media. Podcasts can be delivered automatically, eliminating the time and effort of retrieval.

If you look at successful Internet marketing campaigns, they often follow an email bait pattern: People come to a website submit their email (usually in exchange for what we call "the ethical bribe") and are offered a series of emails that are developed to lead to action.

Email is "pushed" content versus "pulled" content – the information is sent (pushed) to the user without requiring that they visit the Website for more content. In reality, the only feat more statistically difficult than attracting someone to your website is luring them back for a second time. The most successful Internet marketers understand and realize that with so many people competing for our attention, the added power of email communication will make a substantial difference on any online marketing campaign. Whether emails or Podcasts, pushed media (Podcasting) represents a quantum leap over any pulled recorded portable media (Internet Radio or media files made available for download). *Podcasts come to your door. Once you subscribe, it is your choice to open the door and consume.*

A good analogy for this concept is the organic vegetable service that delivers farm-fresh, pesticide-free vegetables to my front door each week. Opening up the box is always a surprise, because we order the service— not the content. We might find fruits and vegetables that we have never seen before in our lives. We have to look them up online to learn how to prepare and cook them. Some experiments are exciting and others prompt an email that says, "Don't send any more of that." Once the relationship with this delivery service is set up, the produce just keeps coming. I don't have to do a darn thing.

On occasion when we have been away from home, we have called the service to say we were temporarily canceling deliveries. The response has always been, "Did we do anything wrong?" Like any successful supplier, they want to satisfy their customers. That kind of dialog can occur with unhappy Podcast subscribers as well. The Marketing Online Live Show is open with few one-to-one relationships, but we still watch our subscriber numbers. Any sudden drop would have us examining the last show or two for some clues. We would probably be saying on the next show, "Okay, we offended a lot of people who left for some reason. Does anyone have any insight to share?" Then a dialog would begin.

Once you click the subscription button, that Podcast will continue to arrive automatically - unless you decide to stop, no other action is ever required. And that subscription can follow you to the ends of the earth. How often has your hometown newspaper been delivered to your hotel room when you were on vacation or traveling on business? What can you do if you want to watch your hometown evening news when you are on another continent?

The equally viable and important inner and outer aspects of Podcasting deal with the bottom-line/top-line elements. Many Podcast elements can be utilized for internal communications. Sam Walton was famous for his video presentations, but they demanded a significant investment in satellite time and the presence of every employee in front of a monitor to make things happen. Imagine every owner and every employee having a small portable video player and being told, "Make sure you watch the update by the end of the week." Could this be why National Semiconductor recently purchased a video iPod for every single employee in the organization?

Internal Podcasts bear similarities to an intranet, but they add the power of time shifting and freedom from the umbilical cord of the computer. In contrast to Sam Walton's video that had every employee coming into the store, a Podcast allows subscribers to plug in and listen whenever and wherever they please. Podcast places the intranet in the palm of the employees' hands.[5]

The outer aspect of Business Podcasting is purely the ability to monetize externally. The next chapter will cover some of the business feedback that has been taken into play, but every touch is an opportunity for monetization. If you touch multiple times, you can touch intimately. You can enjoy a dialog with your base that was impossible in the past because of the expense involved. Every invitation becomes an extremely high-quality touch. One of the best examples is the Big Seminar Live Podcast, reviewed in depth in the case study section at the end of this book. They send multiple hits for preview calls, sneak previews of the event, and post-event content. Each Big Seminar Live listener is hit at least 10 times each month with Big Seminar Live content. No single event brings their subscribers on board or motivates them to pick up the content. These multiple high-quality touches can very quickly enable monetization.

Greatness often means creating something between good and great where the margin is slight. The difference between the person finishing first in the 100-yard dash versus second or third is milliseconds. That goes for the 100-meter butterfly or freestyle or even a marathon. That sliver of extra effort often wins the gold. Podcasts offer the additional power of interaction and access. If you have access from virtually anywhere in any context and you need one extra push for a yes on a financial exchange, a Podcast can take you across the line. Will the only difference between you and your competition be a Podcast to your user base?

Water only boils at 212 degrees. Bring that up to 213 degrees, and you can create the steam that starts a locomotive in motion. In spite of all the energy inherent in 212 degrees, the most you can accomplish is boiling an egg. Even a small difference can be the margin between mediocrity and success, and "champion" business people will be quick to reach for that power. They are challenged with cutting through a world of noise and clut-

---

5. Secure 1-to-1 Podcasting for corporate communication purposes is available today to anyone with security concerns. Audible's Wordcast Program and PremiumPodcasting.com both enable Podcast delivery without the concerns of public consumption.

ter with the most permission based, time shifted, and intimate modality of communication. At this very moment, that means Podcasting.

The question is not whether you should adopt Podcasts, but *how*—a topic covered in detail in Chapter 2.

Podcasting is not an esoteric technology for early adopters or an uncommon luxury. Podcasting is already so mainstream[6] that it is becoming one of the requirements for remaining competitive. Podcasts go beyond boosting the efficiency of communications to creating opportunities for direct monetization. We have generously sprinkled valuable case studies and examples throughout this book, along with theory in application.

Podcasts directly monetized can produce additional revenue streams that do not cannibalize existing streams of revenue within an organization. A Podcast is not a replacement as much as it is an addition. Reading and examining this book with a serious intent and embracing the power that Podcasting enables will give you a clear advantage in using this technology to the greatest possible benefit.

Podcast monetization will be accelerating like lightning in comparison to the same phenomenon with the early days of the Internet. In 1999 the Internet seemed very esoteric to many people, including myself. I was a seasoned direct marketer who couldn't figure out a way to monetize the Internet, so I attended my first Internet marketing conference. I didn't really believe the people who said they were monetizing, but I purchased just under $1,000 of course materials. By the time I returned home and settled down to pour over them about four months later, the content was already obsolete. I was familiar with traditional direct marketing tools like postcards, direct mail and even electronic media like the radio. I just couldn't see how to move those activities into the Internet.

The 1999 holiday season saw little business over the Internet. By 2000, Internet sales took a meteoric ride that gained even more speed in 2001. Even after the bubble with high tech burst, the Internet continued—not an

---

6. At the time of writing the top Business Podcasts in the iTunes Podcast directory included offerings from Harvard Business School, Newsweek, CNBC, National Public Radio and Time Magazine. The mainstream has already embraced Podcasting.

esoteric distribution channel—but as a mainstream distribution channel. Today, the Internet is the definition of mainstream, gobbling up other distribution channels with superior levels of efficiency and speed. Those who see Podcasting as an esoteric form of communication should review the explosive growth of e-commerce on the Internet just five or six years ago. Podcast monetization will progress much more quickly, since the earlier adopters have already embraced the technology. Today, the issue is moving from one source of technology that we are using to communicate to our market and using Podcasting instead.

The catch that holds most people back from Podcasting is a question of gathering subscribers. How can I turn one-time listeners of my content into regular subscribers? How can I crack that code? What these people are failing to consider are the *millions* of new listeners who are silently begging to subscribe but need a program or show that meets their needs or interests. Our Marketing Online Live show is a great example. Even the first few shows had a landslide of difference in the number of listeners with bare-bones marketing. If you just take a look at the number two, three, four, and five shows—the difference is a landslide. The growth of Marketing Online Live has been largely organic.

Beyond our own experience, the show has helped to launch a number of other projects. The opportunity provided by a new audience of iPod listeners looking for content has been tremendous, like low-hanging fruit. iTunes alone can draw a considerable audience if you just have a quality show in the business channel, as their goal is the sales of iPods and will thus push the best shows to the top. Yes, at some point the noise will reach a volume that introduces some real competition. For now, being "out there" and having a quality program is enough to attract a good number of listeners.

Civilizations run through many different patterns, a point well made in "A Study of History" by Arnold Toynbee. He wrote 12 volumes of comparative study of 26 civilizations, analyzing their genesis, growth, and disintegration. Civilization is first obscure, then flourishes, becomes cocky and falls. And it doesn't matter if we are talking about ancient Egyptians or the Romans or Europeans or Americans, the fall of civilization is accelerating.

The timeframe goes from 5,000 years to 4,500 to 3,000 to 1,500 and continues to collapse.

This pattern also holds true for technology, which begins as an adjunct. The Internet was an adjunct that no one took seriously until it became mainstream marketing. Podcasting may still be an adjunct but one that is likely to accelerate in critical mass. The flexion point that Andrew Grove once talked about will arrive much sooner because we are *learning to learn* with this technology. Everyone in the business community should view Podcasting as a current adjunct but also prepare for it to hit mainstream quicker than anyone might expect.

That doesn't mean changing the business model and hiring throngs of new employees and other radical steps that ended in the big bubble burst of 2000-2001. By preparing, we mean *knowing* that a viable distribution channel of communication and commerce can be distributed via Podcast. With a market and a medium—and the Podcast itself is the medium—and a sender with a quality message, any voice has the potential to be well received. Once received, it will begin to multiply itself in every topic of expertise from law and dentistry to information marketers. That powerful evolution will occur simply by virtue of Podcast moving from an adjunct to mainstream.

The question is – will you be part of that move, or will you just sit back and watch that move happen?

Making life better and easier is a critical key to the success of any new technology, a truth that has been illustrated in the evolution of Internet sales. Early in the game, Pets Online offered to deliver a 50-pound bag of dog food to your door for a $40 shipping fee—and not surprisingly, went out of business. At the same time, Amazon teamed up with Toys R Us to provide an online distribution channel for toys. Now that made great sense. The time shifted nature of Podcasting is mirrored in those parents who no longer had to fight the mall crowd and fight Black Friday sales to buy toys for their kids. They could go online and click to their heart's content, sitting in their pajamas and sipping a cup of coffee at 6 AM. If they spent more than $50, which we all know is easy to do, the shipping is free.

Thanks to the Internet, neither of your authors have visited a noisy toy store in years.

The history of marketing absolutely proves and dictates that people will always be hungry for viable content that improves their lives. Any vehicle that frees the consumption of content has to be successful. Such a vehicle would be so empowering that it would transform communication parodies, external and internal. We could muse endlessly about technologies and iPods and Steve Jobs' influence on the marketplace, but making life better and easier is the single most important fact about Podcasting. And it is the one reason that Podcasting should be grasped as important and viable by any intelligent business person.

The Internet experience has paved a solid path of experience if we only absorb the lessons. So many retail players who went wholeheartedly online without dipping their toes in the water ended up diving head first into a block of cement. They thought the technology (being able to ship a 40 pound bag of dog food by FedEx) was the most important thing. They didn't allow the technology and the framework of the distribution channels to grow with them organically. Marketing Online Live is not making that mistake. We are not ready, fire, aiming. We are ready, aim, aim, aim, fire, fire, fire, fire, fire, fire—in the words of Ross Perot. We are growing organically and moving forward based on solid feedback and research.

We recently lost one of the greatest minds in business management of all-time, Peter Drucker. In 1981 he walked into General Electric when John F. Welch had just taken over the helm and asked him two questions. "If you weren't already in your business, would you enter it today? If the answer is no, what are you going to do about right now?" At that point, Welch not only began downsizing, he eliminated every GE business that was not number one or two in its sector. When Welch stepped down, he left a remarkable 20-year run of earnings growth and near cult-like devotion.

We recommend that everyone treat Business Podcasting the same way. Unless you can quickly reach an audience critical mass in a very short time, the fact that a Podcast is free is not a compelling reason to invest resources and climb on board. If Drucker were to ask us the same questions he posed to Welch, the answer would be, "Yes, I would enter this business today." We are ready and ripe to keep going and glad to be in this business right now. Now imagine "no" as the answer. Deciding what to do about that may be a conversation that many people will be having in three years after this book is in its third edition and the landscape has completely changed. In the acceleration of this medium, one year of Podcasting could easily be the equivalent of 10 years offline.

The Business Podcasting Bible basically deals with the *business utility* of Podcast – touching on the technology behind the utility only when necessary. We suggest you take the same approach. With the understanding of *why* this medium is so powerful, the next step will be an understanding of the Podcast consumption processes: Exactly what these online media files really are, who utilizes them, where they are utilized, and when they should be utilized. Part of this process will be teaching how to consume, which goes back to the soap manufacturers of the early 20th century. They actually *taught* Americans how to bathe each and every day. A six letter word changed the face of the shampoo business: REPEAT. Lather, rinse, repeat. Do we really have to use twice as much shampoo or could we get by with just one little dollop? Should we shampoo our hair every single day? Hair-care experts often say that daily shampooing strips hair of natural oils and leads to excessive dryness.

The fact remains that our consumption habits have been trained by advertisers, including the messages on the back of each bottle. That's how the once-a-week bath at the turn of the century turned into three times a week and eventually every single day. Today, we might ask: You don't bathe and wash your hair everyday? How can you live that way? Europeans have a different culturally accepted standard of personal hygiene that does not necessarily include daily bathing or showering. Americans are extremely media-driven, with advertisers dictating consumption.

In Podcasting, information is the medium. And this medium is not simply an excuse for a parasite like an advertisement, just as in broadcast TV. Listeners are actually paying for the show in the same way they do for per-view television—paid entertainment. Although this position might change, we would be vehemently against any advertising in such paid shows. Who can say if Marketing Online Live will someday have sponsors? The topic has not even been discussed.

We are sure of one thing: In our information marketing background, we are all about teaching people how to consume. We teach them to open that "how-to course" box, read the first document, read the next document, go to the next page, then delve deep into the course and find the bonus gift on page 73. In the same way, effective Podcasts actually manipulate the audience—in the positive sense of the word manipulate—encouraging them to open the book and start consuming – in the ways that are most important and most empowering for them. *We can manipulate our audience into making themselves better people and letting us help.*

In information marketing, if the box is never opened, the product will be returned. The same is true in Podcasting. If our listeners lack the knowledge of how to readily consume in different contexts, we can't grow organically. By teaching consumption and delivering high-quality content, we can flourish organically and accelerate any and every business opportunity.

CONCLUSION

Podcasting is not a trend or fad that will quickly be replaced by something else. It is a massive paradigm shift in media communication that puts the consumer in charge. Just like the introduction of the printing press changed the face of Bible distribution, the introduction of the Podcast changes the expectation of how media is delivered and how it is consumed.

Podcasting is a medium that has the potential to maximize business intimacy, accelerate the speed of communication, and boost the bottom line by time and place shifting information content. It places the power of the Internet in the hands of your customer allowing for the promise of this book, *Wherever My Market Is, I Am.*

Businesses that embrace Podcasting and develop strategies for distributing their content and information via this channel will find themselves communicating with their audience (potential and existing) in the most effective and intimate of ways.

AT THE PRIVATE MEMBER SITE

A recording entitled "Monetize Your Podcast in 30 Days or Less" is located at this book's Private Member Website. You can download the recording and transcriptions (and additional content on the "Why" of Business Podcasting) at:

http://www.TheBusinessPodcastingBible.com/why

CHAPTER TWO

"The public, who consume the new commodity or profit by the new invention, are much better judges of its merit than the government can be."

—Charles Babbage

"Wash / Rinse / Repeat"

—Shampoo Bottle

The most basic element of Podcasting from the perspective of the business user is consumption—not accessed feeds or MP3 files and iPods®. *You will never truly understand Podcasting until you start consuming them yourself*[1]. Without a doubt, this is an experiential medium. Anyone who is truly serious about involvement has to begin with his or her own consumption. Many of you who are reading this are already listening to several Podcasts. The others need to take that first step once this book has taken you through the process. And don't just listen from your computer. We want

---

1. If you have yet to consume a Podcast, we recommend the purchase of an iPod before you go any further in this book. The education that will come from downloading a Podcast for yourself and taking the power of the Internet with you on a walk will teach you more than this chapter ever will. It is a highly experiential medium and to understand it, you must experience it first for yourself. Feel free to look up "Marketing Online Live" in iTunes and listen to the very show that launched this book.

you to consume Podcasts during movement as portable media. You want to take the power of the Internet into the palm of your hand.

A real understanding of Podcast Consumption will write your Podcasting strategy for you. It is nothing as simple as *place headphone on head and push play* as it is a vehicle for communication that is far more intimate in nature and powerful in scope.

HOW TO CONSUME A PODCAST

As mentioned in the first chapter, Podcasts are consumed, *when and where the consumer wishes to consume them.* In addition, parts deemed boring or unimportant are quickly skipped.

In addition, the physical location of the consumption dictates response options. A listener consuming your Podcast on the way to work can't visit your Website but can call an 800 number on their cell phone for more information. Another user listening to what you have to say while riding an exercise bike is not going to quit their workout to pick up the phone. Customers on an airplane have no immediate electronic communication option, whether they want it or not. Podcast consumption dictates strategy.

The Business Podcasting Bible is not a book on Podcast creation – it is a book on Podcast consumption. Plenty of fine tomes have already been written on that subject, and we will be sprinkling this book with some of those valuable resources and references[2]. We suggest that even those who feel more familiar with Podcasting approach this book as if you know nothing. We are going to begin with the lowest hanging fruit, giving you everything you need and walking you through the process. This *how* chapter defines the consumption of a Podcast as it differs from all of the other audio options currently available on the Internet. That basic but critical

---

2. Visit our Appendix "Podcast Creation Mentors" for a list of some of the top teachers in Podcast creation or log into the private member site at http://www.TheBusiness PodcastingBible.com for a frequently updated creation reference.

knowledge of consumption will be the key that allows you to leverage this medium to your advantage.

WHY IS AN UNDERSTANDING OF CONSUMPTION SO IMPORTANT?

Consumption tells us how consumers are utilizing a product or service or software. Walking in the shoes of your target market tells you how those people are consuming, what technology they are utilizing to consume, where they are consuming, and most importantly—*why*. The *why* is actually the easiest to ascertain in advance.

Where are Podcasts consumed? The answer could be on a subway, in a bus, in front of a computer, in bed with earphones, on a commuter train or airplane, by laptop or media player. *Virtually anywhere* is the answer that gives Podcasting such a powerful advantage (but provides the biggest challenge in directing a response). Answers to the *how* question could include a media player, the Internet, a computer where a Podcast has been downloaded, or even iTunes®, Yahoo!®, and other Web-based platforms.

Where remains the most important aspect of consumption because of the time-shifting element and the subset of convenience. *Where* is the power core of Podcasting. The Podcast receiver can consume information from virtually anywhere, creating a quantum leap over other modalities. Can you send an email or read a letter during your daily commute? No. Can you listen to Podcast while you're driving? Yes. What other element of the Internet can be brought into a daily workout?

From a business and educational perspective, audio Podcasts and video Podcasts live in different worlds. Video Podcasting is currently generating hype but fails to provide dead-time learning technology. I can't watch a video Podcast during my morning commute, but I can think of no better way to feed my brain in slow traffic than listening to a quality audio Podcast.

The issue also boils down to entertainment versus education: An audio-passive source of information versus an active source that demands visual attention. The far-reaching power of audio-passive cannot be overstated.

You can still hear a TV commercial if you walk into the next room for a snack. Knowing that audio Podcasts can be consumed from literally anywhere is the key to understanding your listeners. Grasping the *how* behind their consumption allows you to begin writing copy and content that encourages your audience to buy into your Podcast message.

Imagine being on an airplane with a Podcast that you downloaded about two hours ago. You can hardly wait to listen to the next issue of Marketing Online Live, because it's going to be all *about you and what is important to you.* In the dead time of air travel, you are suddenly listening to the Podcast you downloaded when you plugged the umbilical cord into your tower or laptop. The time shift of two hours has everything working to your advantage. The more clearly we understand the *where and how* of Podcast consumption, the more traction we will have.

Those who listen to Marketing Online Live have heard the same scenario on many occasions. You wake up in the morning, yawn, and walk over in your pajama bottoms to plug your media player into your tower. Whether your media player is an iPod, a Zen, or anything else—our Marketing Online Live Podcast is waiting for download. Once you are dressed and on the road, you find an open FM station and start listening to Alex and Paul in the middle of rush-hour traffic. That image conveys the power of Podcast and the power of understanding consumption. People can easily integrate these behaviors into their daily lives. Virtually anyone can be a Podcast receiver.

THE PODCAST CONSUMPTION PROCESS

The first necessity for consumption is some form of Internet access— usually high-speed and broadband[3]. Nighttime downloading options make it possible for someone with a traditional dial-up connection to access their Podcast as well.[4] The next requirement is a Podcast aggregator, more

---

3. And not necessarily by the Podcast consumer. We have received emails from subscribers who have their secretary burn Podcast content to CD so that they can listen in their car stereo on the way to and from work.

4. Broadband Internet access recently passed the 75% penetration rate so slower connection options are quickly becoming moot.

popularly termed a "Podcatcher" or just traditional web access.

iTunes from Apple, Inc. represents the 800-pound gorilla of the Podcasting aggregation because it is the only means to (legally) put any form of content on the Apple iPod. It is by no means, however, the most powerful and not even the easiest to use. Still, at the time of this writing, iTunes claims an 82 percent market penetration. Talking about other podcatching clients is risky because the industry changes at a lightning pace. We will mention a few top dogs, but who knows what their fate will be even by the time of publication (but they will, of course, be tracked in the Private Member Site (http://www.TheBusinessPod castingBible.com/how).

Podcasts.Yahoo.com is a great Web-based Podcatching and listening system that integrates with Yahoo!'s subscription music system through a Podcasting plug in. Odeo.com offers a Podcatcher and a player that are both web and desktop-based. Juice; formerly the iPodder Lemon product, went through a name change under pressure from Apple's litigation process relating to all websites that included the name iPod. The remaining contenders are many but have failed to penetrate the market at a depth worth mentioning.

Within this Podcast aggregation world are web-based versions for desktop listening, those for laptop consumption, and

iPod as the platform

There are still a lot of buzzwords and jargon surrounding the Podcasting space. The explanation of Podcasting is so much easier without including the terms: podcatching, RSS subscriptions, downloading, or multiple player types and models.

You can do that with what we call the *iPod as the platform* strategy.

In short, if your Business Podcasting language is simply that of iTunes and iPods, everything get a lot simpler for everyone involved. In fact, some people will be considering the entirety of their Podcasting infrastructure and strategy only on Apple's platform because of the very simplicity that such a distribution mechanism enables.

Instead of detailed subscription directions, a simple "Click Here to Listen to This Podcast On Your iPod" button could simplify the process considerably (and push the "best" consumption strategy mentioned earlier in this chapter).

Keep in mind the following: iPods work on both Mac and PC platforms. The number one portable player for the PC is the iPod. The number one Podcatching client is iTunes. The penetration of iPod and iTunes as platform is greater than 80 percent[5]. These products have a hold on the industry that compares to no other, and we see no reason for this to change. The iTunes platform enables

---

5. At time of writing, 88.4% of the Marketing Online Live audience downloaded our show on iTunes (Mac and Windows).

portable media players. Some web-based applications allow click-to-play, including Yahoo! and Odeo. Many specific Podcast websites also provide click-to-play options.

There are, as you can see, many ways to consume or catch a Podcast.

Click-to-play Web-based strategies present an interesting sidebar for Business Podcasting initiatives. In short the problem is this: if they don't have to subscribe to listen, what reason will they have to subscribe? If they don't subscribe – you don't have the power of Podcasting, you merely have the power of online audio.

Begin with the simple question: Do I want to discourage subscriptions by enabling a click-to-play strategy? Making the process easy is a good way to draw larger numbers of initial listeners. However, the typical consumer's thinking runs along these lines: "I can always come back; I don't need to subscribe." And statistically, most never return. You must decide whether you want a web-based playing opportunity or subscriptions only. One strategy is to have only the most recent episode or even the first five minutes of your most recent episodes available for click-to-play. Fill the first 10 minutes with plenty of juice and nectar then create an option strategy.

Giving your audience something that is useful but incomplete is known as *cognitive dissident* in psychological terms. It may be incomplete, but listeners have access to it without having to subscribe and can make their decision based on what they know, not what they are promised.

Subscribing is a decision—good or bad. Our strategy encourages them to play a little bit with a single click and then we create an option to subscribe with a clear description of the benefits if they do. Certainly, with Business Podcasting, this teaser approach is likely to be the future of single-click play. Right now, the standard approach with Yahoo! and many popular websites is the ability to click-to-play without subscribing. You'll need to determine the weakness or strength of this strategy.

We are also talking about free content up to this point. Moving into paid content will polarize our audiences. Our business-to-business focus will polarize into business-to-consumer, which seems to be all free right now. What is B-to-B? A good example is teaching another business how to Podcast. Entertaining a businessperson at home the way *Newsweek* does would be classified as business-to-consumer. Teaching someone how to lose weight is another example of B-to-C. However, teaching people how to utilize a technology that is specifically designed to help their business make more money falls under B-to-B. The gray areas in the definitions of B-to-B and B-to-C cause a great deal of confusion. Today, the overwhelming majority of Podcasts are perceived as B-to-C.

the burning of Podcast CDs for free – a strategy that should not be undervalued.

Finally, iPods are available for less than $100. Although the iPod Shuffle currently lacks a screen, the affordability of these products is very appealing.

Those who are seriously considering a Podcast delivery element to their business need to examine the possibility of iPod and iTunes as the entirety of their platform.

Along with Internet access and Podcast aggregation is a requirement that many people overlook: *a computer that plays audio.* This is especially critical within the B-to-B community. Audio is traditionally achieved through a sound card. Most computers including laptops, which tend to be a business asset these days, provide built-in sound cards, but they are often muted out of respect to co-workers (or as a matter of corporate policy). The sound might be muted by default or just turned off. Some organizations prefer this silence to the din created by 200 computers all making noise in one large room.

Although audio capability can be built in or added on, Podcasters cannot assume that their base of listeners have access to it. That fact must be taken into account. If you create a video Podcast, your audience obviously needs software that can play Internet video. Potential Podcast consumers who can meet the two relatively simple requirements of audio and video can use a podcatcher to download a Podcast and consume it via personal computer. Having a high-speed Internet connection allows them to surf the web and click to listen to any Podcast. *However, that access remains stationary.*

IS THE CONSUMPTION EXPERIENCE GOOD, BETTER, OR BEST?

All Podcasts are not created (or consumed) equally. A Podcast consumed at a desk with the volume turned down low is only a percentage as powerful as a show taken to the gym or in the car. As you plan your Podcast strategy, an examination of the consumption experience is mandatory.

The *ideal* vehicle for Podcast consumption—which is especially true of the Business Podcasting we are examining in this book—is a portable media player that provides *mobile access which allows consumption on the consumer's terms.* Once consumers start using that PMP to move content from their computer terminal into any desired location, the power of the Internet is suddenly in their hands[6] (and yours to harness).

---

6. PMPs are by no means synonymous with the term iPod. Portable media players range from $30 discount models that can play a five or six-hour Podcast to $400-plus iPods from Apple with 60 GB of video.

The PMP is such a vital element to the ideal consumption experience that those who are producing a premium[7] or highly monetizable Podcast may want to consider free distribution of the media player. Consumers who aren't willing to buy a media player will often take one, place content on it, and take that jump on your behalf. The investment will make financial sense if consumption of the product continues (and monetization ensues). You can see examples of this promotional approach everywhere. Cell phones are free with activation. DVD players are sometimes sold for less than the DVDs themselves. The Tivo unit is now free with a year's subscription. The concept of a free portable media player as part of a paid content subscription is completely realistic (and strategically viable)

One word stands above all the others in relevance to consumption. The same word made the invention of the telephone so revolutionary and gives mobile phones and the Internet such incredible power. That word is *access*. Podcasts offer access to important information that can be consumed in nearly any way imaginable. Furthermore, you subscribe to this information from anywhere in the world. Podcast access is wider and enjoys a much larger reach of context than any media form we have seen to date.

While context is decisive, receiving information depends on access. Tivo gives me access to my favorite TV show even when I am not around. Sure, that access is later than actual air time, but the technology still allows me to consume it. Access is the key that empowers GoToMyPC.com®. This remote PC access tool made it possible for me to step off the airplane in Singapore, walk up to a free terminal and write the words "I love you" to my wife on a Microsoft Word® document in my home computer. Then I sent her an email that told her to check my computer. We are not only talking about access—we are talking about instant access, and, in many cases, *free instant access*. The power is in the hands of the consumer.

PMPs with a hard drive offer the *best experience*. Instead of storing four shows you think you might want to consume, you can store 400 hours of

---

7. For more information on Premium Podcasting, see our Appendix: Charging for Podcasts.

The Apple Enhanced Podcast Format

In addition to the traditional MP3 file format, Apple offers a file format for "Enhanced Podcasts." To use an Apple-enhanced Podcast, you have to play it on an iPod or in iTunes. The trade-off is a number of features that are not available in the MP3 format, such as the use of chapter marks and images.

When you break a Podcast into chapters using this format, the fast-forward and rewind buttons on your iPod become chapter skips. This chapter functionality has tremendous power in situations where a listener has no interest in a specific topic or wants to quickly find the section where they previously stopped. It also puts the listener in additional control as they can quickly find

shows to pick from when inspiration hits. The consumption paradigm then completely changes. For example, four shows on a flash player in our first example would easily take you through a traditional airplane flight. However, a hard drive filled with content would give you a chance to catch up with additional information during that unexpected layover in Denver. Now we have moved into *best experience*.

Best experience encompasses the subject of great headphones, and cheaper players tend to produce tiny audio. The iPod quality is acceptable, but headphones are available that make the experience considerably better. Noise-reduction headphones offer an entirely different way to experience content. It may seem odd to have headphones fives times the size of your media player, but using that noise-reduction headphone set on the plane will offer an entirely different Podcast experience. The last element of the best experience is the FM transmitter that enables you to play that Podcast from your car stereo with the click of a button. None of these enhancements are necessary for portable access via a PMP, but they certainly do provide the best experience.

Even technophobes who are already used to listening to their radio can appreciate the transition from something haphazardly coming over the airwaves into a permission based Podcast that they really wanted to hear. This power of self-direction is inherent with

Podcast consumption. First is the visual experience as they plug in to retrieve the information. Once in the car, they find an open FM station and begin listening to their heart's desire. The difference is predictability—of knowing what is going to be on versus wondering what kind of content will come through. Will it be a repeat? Is the guy in a bad mood? What does Paul Harvey have to say today? When will this annoying commercial end?

Using the example of the car and the antenna has drawn criticism from people who point out the many steps that have to be taken to make this happen and the equipment involved. Some people even question if we are receiving an affiliate commission from the antenna company. In spite of any complications, this is still the least resistant way for someone to enjoy access to a Podcast in a car[8]. It is the easiest way for a person to jump from what they are already doing into where they would like to be. That's why we repeatedly use this example.

The difference between the FM transmitter and the cassette adapter is really quite simple. All car stereos have radio—not all cars have cassette these days. You may have cassette capability at home, but

their way through any particular Podcasts.

Another advantage of these enhanced Podcasts is a multimedia presentation with images that serve to illustrate the spoken word. These images can be hyper-linked, enabling a call-to-action opportunity such as *Click here for details* or *Click to subscribe.* In the extremely popular program with host Adam Curry called The PodFinder Podcast, iTunes actually offers the best of selected Podcast shows. The iTunes screen presents an image of the show on your iTunes screen that offers and promotes automatic subscriptions. Part of the power of this approach is the simple call to action.

It is important to note that images that are stunning on the desktop screen become very small on the smaller

---

8. More and more cars are being built without cassette desks – yes, we are familiar with the cassette adapter option but have rented too many cars without the option to recommend it as the standard.

iPods—especially the Nano. Limited content from a consumption standpoint can be placed upon it, but it remains a powerful one-up for the enhanced Podcast format.

Audible's Spoken Word format, used for ebooks and their Wordcasting service, enables chapters and associated images but does not enable click-to-image and other advanced features.

Is the Apple-enhanced Podcast worth examining for those who want to add some level of interactivity into their Podcasts? Definitely. Just keep in mind the two major limitations. First, you are confined to the iPod. When enhanced Podcasts are your only mechanism of publishing, you are essentially forcing people to use the iPod. Secondly, any click-to-call action will mean

you can't bank on that rental car you pick up at the airport to have a cassette adapter for an iPod. If you take an FM transmitter, you are good to go. Lately on the road, I have noticed people with little singer headphones and wonder how many are hands-free telephone options and what percentage are actually MP3 players.

As you can see, we are really looking at good, better, and best consumption experiences. The *good* process is web-based. You discover a Podcast through a friend's recommendation or via a Podcast search engine like My Podcast Center, Yahoo!, or other websites. Whether you click-to-pay or download at that point, web-based consumption offers *only stationary access*. Not only does the Podcast lack portability, it is not automatic. You have to repeat the same steps each time that you listen. Silly messages like *Check back often!* or *Bookmark this website!* are ineffectual. People are not going to return without a good reason. That's why the web-based process is in no way desirable. Podcasters are faced with grabbing email addresses just to ping people accordingly whenever the show changes.

For whatever reason, if all you can get is "good," go for it – but aim for better or best if at all possible.

Now let's review *better*: The access point is a podcatcher that pushes content to subscribers. They no longer have to go out and pull down content on a regular basis through a web connection (or repeat the steps every time you wish to lisen). Subscriptions can be handled in various ways. The Yahoo! Podcast directory and the iTunes Podcast search engine are single-click interfaces. Click on the button and that subscription is automatically added to your system. That simple approach is the ideal and what many people already expect.

Another approach is to ask subscribers to cut-and-paste an Internet address in order to bring the show into the podcatcher. Each Podcast has a web address similar to a web page. This is obviously much less desirable than the one-click interface. Reconfigured podcatchers are another option, where subscribers download pod-catching software that is preconfigured with existing shows.

For all Podcasters, the true automatic (and portable) subscription is the *best* option. When a podcatcher-based subscription offers automatic downloads, usually in the background at a self-determined time, that are transferred to a portable player, the Podcasting process has become so easy that it almost becomes hard not to consume the content. Now you are free to roam about the world and consume that Podcast anywhere, anytime, when the mood strikes. No prep time is required – minus having to grab your iPod on the way out the door.

The last important question deals with consumption habits: Are they regular and nothing if your listener is taking that iPod on the road or consuming the media on a portable player. Rather than catering to the mainstream, the enhanced Podcast appeals more to early adopters and those who just want the extra glitz.

Which introduces the question: What are the options for non-Apple listeners? Many Podcasts with enhanced Podcast feed also provide non-iPod users with the traditional, non-enhanced feed. If your personal Podcast strategy depends heavily on enhanced features like calls to action or clicks and images, a stripped-down version would be self-defeating.

Because the Apple-enhanced Podcast is certainly not in its final revision and will change through time, it will be interesting to see what direction it takes.

Certainly, it has value from a forecasting point of view. Enhanced Podcasts may be 180 degrees from the garden variety of boring Podcasts, but neither one of these extremes are ideal for monetization.

Note: At the private member site for this book, we will continue to track the implication and penetration of the Apple enhanced Podcast format and the competitors that are sure to follow suit. For more information about the private member site, please see our appendix, "About the Business Podcasting Bible Member Site"

routine? If so, how will changes in that routine alter consumption? With proper set up, you can change email software providers and still receive your other email. It doesn't matter if you have upgraded to a new version of Outlook™ or changed to EUDORA®. If people change their consumption patterns for your Podcast, will they suddenly decide that they no longer have the time or the ability to listen to your show? Maybe their work-time commute changed or the dog mangled their iPod.

The ultimate power of Podcasting—the power of the Internet in your hand—introduces a wild card in terms of consumption. Television producers know *exactly* how their content will be consumed—the audience will be sitting down and passively watching from a short distance. Podcast content can be consumed in very different ways, opening the door to an entire world of unique opportunities.

PODCAST CONSUMPTION SCENARIOS

This examination of Podcast consumption actually covers nine different scenarios—each one with varying consumption styles that result in different production strategies. This list is not end-all inclusive, but it does represent the lion's share of options that the business community should be examining. The first critical issue affecting these scenarios is direct Internet access or some form of

Internet-based call to action. Podcasters who want listeners to interact are going to need a two-way communication vehicle. If the majority of their listeners are lacking that capability during their consumption process, interaction should not be part of the process. Other "calls to action" might take the form of 1-800 telephone access. The question to ask: What percentage of the listening audience will be able to take advantage of that?

1. Computer work time

Particularly within the business community, work-time in front of a computer is still the prime time of consumption for Podcasts. Whether web-based or podcatcher-based, Podcasts are consumed while someone is checking email or working on the computer.

2. Non-computer work time

The computer is still involved but the Podcast show is just playing in the background. The listener is busy eating lunch, filing, sorting mail or some other non-computer activity.

3. Commute time

The drive time to work is defined by a regularly scheduled, predictable situation. The average 20- to 30-minute, one-way commute provides four to five hours of potential consumption time every week.

4. Unplanned down time

Completely unexpected delays like a four-hour traffic jam or an unplanned layover create a window for extended consumption. Now you can take advantage of the additional hours of content that you placed in the queue without knowing whether or not the opportunity to consume would arise. Of course, this would be impossible without the power of the Internet in the palm of your hand.

5. Exercise time

Why do so many people love to consume Podcasts during exercise? Sure, they can feed their brain while they work their body – it is the ultimate win/win. The mind set during those more excruciating moments as the sweat pours down is similar to that of a commuter in traffic: I have nothing better to do than throw myself into this Podcast.

6. Chore time

Many people like to consume Podcasts as a diversion during their chores—cooking, mowing the lawn, or painting the fence. As a culture, we are already accustomed to listening to music while we work and Podcast consumption can often enhance and enrich that content.

7. Travel time

Less predictable than commuting time, travel time—once it has been set—provides a longer stretch of time for consumption. Someone who regularly consumes Podcasts might bring as many as eight hours of play time for a four-hour flight—just in case. Look at the rate card for any in-flight magazine to realize the power of a potential customer with little distractions and a lot of time to consume a product.

8. Entertainment time

With the rise in Podcast quality, many people are turning away from the consumption of traditional media during their leisure hours. Instead of watching "whatever is on TV" for an hour, they are enjoying a video Podcast or listening to a standard Podcast from an easy chair. Imagine customer loyalty if you could take the place of the "idiot box" in their life.

9. Planned time

The last, and possibly one of the most exciting, consumption scenarios—particular for those reading this book—is planned time. Listeners now have a compelling *reason* to consume. Because of a specific training program or some subscription service, they are devoting Monday nights at 8:00 PM to consume a Podcast.

Each one of these scenarios elicits a different interaction, a different level of intensity, and different levels of predictability. Yet, they are all important and part of the game.

What, when, where, who, why, and how are all encompassed within the universe of Podcast consumption:

- *What* simply refers to "which Podcast?"

- *When* and *where* are closely related but *where* is more pictorial, more visual. After all, *when* is anytime. *Where* might be while riding my John Deere mower.

- *How* relates to access: via computer or media player and other options.

- *Why* is extremely important.

We are educators, not entertainers. We are saying, "Show me what you do with your dead time and I can show you how successful you can be. If you prefer to listen to U2, fine. But many people want to hear something that can motivate, educate, stimulate—something with the power to move their lives or careers forward. Certainly, most corporate executives and entrepreneurs would prefer to transform dead time into time spent feeding their brains.

We certainly do that. For longer commutes like driving from Los Angeles to San Francisco, my stack of CDs has become a lineup of Podcasts. In my office at lunchtime while I am chewing a sandwich—I am digesting the latest message that I missed yesterday from the CEO of my company on my iPod or iPod Nano. I need to "cheat" before the meeting scheduled immediately after lunch.

STATIONARY VERSUS PORTABLE ACCESS

Access begins to change form in definition. What is a PDA? What is a BlackBerry™? What makes these tools so powerful? Access, of course—sometimes to the point of obsession. Users of these technologies get access to content in places they never would have before. Stationary access means a computer, the Tivo, or the home media center that requires a listener to go to a certain place to receive the media content. Portable media player options, both audio and video, change that scenario by offering portability – access where you choose.

Preconfigured pod-catchers

Considering all of the headaches associated with configuring and loading content with an iPod or PMP, there is nothing more valuable than a preloaded media player. The media player alone is really a host without little value of its own until it begins to communicate information *on demand*. Audio players, DVD players, CD players—none of these electronic devices have value beyond the data or information you choose to put into them. Preloading an iPod is analogous to placing a blade into your razor. Not only does preloaded content offer a critical measure of simplification and convenience, it opens the door to monetization.

To give you a sense of just how powerful this can be, let's review an

Portable access has a great impact on the volume of consumption that can take place. The hours spent in front of a computer each day are limited, but we can carry a 1.5-ounce iPod Nano almost anywhere.

VIDEO VERSUS AUDIO CONSUMPTION

Video Podcasts are enjoying a great deal of attention. Simply stated, they "sell" well and are easy to consume (although their role of one-off replacement or consumption alternative has yet to be proven). The impulse buy of 1 of (at time of printing) 150 different television shows on iTunes has made the option of portable video consumption an attractive one to many. Admit it, the video iPod is a very good looking device.

The image of a DVD springs to mind with the mention of the word *video*. As much as we love DVDs, they require a DVD player. We are back to *stationary access*[9]. Being able to play that DVD in your iPod is real power – being able to take multiple movies with you on a trip in a form factor the size of a deck of cards is suddenly extremely attractive. And, in terms of video and audio, we want capability and access from the same player – the iPod gives that to us.

---

9. Yes, there are portable DVD player options but they represent a tiny percentage of overall DVD consumption.

I personally use 10 times as much audio as I do video. Bad hair days, poor lighting, or any number of factors may exclude the use of communicating through video. Video tends to be more polished and requires more preparation. Those who have edited video know how many elements are involved and how expensive the job can become.

From the perspective of an information marketer, video means a keynote speech. Video means—something more than just a talking head. Perhaps it means a Webinar recorded for later consumption. Regardless of the form, video is not as *accessible* as audio. Many activities that demand our attention like driving a car exclude the use of video. We can't watch video in the background in the way we can listen to audio and still be able to pay attention to whatever else we might be doing. Illustration: the next time you stroll by a large television display at the store, try to watch two different TV programs at the same time. We inherently know how much of our attention is captured by video versus audio. The same boss who doesn't mind you listening to soft music in the background is not likely to tolerate you watching a video on the computer screen.

The initial reaction of business users to Podcast video is the ability to insert a traditional commercial piece into the media. Traditional commercial insertion, although fully capable within video Podcasting, should be limited. The iPod scroll option

example of the way we are currently working with the Apple iPod. Granted, Apple is not the easiest company to deal with because of its size, the technology, and thin margins. Companies like Keystone Electronics have a typical two-times retail margin, while Apple margins range from 10 percent to 30 percent tops in most cases. So our strategy involves buying the media players at retail and engraving *Limited Edition* on the back.

Apple is offering the personalization for vanity reasons so buyers can have their iPods laser-engraved with a name or some brief greeting. We are successfully leveraging this option to create our own *Limited Edition Alex Nano, 1 of 39.* We just slice open the box in a very clean, convenient way and preload the iPod. We can load 21 hours of content on an iPod Nano. Furthermore, we can Podcast even more information on that Nano, later, after they've experienced the value of the content. Beautiful!

Basically, we have created a subscription base to monetize. The value of the iPod Nano is now set by the Podcaster, so cost is not $100 or even $1,000. The price is $1,997 and worth 10 times that amount in valuable content. So the strategy involves giving away the preloaded Nano, which has been repackaged with a sticker that reads: *Before you break the shrink-wrap, call this 24 hour recorded message.* The voice of Alex Mandossian is waiting to greet them and tell them exactly what to do.

This approach frees the consumer from searching for CDs that

makes it extremely easy to fast-forward through anything. Commercial or content, the user remains in complete and total control. That's why subsidizing a video Podcast through the traditional commercial insertion is ridiculous—those commercials will never be consumed – let alone acted on.

Advertising has even coined the new term, "Tivo Proofing," where product placement within the content becomes part of the strategy. We are seeing good use of this technique on a regular basis in reality shows such as *The Apprentice* and *Survivor* and only expect the trend to continue to grow. Tivo Proofing represents a real shift in the relationship between commercials and video content, and video Podcast should absolutely learn from what is happening in the television industry. On the other hand, the elimination of traditional video delivery channels is extremely exciting. We now have the freedom to deliver video content without pressing DVDs and making sure they reach the intended recipient.

Along with iTunes Podcasting and the ability to communicate via video Podcast, products such as Tivo and Akimbo® make non-traditional distribution channels for video content very easy and doable. Many people are concerned about the battle associated with web video. Does it have an associated monetization angle? The cost of providing a two-hour lecture via Internet video will always be less than the cost of pressing and mailing out a DVD. When video is advantageous as part of the consumption process, the distribution to the Podcasting channel can be an incredible asset. Still, the impact and role of video and the emphasis it should receive must be determined on a case-by-case basis.

Now let's flip to the audio consumption side of the house and use a commonly understood analogy: television versus radio. Most people consume a considerably different amount of television over radio during an average week. This consumption disparity is the underlying reason that we need to closely examine audio versus video Podcasting. Audio Podcasting is going to exponentially reach more people, more often, and usually more effectively.

Video is doable, obtainable, and very attractive through this channel. But from the pure vantage point of effectiveness, audio always maintains the upper hand. Audio provides greater access in more places with more ease and convenience. Sure, video adds a new dimension of sensory stimulation. But it lacks the power of passivity and the intimacy that is created by *unlimited access*. Audio access can be more frequent, faster, and easier. Consumption can be literally anywhere, in any circumstance, including those times when our attention must remain at least partially on something else.

Audio certainly holds the greatest power for us as business professionals. Audio is the

fell through the seat of the car or lugging around cases of DVDs and CDs. No more worries about cracked jewel cases or annoying scratches. All the listener has to do is carry that convenient little iPod. Hopefully, it will be the Alex Mandossian iPod Nano.

We believe this approach is the future of information marketing. The people who will be making the big money will be those who are creating the stands on the wall that hold the various iPods with names like Mark Victor Hansen, Alex Mandossian, Paul Colligan or other leading information marketers. Each iPod Nano will feature a unique player, person, or talent. Filling up 2 Gig with valuable content, which is easy for us to do, is worth several thousand dollars. With 4 Gig, the cost would go up to $5,000. Why not? The price includes free updates for an entire year.

The benefit to consumers is a constant flow of *worthwhile information marketing content* that does not require a stack of CDs or DVDs that stands taller than they do. A consumer can hold an iPod Nano as thin as a pencil in the palm of his hand and carry it virtually anywhere.

It also teaches them the value of portable media content first, without requiring that they go through the hoops of downloading a Podcatcher, connecting to the Internet, etc.

Preloaded portable media players offer a real object lesson in the potential value of content over the media player. What value is an iPod? If a song sells for 99 cents and the entirety of a band's career can be placed on an iPod for half

answer when we need to develop a consumption strategy that reaches the most people in the widest possible number of places. Dead-time learning does not require video. "Prime Time" entertainment is dead without it. With enough valuable input headed for the brain, dead-time can even be monetizable. Would the CEO of your company mind if you listened to his message in the dead-time of commuting or flying on an airplane or eating lunch? "Hey, what are you listening to?" The answer would be "You."

Most companies today are thrilled to hand laptops and cell phones to their employees because of that very reality. Perhaps you will catch up on a report or follow up on an important phone call during the dead-time at the airport. The price tag for providing that technology is well worth the cost. Sure, an employee might use the portable laptop for personal email and occasionally make a phone call home on the corporate cell phone. Executives and managers have run the numbers and know the value of enabling their employees. The same approach is easily transferable to Podcasting.

SUBCONSCIOUS MODALITIES OF PODCAST CONSUMPTION

The subtitle may be a tongue twister, but we need to consider four subconscious modalities of Podcast consumption that are considerably different from other "traditional" forms of media. We have already made many comparisons to radio versus television and CDs or FM stations. However, these four areas of Podcast consumption are unequaled. Embracing and understanding these subconscious modalities will bring you to a new pinnacle of communication that will make a world of difference in your Podcasting corporate strategies.

NUMBER ONE: PLAY-BUTTON POWER

Users who are in control of beginning, ending, and taking a break are truly engaged in permission based consumption. The freedom to decide *what*, *when*, and *how* we will consume places us in a position of power. The originator of the message has subconsciously enabled that level of control and the listeners will express their gratitude—consciously or subconsciously. If I have to choose between a program that requires stationary consumption versus one that I can consume when and where I please, I will choose B every single time. That's play button power.

NUMBER TWO: EARPIECE INTIMACY

Earpiece intimacy is a vital element of Podcasting as an intimate form of communication. Nine times out of ten, listeners will plug a piece of plastic into their ears. Now you can speak to them directly while they are

the price of the cheapest iPod, the value may be significant. However, the caliber of training materials and information marketing content within our industry carries an intrinsic worth of $5,000, $10,000 or $20,000. The value of *that* iPod is absolutely insignificant in comparison to the content it holds.

As long as the content paradigm remains focused on free Podcasts and 99-cent songs, the value remains in the player. When the content paradigm shifts to a highly valuable information marketing network, the player becomes a mute point. One of the most exciting elements of preconfigured media players is their potential to have everyone pointed and thinking in the right direction.

exercising or strolling through the park. If you are not talking to them direct-ly through an earpiece, it might be via the FM transmitter on the drive home from work. In that instance, you could easily be the person who is sitting beside them in the front seat and carrying on a dialog. Think for a moment about the sea of faceless bulk email ads, junk mail, and billboard ads that remains so distant. Podcasting enables earpiece intimacy that is simply and completely without comparison. Any Podcast that sounds like every other broadcast is failing to utilize its own inherent power.

We all know the experience created by headsets or earphones that block out all other stimuli. No matter what the medium, when outside noise disappears, intimacy increases. If you listen to a Podcast on your stereo or computer, you might be distracted by the rumble of the trash truck outside your door. Not so with a headset. Now the Podcaster is your sole stimulus and the two of you are married in a dialog, and dialog encompasses *listening*.

That earpiece provides incredibly powerful access to the person who is using it. As a Podcaster, that simple tool gives me permission to date the listener—first casually, then more frequently, and finally exclusively. Eventually, we might become engaged and get married. Divorce in this case would be analogous to unsubscribing or asking for a refund.

NUMBER THREE: TIME SHIFTED THANKS

In many respects a subset of play-button power is time shifted thanks, which is important enough to receive unique consideration. Play-button power relates to the remote-control mentality. The person who holds the remote has the power of decision, although those decisions are limited at any given moment by the available channels and programs.

The best analogy for time shifted thanks is the additional freedom offered by VCR and Tivo remote controls. Now the consumer has complete control of the time and sequence: Start, pause, fast-forward, rewind, stop, or start over. Unless competitors are offering that level of control, it places your consumers in a position of subconscious gratitude. We live crazy lives filled with unpredictable twists and turns. We appreciate the chance to participate in something that only requires 15 minutes out of our day in the time and place of our choosing. That might be during our daily commute, our weekend housework, or the one day a month we set aside to tie up loose ends. The appreciation we feel is time shifted thanks—which is considerably more powerful than play-button power.

Time shifting places the level of urgency in the palm of the hand or in the mind of the consumer. The person who is doing the consuming is ultimately accountable for listening or viewing. I might want to use my Tivo to record the Super Bowl so that I can review plays after the fact. If I want to participate in the "who won" surprise, I need to watch the Super Bowl on television when it is actually aired. The cost of Super Bowl advertising is a living testament to the urgency that most people feel about that element of surprise.

The person who is consuming the Podcast controls the sense of urgency. What makes that so intriguing? The more principal-centered the Podcast becomes, the more ageless its content and the greater the time-shifting impact. Our Marketing Online Live Podcast, which is really a news piece with a principal-centered duo, integrates personality with character. The hot news story is the sexy part, the sizzle. The principle-centered marketing angles that we discuss are the backbone; the roots of the tree. The character behind the personality is the element that attracts listeners and subscribers. We constantly get emails from new listeners who "just heard" a show 6 months old thanking us for the content.

Time shifting determines content. A time shifted newspaper is completely irrelevant. Knowing yesterday's stock quote is probably of little consequence if I am buying that stock today. The bottom line is consumer control: I will act when I am moved to do so, and that is highly intimate. The consumer is saying, "I want to listen to you when I want to listen to you." Typically, that translates into *when it is convenient for me to listen*. It would be interesting to evaluate the behavior patterns of our listeners if we announced a specific time when our Podcasts would be available. The faster the download, the more keenly interested that person would be in our content.

When the two of us recently returned from a vacation, we were buried in emails and physical mail from people who were clamoring for information that they wanted last week. At the same time, we both wanted to listen to a series of Podcasts. While the 32 clamoring customers represented a level of frustration, we were totally in control of our Podcast consumption. If those Podcasts could have left a message, it would sound like this: "We'll just be waiting here on your hard drive when you are ready to listen—no problem." Some we listened to immediately because we needed the information. Others waited for a more opportune moment. That sense of time shifted thanks is a level of gratitude that traditional media lacks. The same person who is thrilled by immediacy one moment is elated to delay consumption the next.

NUMBER FOUR: ANONYMOUS CONTROL

Anonymous control is subconscious yet extremely real. Most people who read commercial email know that some sort of tracking is in place. They realize that a visit to a commercial website will generate certain statistics about their computer. This level of *watching* has nothing to do with invasion of privacy or spyware. It is simply an integral part of Internet marketing.

Today's Podcast consumers have knowledge that is hidden from the Podcast originator. With existing technology, Podcasters have no way of knowing whether or not a consumer has truly *listened*. Someone might fast-forward through most of the program or listen to one part repeatedly with the rewind option. If a consumer found the entire 30 minutes in the middle to be worthless, the Podcaster would have no clue.

The anonymous user is in control.

Consider double-time listening. Most portable media players now offer the ability to listen to the spoken word at 1.2 or 1.5 times the normal speed. One of our Marketing Online Live listeners might decide that our 30-minute show is worth only 15 minutes of his time. Nothing is in place at this time that would give us any knowledge of that type of control and response. We do the same thing when we try to cram four hours of Podcast time into two travel hours. Is it possible? Sure, that's why people teach speed learning— how to turn up the MP3 speed and actually listen and absorb the content. We have the ability to consume any program the way we want without the Podcaster's knowledge.

While Podcast consumers can enjoy a conversation that is extremely intimate, they still maintain the upper hand of anonymous control over the play button. We have essentially added *play shifting* to the ultimate control of time shifting by allowing listeners to select the sections they want to hear and at what speed. Now we have a consumption model that puts a smile on our face. Everyone out there enjoys this feeling of control—a fact that is extremely important to understand as you begin to build a Podcast for your audience.

The anonymity factor has great appeal for the same reason that many philanthropists prefer to give without fanfare. They want to be part of the virtue of giving and enjoy all of the associated good feelings without being constantly hounded by people and organizations who want money. The same principal of anonymous control holds true in the world of spam versus subscriptions. The latter allows you to be an invited guest in a home with a host who appears at your whim. That power simply does not exist anywhere else.

REAL UNDERSTANDING OF CONSUMPTION WRITES STRATEGY

So much space has been devoted to consumption models and modes in this chapter because this in-depth understanding is critical to Podcasting success. Some factors will impact your strategies on a simple or mechanical level. For instance, creating anything longer than a 30-minute Podcast for a commuting audience is ridiculous. If your Podcast includes a call to action, you must provide a means for your audience to respond or at the very least offer a compelling reminder.

The more complex considerations revolve around the *mindset* of the listeners. People absorb information in many different ways for equally different reasons. After a long day of screaming at the kids, your wife will have a completely different mindset than she will after a week-long romantic beach vacation. Listeners who are battling rush-hour traffic can be easily frustrated. Those who are exercising or doing yard work or cooking can be distracted. If the theme of your Podcast is entertainment, your audience may have definite expectations. Unlike traditional media including television, a single Podcast often has multiple listeners with multiple consumption scenarios.

Do you have something for everyone? What is the mindset of consumption and are you performing to that mindset? Do you truly understand your audience and are you planning accordingly?

Remember: What is simple to understand will be consumed and utilized the most. Microsoft Word has been around for years, but most people only utilize a fraction of its power. Rather than taking advantage of the many advanced features, they just stick to the basics. The very simplicity of generating and initiating a communication in a Podcast makes it a powerful medium. Simplicity of access translates into anyone, anywhere, anytime.

We need to teach people how simple (and powerful) Podcast consumption can be. They can do what they are already doing with a minor difference but a major impact. They might need to plug in with a digital umbilical cord or USB connection and download into their portable media player. Maybe they will have to add a small antenna, go to their car and attach the antenna onto their iPod and then find an open FM station. That's exactly how Marketing Online Live successfully competes with morning radio for numerous CEOs, by offering permission based radio that is Podcasted and time shifted with the user in complete control.

At this point in the book, you've probably notice very little talk of the technologies at play here. A true understanding of consumption is much more important than a dialogue about the bitrate that your MP3 should be recorded at. In our appendix, "Podcast Creation Mentors" you can find all the technology information you need – just understand the consumption process first.

CONCLUSION

Before even the title of a future Podcast is conceived, a plan for optimizing and encouraging the best possible consumption experience should be developed.

A solid understanding of Podcast consumption writes the business plan for anyone who desires to launch a Business Podcast. A great consumption experience, mixed with the proper leverage of the subconscious modalities of the consumer will result in the ideal outcome for the Podcaster.

AT THE PRIVATE MEMBER SITE

A video walkthrough of the Marketing Online Live Podcast Website is provided at this book's Private Member Website. The video explains how we encourage and teach the best possible consumption strategies for the Podcast. You can view the video (and additional content on the "How" of Business Podcasting) at http://www.TheBusinessPodcastingBible.com/how

CHAPTER TWO   59

THE BUSINESS PODCASTING **BIBLE**

CHAPTER THREE

"Everybody who is incapable of learning has taken to teaching."
—Oscar Wilde

"That's the simplest way to explain it ... Podcasting is a factory that produces apple pies for whales."
—AskANinja.com, Special Delivery #1, *What Is Podcasting?*

Before we go much further, we need to understand what a Podcast actually is. In this chapter, you'll find that it is in fact two things: a *channel* and a *medium*. Understanding this duality in Podcasting is vital in developing a business strategy for the technology.

And, unlike what Ninja, one of the most popular video Podcasts on the planet says; it is a lot more than producing apple pies for whales ;-)

THE *WHAT* OF PODCASTING

Believe it or not, the geekier[1] element of the Podcasting community still argues about the "true" definition of the term Podcasting. Find five

---

1. In this book, and in our professional lives, we don't use the term geek as anything but a term of respect. Paul considers himself a geek as much as Alex considers himself a technophobe.

Podcasters, ask them to define what a Podcast is, and you'll actually get five very different answers. We, in fact, offer Ninja's definition to show you how broad the dialogue has gone (and to have a little fun with the process).

At the time of writing[2], Wikipedia, the open-source online encyclopedia defined Podcasting as follows:

> *"Podcasting is the method of distributing multimedia files, such as audio programs or music videos, over the Internet using either the RSS or Atom syndication formats, for playback on mobile devices and personal computers."*

What is even more important for the business community is the second sentence in the definition:

> *"The term Podcast, like 'radio', can mean both the content and the method of delivery."*

We cannot stress this fact enough: **This duality in the definition of Podcasting is the source of the Business Podcaster's power.**

This technology duality is not just found in Podcasting: Those who have listened to Alex's Teleseminar Secrets™ (http://www.teleseminar-secretspodcast.com) have heard this repeatedly: The telephone in your home is (for most people) a consumer product, just like your coffee maker. Most people don't make money from their home coffee maker. They just brew and consume and enjoy. That same coffee maker in a Starbucks has the potential to generate tens of thousands of dollars—perhaps millions. The context has changed, so the *what* is redefined.

Teleseminar Secrets™ teaches people how to use their home phone as a tool for monetization. Sure, the telephone is a channel of communication. But it can also be a distribution channel and a medium that enables you to monetize your voice and your content. Podcasting shares that paradigm. The

---

2. Wikipedia (http://www.wikipedia.org) is an "open source" online encyclopedia, that allows, truly anyone, the ability to edit and modify any entry at any time. It can, at times, be the ultimate online resource guide or the world's largest argument. At time of writing, we agreed with the definition offered but warn our readers that, at any time, their definition might change.

Podcast definition of *what* needs to encompass business purpose—not just consumer value but commercial business value.

In the case of Teleseminar Secrets™, the phone is many things. In the case of Business Podcasting, the Podcast is many things.

As suggested by the Wikipedia definition, we see the duality in radio as well – it is both a media format and a way of delivering that media format.

If the name of this book was *The Podcasting Bible*, we would be writing a 700-page tome. The *Business Podcasting Bible* defines a commitment to the *business* opportunities in Podcasting. These businesses might be selling to other businesses or to consumers, but we are speaking directly to the business person. We want our readers to don their business hats as they examine the value of *what* in this book. We want everyone to look through the business lens—not the consumer lens.

So, our definition of Business Podcasting is as follows:

The strategic leveraging of the Podcast channel and/or medium to expand your business.

CHANNEL OR MEDIUM?

Just because a communication is *delivered by Podcast* (or down the Podcast channel) does not necessarily mean that it *is* a Podcast, nor does it mean that the creators have any real understanding of the Podcast medium. Alex's Teleseminar Secrets is offered in (Premium) Podcast form, but it is the recordings of his 2 hour plus teleseminars. His production of the class doesn't spend a minute of time worrying about Podcasting – their goal is valuable audio content that is later delivered via Podcast to those who prefer to hear the content at the time and location of their choosing.

Another example of Podcast as channel is the extremely popular IT Conversations (http://www.itconversations.com). This aggregator of recordings from technology events serves tens of thousands of listeners with the recordings via multiple delivery formats, including the Podcast. IT Conversations wouldn't be where it is today without the technology of

Intimacy Demands Quality

Interruption advertising works when viewing from a distance – *yes, tens of thousands are watching (or listening) right now, and I'm sure some of them care about this product (or content), so I understand why they're doing this.*

It is ineffective, but tolerated. How many hours of radio traffic reports for freeways you'll never drive on do you tolerate to get that 15 second nugget on the road your about to turn on to? How many ads are inserted during that time frame?

Not true for a Podcast, *it's just me listening and if you aren't talking about what I am interested in, I'm leaving.*

What is the *real message* of your Podcast? If you are barraged with ads during the first

Podcasting, despite the small percentage of content at their site that is a true "Podcast."

In the example of Podcast as medium, I refer again to our Marketing Online Live Podcast (http://www.marketingonline live.com). The format, style, length and approach is entirely developed (and optimized) for listeners consuming the "show" on a PMP at the time and place of their choosing. We've received letters from very busy CEOs who listen on the ride into work and others who consume our show during their daily walks on the beach. This penetration never could have happened with a teleseminar, or live event, and we are thrilled with the results.

Another example of Podcast as medium is the extremely popular "This Week in Tech" (TWiT) Podcast (http://www.thisweek-intech.com). This show by technology writer and radio and television personality Leo Laporte is believed by many to be the most popular Podcast in the world[3]. Where the implications of TWIT are profound enough for a book of it's own, we point out a few things that help explain why TWiT could only happen in Podcast format: A) The show is never a set length in time (although they are usually around and hour long).

---

3. As will be discussed later, the very nature of Podcasting, unlike Internet radio, prevents specific listen numbers. Leo's show is, however, downloaded hundreds of thousands of times per episode and his impact in the "Podcasting Space" is uncontested.

They run it until the content is done, and then they close. No padding on this show. B) The same "gang" behind TWiT (remember, this is probably the world's most popular Podcast) came from a cancelled television show. What "didn't work" in the broad nature of cable television is extremely successful in the niche world of the Podcast. C) Although there is a constant call for fans to "bring back the old show", the freedom offered by this format has produced a show considerably better than anything they had on television.

While we try to make a distinction here, in the emerging world of Podcasting, the edges between the channel and the message tend to blur. As we discussed in Chapter Two, the Podcast channel simply relates to Podcast delivery, which provides a wealth of benefits over traditional channels. Podcasts are cheaper, faster, more convenient, and offer a time-shifting advantage to the consumer. People have the freedom to listen whenever and wherever. However, the channel is not the medium and the medium is not the channel. For example, if Teleseminar Secrets were ever delivered only by Podcast, the entire format for the class would change.

Podcast is first and foremost a communication medium just like television. With as many as 500 channels on cable, TV is a tremendously broad medium where channels act as subsets. Podcasting can be utilized as

minute of one, the (real) message is, "We are using this Podcast thing to lure you into spending money with our sponsors. Thank you for participating. We can click you off as a subscriber." Their *real response* is, they will never listen again.

If the first minute of the Podcast gets directly to the point — and that point is something very important to you (and the listener) — you have their complete and total attention.

People may visit an ugly website, but will they stay and linger — let alone buy something? Back in the early days of web design, one of my competitors bragged about 5,000 visitors a day. Truth be told, he had an army of interns who spent all day sending people to his website. Because his stats were open and accessible, I was able to confirm the 5,000 count—but only for the home (doorway) page. Less than 10 visitors a day were clicking through the informative pages on his website, so he was essentially offending 4,990 people and bragging about it.

If they download a Podcast but don't listen, who cares?

The very intimacy of the Podcast medium means that consumers will not listen, unplug and unsubscribe faster than ever before. That fact is very important to remember.

With Tivos and VCRs, we are a society trained to fast forward through commercials, yet a surprising number of Podcast pontificators claim ad revenue is the clear model for Podcasting. This paradigm is simply ineffective in the immediate intimate

an adjunct, as it is in the Teleseminar Secrets class. However, our Marketing Online Live program is a good example of utilizing Podcasting as a *primary communication channel* through the Podcast channel. Seen as a communication medium, Podcasting takes on a much broader view. The Internet began as a medium of communication and has now shifted into channels of distribution.

Some of the most successful Internet marketing endeavors have been launched by those who took a traditional medium and translated it to the web. Every element of an old-fashioned, direct-response marketing piece had a direct effect on cost, from the number of pages to the insertion of bulk media. The first folks who took that medium out to the web met with some success. But it was the next-generation of web sales letters that incorporated audio, video, and interactive elements that managed to draw considerably higher results. People began to see a much better conversion when the sales letter was translated into the Internet medium, and we are likely to see the same phenomenon with Podcasting.

One of the beautiful aspects of Podcasting is the opportunity to combine education and entertainment as *infotainment*—even within the business arena. You could hire someone like Colin Powell to speak directly to your constituents for $100,000. You can also hire a consultant to work with your sales staff and lower management on building viable strategies for the next 12 months. Either way, the investment of time and money would be substantial. Podcasts nearly eradicate that education and entertainment value. Even if Colin Powell were to develop a Podcast specifically for your company, the price would probably not be $100,000 as the "recording studio" could be delivered to him at home.

Media delivered by a "valid" channel will always have some merit. But the pot of gold at the end of the rainbow is media that integrates an understanding of the way people are consuming it with the actual content. Too many people view Podcasting purely as a channel and then argue that it must remain open source and free. Well, the channel *is* open source and free. We pay no royalties or licensing fees to utilize the channel. Even in terms of server hosting fees, our terabytes of Podcast bandwidth have yet to cost us more than $30 on any month. The channel is not the medium—it enables the medium, and the medium does not have to be free.

We don't want to own the channel or label it with our own names. We are just thrilled that the channel exists and allows us to tap into a virtually unlimited distribution field. Without an open channel, Marketing Online Live as we know it would not have been possible. Instead of doing an Internet radio show that would require everyone to be online at a certain time and raise audio capability issues, we had the opportunity to

communication form that is Podcasting. They have plugged you directly into their head, don't even try to give them anything but the best.

As a result of these facts, we don't see (traditional) ads supporting Podcasts as the eventual direction of this industry. There is too much room for a considerably better rate of return in providing the right message to the right audience at the right time. Simply stated, we believe that the money lies in Podcasts where content is not interrupted by advertisements from sponsors – but where the sponsors, if any[4], are part of the content. The great challenge that faced e-zine

---

4. With Premium (Paid) Podcasting and internal/external product/company support Podcasts, there are unlimited opportunities for extremely profitable Podcasting without a single ad embedded.

publishers was the tendency for people to focus on advertising instead of content. If Podcasting can remain clean—and certainly it can do that within the business world—sponsors are not necessary or even desirable. Remember, the Podcast medium is unlike television, where couch potatoes who are continually cycling through the channels will often stop more than once on a particular show. When your Podcast consumers unsubscribe, you have lost any chance of regaining their attention. The very immediacy and intimacy of the medium dictates that your listeners will unplug in record time if you are lacking a solid strategic message.

My own approach to listening to a new Business Podcast usually begins with travel time. Prior to boarding the airplane, I have

Podcast our show to anyone with an MP3 player (or an internet-connected computer). By utilizing the channel, our listeners could pick us up anywhere, anytime. *That* is the channel, and the power of the channel. Now let's delve into the medium.

With the exception of VCR tape delays and Tivo® time shifting, television programming is traditionally consumed from across the room at a specific time. Length is also very specific, from a 30-minute sitcom to a one-hour drama or a two-hour movie. The format is very predicable: Fast cuts, precise edits and commercial interruptions. Podcasts are not restricted by any of these elements, yet it could certainly make use of them.

Radio is an auditory communication medium that arrives only by sound. Like television, radio is not designed as an interactive device. Radio also deals with specific times and events. Even long stretches of musical programming are precisely executed to include the news, weather and traffic reports, commercials, announcements, self-promotions, and other station format needs. Public media like radio and television, fall under the scrutiny and regulation of the Federal Communications Commission.

Howard Stern moved his show from traditional to satellite radio to avoid certain FCC obscenity restrictions, but his program is still broadcast via radio. He still goes to the station to broadcast and his listeners have to catch his show during that exact timeframe. While some devices promise to time-shift satellite radio content, the restrictions at this time make it more complicated than it's worth.

Technology has greatly expanded the consumption models for motion pictures. The first release of a movie is on a tremendous screen in some theater that probably offers stadium seating. That scenario probably includes your sweetheart or friend by your side, the aroma of popcorn, no commercial interruption of the film, and a shared viewing experience with an entire room filled with other people. Movies have their own time-limit tradition: About 90 minutes for a comedy and two hours for a drama. Longer comedies tend to choke and epic-length films are too easily dismissed as tedious. In the theater or at home on DVD, the movie format is considerably limited by restrictions and expectations—including the requirements for a specific rating. Filmmakers are often faced with cutting or editing if they want a G for general audiences rating or even an R for restricted to adults.

Radio is a medium. Television is a medium. Film is yet another medium. Podcasting is a completely independent medium. From the perspective of the success of Teleseminar Secrets, a teleseminar is an extremely profitable medium that utilizes an incredibly simple channel. The widespread ownership of portable media

already researched any new Business Podcasts at iTunes®. The downloaded episodes are cued and waiting for me in a play list. As the consumer, I listen judgmentally and skip over any Podcast that fails to pique my interest within the first 45 seconds or so. For a typical trip, I might have subscribed to 15 Podcasts—lucky to find one that interests me.

What is the answer to the issue here? Quality. If you produce content that people *want*, as opposed to *are willing to put up with*, you'll have an intimate connection to an audience hanging on your every word.

And that, dear reader, is the power of Podcasting.

players, computers, and telephones is integral to that success. Converting a teleseminar into a Podcast as we did with Teleseminar Secrets—or supplying it on CD like our home-study course—requires editing. The opening disclaimer states that the content was originally taken from a teleseminar. When consumers understand the nature of the original medium, they are able to translate accordingly, and do so willingly.

With the exception of fewer FCC restrictions, Internet radio is similar to traditional radio. Listeners are still tethered to their computers, confined to a specific time and space without the benefit of time-shifting or portability. The use of CDs, DVDs, and videos provide a measure of those advantages but have their own limitations, including run time and very specific consumption strategies. Podcasting, as a separate medium, is not without restrictions. At the same time, it offers a new paradigm with an extraordinary measure of freedom and some very real and exciting opportunities. A Podcast places the power of worldwide broadcasting into the little guy or gal's hand.

While broadcast television is not a true monopoly, it could be classified as an oligopoly. Cable television is also driven by subscriptions but primarily by advertising. The cost of advertising varies with time slots and viewer popularity, but any form of television is a medium where the interruption of an advertisement pays for the entertainment. Airwaves are not free, so radio follows the same pattern. Movies also involve commerce, whether you see them in the theater, buy the DVD, or subscribe to Netflix.

Podcasting is a medium that empowers anyone with a voice, much like, as we discussed in our introduction, the revolutionary invention of the Gutenberg Press. Anyone who was literate had the opportunity to create a huge ruckus in their own village or far beyond. The written word has launched entire wars. Podcasting has as much power.

Podcasting allows nearly anyone to say almost anything without the censorship of a third party like the FCC. Howard Stern created a wave of curiosity just by abandoning radio that is governed by third parties and embracing the more open and free medium of satellite radio. People were just dying to know what he wanted to say. How would the medium change? Was the "real Howard" hiding behind those restrictions? Will uncensored-Howard have anything new and different or louder and more profane to say than censored-Howard? The public is already fascinated by the move, and moral implications aside, the technological and media aspects at play are absolutely fascinating.

Podcasting is also self-governing and provides the same freedom of expression. Just look over the wide range of Podcasts available on Yahoo! and you'll find every imaginable subject including explicit sexual content.

Podcasts can be offered as a paid subscription or given away. Maybe your consumption strategy will begin with a free content that seduces listeners into subscribing laterto a paid Podcast. As the technology and user base matures, more and more Podcasts will be on private platforms that are not available for public consumption.

Communications media can be auditory or visual, entertainment or education. The significant differentiation is *public* or *private*, and Podcasting can be both. Anyone can offer a Podcast to an audience anywhere in the world. Production costs are relatively nothing. The *value* of that Podcast is the intriguing issue. The value of ones and zeros or content and information has been the theme of science fiction speculation for decades—describing a world where the true economy relies solely on ideas. Consider that theme in the present: A million people working on a bad idea produce nothing of value. However, a great idea requires but a single innovator[5].

Those who are interested in developing a strategic Podcast message need to be clear on the difference between channel and medium. That's why so many people express frustration with Podcast monetization. They see the channel as completely free and open and have no concept how to monetize what everyone else is giving away for free. Once it is understood that the value is in the content, the medium, the path to monetization becomes much clearer.

---

5. For a brilliant, pre-Internet discussion of this phenomenon, we recommend our readers pick up John Naisbitt's brilliant book "Global Paradox" where he expounds on the concept that "The bigger the world's economy, the more powerful its smallest players."

Justifying Internal Podcast Strategy Expenses

Within the right companies, can portable media players be placed in the same desirable category as laptops, cell phones, and PDAs? Cheaper media options are certainly available. In short, business can, and should, no longer be confined to the office. Employees who are able to use and take home these electronic tools have been proven to be more productive. They tend to bring some of their work home and give more of their time to the business, which makes the associated expense very worthwhile.

Companies who are reviewing the value of external or enhanced communication need to ask themselves if time-shifting would give their employees a stronger

Most of the failures seen in the early Podcasting game can be attributed to confusion over channel and medium. People began launching Podcasts simply because they could and it was free. The channel made that possible. Literally anyone can put up a server or access to a server. With folks out there willing to host for free, you don't even have to pay a nominal access fee every month. No wonder people have been launching literally anything at all—chopping it up and delivering it down the pipe. I have to chuckle each time I see a television show Podcast that lacks any commentary or extras but only provides a "best of." How many of us want to follow an hour's TV show with a five-minute clip of something we just watched? The content was pathetic, and lacked interest (let alone value) and was quickly dismissed by anyone who consumed it.

A similar scene occurred when desktop publishing programs were financially viable for the "non-professional." Suddenly a generation of "graphic designers" who mistook the technology for talent offered their obviously valueless services to a public who saw the results and decided not to buy. It was almost as if the (popular movie) "Field of Dreams" mantra *"If you build it, they will come"* was a promise for everyone, not just the film's protagonist.

Right now, Microsoft® Publisher allows anyone to produce a brochure with its wizard and then launch a website with a single click a few seconds later – but any examination of the results negates their use in a business environment – for but a few talented users.

That's why the development of a strategic Podcast message requires a solid understanding of the difference between the channel and the medium. In the world of Podcasting, the *what* question should be the easiest to answer. Instead, it is the most difficult (for many) because of the duality of the term.

In short, the value proposition of the Business Podcast is in the *value of the content*, delivered and consumed via *a very inexpensive, and extremely powerful, channel*.

THE ART OF STRATEGY CASTING

In our teleseminar series Podcast Secrets (http://www.podcastsecrets.com), we discuss a concept called the Podcast Monetization Roadmap™. The first step in the Roadmap is called "Strategy Casting." A full graphic of the Podcast Monetization Roadmap can be found in the Appendix section of this book.

In a nutshell, Strategy Casting is the art of launching your Podcast with a plan. In the first stage of Internet media, we saw millions spent on launching Websites without a single end-game in mind (claiming to hope they'd eventually find it in the process).

focus. Would the consumption of a "what's happening this week" Podcast during the commute to work on Monday morning change the experience at the office once they arrive? Would eliminating excuses result in better communications? An employee who misses a regular weekly briefing because of a doctor's appointment or an office emergency could catch up to the rest of the team through the time-shifting power of Podcasting.

Just having the ability to keep everyone playing from the same sheet of paper would result in better communication. Time-shifting important communications would also reduce a great deal of the stress created when busy people are constantly juggling their schedules around rigid meeting times. The last question that employers should consider is quite simply: "Could we boost morale by giving our employees an iPod?"

Any corporation that requires an internal communication strategy needs to examine the far-reaching advantages of Podcasting and examine the cost and value accordingly. The cost can be easily justified if the end game is planned, and clearly presented.

We're seeing the same in the early days of Podcasting. Any reader who has gotten this far in the book would realize the futility of such an approach.

Strategic Podcasters enlist two types of strategies: internal and external. Internal strategies revolve around the translation of existing *internal* messages or communications into a Podcast. Those who are thinking strategically about internal communication should be asking, "Could this content be as effective or possibly even more effective when delivered via Podcast?" The only way to answer that question is to solicit and test individual responses. The proof is in the pudding.

From a strategic viewpoint, internal Podcasts have the advantage of playing to a captive audience of employees. Even if you make a mistake the first time around, you have the opportunity to discover what went wrong and adjust your approach. Enlisting some simple tracking tricks is the best way to test an internal Podcast. At the end of your Podcast, send your listeners to an internal site or request that they dial up a telephone extension to confirm that they have listened. Simplicity is the rule, but be careful when comparing results. Let's face facts: Many corporate communication mediums are ignored when employees have that option.

Internal Podcasting has the potential to create entirely new communication opportunities. As a fresh, new corporate communication vehicle, Podcasting can be amazingly fun and exciting. Case in point:

Novell® telephone support. Everyone knows that tech support is hell. First you call in and then you wait in a cue. Novell once diffused that frustration by hiring a comedian who provided funny "traffic reports" and cracked jokes, turning a traditional and extremely stale communication vehicle into a smash hit. Some people actually called in just to listen to the guy. And what comedian wouldn't jump at the chance for 20 minutes with an audience who is absolutely trapped? Internal Podcasting has that same possibility.

Imagine being able to *listen* to the content of some boring interoffice memo with the addition of wacky sound effects. "How are the sales doing today?" might be accompanied by the sudden flush of a toilet or the roar of a rocket launch. The addition of sound and a little verve—more "cow bell," as they say—can transform the nature of internal communications. Corporate communications today are relegated to interoffice email or written memos, corporate newsletters, and the intranet. Instead of reading the memo with the 800 other pieces of email in the inbox, it can be consumed in the car on the way to work through a company iPod or even a Podcast to cellphone interchange.

Microsoft® loves to brag about the success of SharePoint, which was a product designed and developed for corporate internal (intranet) use. SharePoint basically provided a communications website where people could collaborate, share information, and work together on projects like task lists or consumer lists. It also provided a base camp of sorts where important information and documentation could be stored. Before long, tens of thousands of SharePoint websites popped up at the Microsoft intranet because, quite simply, internal communications need some excitement to be effective. SharePoint represented, at the very least, something different, and was embraced (at least, internally, accordingly).

Internal Podcasts have the potential to serve as an amazing new communications vehicle for management, sales forces, human resources, new employees—virtually *anyone on the inside*. As an employee, or part of "the team," you can have access to a Podcast that is not open for public consumption. Maybe it's a private memo to upper management with different levels of confidentially. Internal Podcasts can operate like an email broadcast with audio, which makes them a very powerful intranet memo and commu-

Finding Your Voice in the Podcast Space

Caution: In the Podcast "space", those who unsubscribe are essentially lost. The good news is that domain names in Podcast titles are disposable. If you launch a Podcast that falls flat, do not attempt to resurrect it. Start over. Domain names are approximately $7. With products like Podcast Cover Producer at PodcastCoverProducer.com, a new graphic is less than $50.

To avoid losing your audience, stats are not enough. As you find your voice in the Podcast space, encourage your audience to communicate with you. Right now, we have no way to automate this communication process. Communication has to be initiated by the Podcaster, which can be

nication modality that has yet to be seriously explored. The issue of monetization further blurs the edges of this new and emerging paradigm as the profit comes from better communication, which can often lead to more sales. You can conceivably provide Podcast services that cater only to the business intranet community—something that Audible, Inc., has been doing for years with Fortune 500 companies before Podcasting was even a word.

Within this context, Podcasts represent a closed channel for an internal medium. The platform would remain closed to those who are not invited but open to those who enjoy access—similar in spirit to a security clearance. Once again, these Podcasts are a communications medium and a channel. While not necessarily monetizable, closed-channel Podcasts provide a great delivery vehicle for private information to a select audience. Security controls like the Net Nanny® that are used by parents to keep their kids safe online do the same thing: They simply close the platform. Podcasting allows that to happen in a time shifted way, although few companies have yet to take advantage of this new paradigm.

Some of the Fortune 100 companies have warmed up to this new Podcast technology, if only for voice memos. We already have the technology to replace the traditional memo through the exchange email system, but the plug-ins tend to be clunky and we are stuck with a third interface. With this new

CLAIM YOUR FREE INSTANT ACCESS TO HOURS OF EXCLUSIVE PODCAST TRAINING

Plus Enter to Win a FREE Preloaded iPod.

Register Your Copy of *The Business Podcasting Bible* at http://www.TheBusinessPodcastingBible.com/members Today!

accomplished with a website. Take a look at MarketingOnlineLive.com and you'll see billboards, interactive blogs, and forums that encourage communication with our user base. Integration with the web surveying system using tools like Ask Database™ begins to make sense as well. Usually an ethical bribe entices the listener to come through and communicate with you.

Providing original content that supplements our existing audience base has always been the goal of MarketingOnlineLive.com, and that will probably continue for some time. We wanted to offer something worthwhile that not only brings them on but secures them for what might be coming next. Sure, we would love to bring new customers into the fray. However, our primary goal has

Podcasting option, employees can listen to the corporate announcements on the same media player that pumps out the latest hit tunes during their workout at the gym. Most people would see that as very intriguing, and at the very least are worth exploring, before launch, in the Strategy Casting process.

Using Podcasts for external communication brings us to four content options:

1. Marketing communication

Particularly for those who are interested in direct monetization, the utilization of Podcasts as a distribution channel for great marketing media is truly exciting.

Respect for the medium dictates the strategy, beginning with the issue of advertisements. Inserting ads within the Podcast, which is typical with other media, will not be as effective as other marketing options. People will unsubscribe and never return – because they know they are being marketed to. Conversely, a strategic, well-planned and well-executed marketing communication piece can be extremely successful – if the medium and consumption process is understood.

2. Supplemental communication

Unlike marketing Podcasts, supplemental communications deal with products or services *that have already been purchased* and the goal of the communication becomes a stick and/or support strategy. Technical products or those related to an event are great examples. One of the largest of these events is Microsoft Tech Ed, which attracts thousands of developers who want to learn more about Microsoft products. Instead of multiple tracks, this event utilizes literally hundreds of tracks. Pleasing everyone is impossible, so Tech Ed utilized Podcasts that enabled attendees to pick up whatever they might have missed. They could relax in their hotel room, engage in dialog, and consume more than they have ever been able to do at Tech Ed events in past years. Could someone who did not attend Tech Ed log onto that Podcast? Sure, but does that matter? The Podcast was a supplement, and consuming that supplement without attending Tech Ed would not make sense. In the case of Tech Ed, Podcasting was used to make a good product better.

The supplemental Podcast is similar to a DVD director's commentary but is more specific in content. Maybe you have invented some incredible espresso machine or a new specialty food item. A Podcast that teaches your customers how to use your invention or gives them tips on creating gourmet delights with your food item is definitely a supplemental communication. Imagine a sale that offers not just the product, but a year of video content on how to use it. Yes, marketing could still be a subset of that Podcast, but it won't be the most powerful element of it. Others might peek in to hear more about the things that are possible with your products. Episodes might be passed on. But in the end, the supplemental Podcast communication is

been to supply original content to supplement our existing base—not to sell the Podcast or close it out. In fact, we wanted to open it up. We tried different lengths and different delivery mechanisms but found 20 minutes to make the most sense. From day one, communication with our audience was encouraged through the website and the "calling out" of the show email address during every Podcast episode.

If you encourage communication from your audience and they don't respond, you still have feedback. One fellow was complaining that he had several hundred downloads of every one of his shows but no one was answering the request for email response. "What does that mean," he asked? Well, it's very clear what that means: His audience did not see him as worth the email. An entire book or an entire course could be devoted to the tricks of the ethical bribe. Suffice it to say that people naturally enjoy sharing their knowledge, and "ask surveying" can be tremendously valuable.

fundamentally different from marketing and must be understood accordingly.

3. Repurposed communication

Most television productions, movies, and radio Podcasts do a poor job of following this model, as we touched upon earlier in the chapter. Most of the time, the Podcast regurgitates a chopped-up version of the original and shoots it down the channel. Teleseminar Secrets provides the ideal example of repurpose communication. This Podcast was never intended for those who were not a part of the Teleseminar Secrets class, and each Podcast episode bears the reminder that "this is a recording of a teleseminar." The Teleseminar Secrets Podcast is designed for attendees who could not consume the class event at a particular time, for whatever reason. Many people will undoubtedly log onto the call to have the backup recording shot to them as soon as possible just to speed up their rate of consumption.

Strategically designed, effective repurpose communication can take on a multi-dimensional consumption strategy that can only benefit your existing customer base. Delivery of existing content through the Podcast channel has the potential to add tremendous value to what you are already doing with very little additional work. Seminars, information products, earnings calls, independent films, concerts, shareholder updates, and other special events are a few of the viable opportunities for repurpose Podcasting.

We believe that significant revenues will be generated by those who truly understand the power of effectively repurposing content and shooting it down the Podcast channel.

4. Original communication

Some of the most incredible, revolutionary Podcast content will be completely new material that embraces both the channel and medium. AffiliateGuyPodcast.com, a Premium Podcast for people in the affiliate marketing industry is an ideal example. This Podcast could have been packed in a CD training series and mailed on a monthly basis as many premium content packages are. However, the monthly Podcast content often extends beyond the capacity of two CDs, which creates packaging issues and other headaches. Delivering this content as a Podcast makes perfect sense. The audience knows that each Podcast is as long as necessary to delve just as deeply as it needs to go. Every Podcast delivers the *complete message* contained in the monthly episode. Nothing has to be edited, cut, or omitted. In addition, the content is delivered minutes after completion, not having to worry about the delays associated with mail delivery.

We have a fitness industry client who utilizes the Premium Podcasting system to teach body-building techniques on a paid Podcast venue (read about him in the Appendix). He

Three Steps to Making an Existing Podcast Better.

Those who have already launched a Podcast have a viable mechanism for enhancement. Even if you launched without Strategy Casting, you are already in motion and can improve what is already there. What three steps can you take to improve your intended Podcast results?

First, *ask your audience*. Find out how your audience feels about what you are already doing. See if a "best of" would suit their taste or needs. Maybe they are more interested in having your content in its entirety or having access to new, supplemental content. It doesn't matter what the answer is, just ask the question. You may find that you are already giving your audience everything they want. You may also find that you are missing the mark entirely but that your audience is more than willing to point you in the right direction.

Once you have tallied the poll and understand the needs and wants of your target audience, you are ready for step two. Second, *examine your monetization options and numbers accordingly.* If your Podcast is a marketing vehicle, how could you draw more customers? How can you track those results? Spending an entire year producing a high-level, high-profile Podcast from the perspective of marketing monetization without knowing whether or not it is effective is just silly. If your Podcast is a stick strategy, does it truly help customer retention? How can you test that? Again, you have to be able to track results.

can devote as much time as necessary to cover the content through this channel. Sending someone a CD of a workout is ineffective. And who would want to watch a workout at home on TV before heading off to the gym? However, someone can strap something like the flash iPod® Nano on his or her arm and lift weights at the same time. Now we have something new and exciting.

We are going to be seeing more and more original communications that embrace the Podcast channel incredibly well. In fact, this approach may well represent the future of Podcasting or at least the ultimate value of the technology. After all, original communication allows you to take an existing commodity like a body-building program and deliver it as an entirely original product through a new channel. The exercise may not be new but delivery via Podcast suddenly creates a fresh cache.

With all four of these external Podcast communication vehicles, physical limitation is no longer an issue. The attention span of the consumer is really the only restriction. And if you look closely at the trend in the parade of new technology, capacity is always increasing: Audio tapes to CDs, video tapes to DVDs, and DVDs to portable media players. Podcasting allows the strategist to focus solely on content because capacity is unlimited.

Podcast gives you the freedom to provide as much information—whether marketing, supplemental, repurpose, or original—as you desire. Taking complete control of program length is one of the most significant aspects of these new communication forms. You can do a five-minute Podcast or a 500-minute Podcast. Editing and cutting to meet capacity limitations are obsolete activities in the world of Podcasting.

Strategy Casting dictates that you understand that you are no longer bound by the *physical limitations* shared by all previous traditional channels but have new limitations imposed by the consumer. In short, the program ends when your consumer decides it does.

Many 90-minute Podcasts have less than 30 minutes of content value. Many 30 minutes Podcasts can be summed up in 30 seconds of meat. Mom was right when she said, "*Just because you can doesn't mean that you should.*" People are constantly asking us how long a Podcast should be. Everyone is looking for the magical formula. The answer is a simple one: *A Podcast should be as long as it needs to be and not one minute longer.* In addition, an understanding of the consumption of your audience might quickly make that decision for you.

Some episodes of AffiliateGuy Podcast.com have clocked in at 1.2 minutes. Others require as many as three hours to cover the topic. The line may be a delicate one, but one fact is sure: Freedom from physical restrictions enables the Podcaster to focus on *content value* in a way that no other medium can provide. Musicians enter the studio knowing that they need about 12 songs for a 60-minute album. Sitcom writers

Direct monetization Podcasts are the easiest to track—just count the incoming revenues.

Third, *relaunch your Podcast with predetermined* metrics that allow the tracking you will need. Once the feedback system is in place and you start responding to the requests of your audience, you will be in a very favorable position.

Medium as message

Traditional media carries along the subconscious expectation of wasted time. Listening to the radio includes commercials, annoying disc jockey banter, and traffic reports you may not need. Technology has not only placed the control in the hand of the listener but made that control remote. Tivo has created tremendous issues in the world of traditional media content because it places the control in the hands of the end users—not advertisers or sponsors. So, this subconscious expectation of wasted time is based on reality.

The effective use, with the near elimination of wasted time, of Podcasting as a medium respects the listener on multiple levels. The medium of Podcasting understands that end

have to drag the laughs out another four minutes before the next commercial break. Movie directors end up slashing scenes to keep their film from extending beyond a reasonable timeframe. Only the Podcast medium truly gives free rein to creativity and strategic genius. The 20-minute timeframe that we set for Marketing Online Live Podcasts is based solely on the consumption habits of *our own listening audience*. Nothing about the channel or the medium represents a limitation, which gives Podcasting tremendous power.

Sometimes Podcast content will run longer—particularly in the educational and the business arena—because the topic is embryonic and concepts are still emerging. The Podcaster leads an almost cathartic journey into a search for clarity or truth, which often takes a meandering path. Still, the length must be comfortable to the consumer and be quality and content rich. Podcasting is in the genesis of its evolutionary process. After 10 years of looking back at the Internet and trying to grasp all that it can be, we are just now making paradigm shifts that are bringing about considerable improvements.

WHAT IS THE "RIGHT" CONTENT

Once you have a clear understanding of channel versus medium, you are ready to develop Podcast content. Start by answering these five questions:

1. Who is your audience?

We never fail to be amazed at the number of people who actually deliver Podcasts with no understanding of their audience.

2. What is the value or purpose of your content?

The communications goal behind a marketing message is the generation of sales, the acceleration of consumption, the building of a new client base. When enhancement is the desire, the Podcast can provide a successful stick strategy. What is the value of purpose of your content?

3. How will it be consumed?

The consumption of a Podcast dictates how it will be produced, as covered in detail in Chapter Two. If the traditional commuter is your consumer base, it makes very little sense to create a Podcast longer than 30 minutes. Podcasts beyond three or four minutes in length might be inappropriate for a consumer base of teenagers. How will your content be consumed?

4. Is your content time sensitive or evergreen?

Determine whether the value of your content is dependent on consumption within a specific time period or if it could be consumed at any point. Production issues, the naming of a show, and the introduction are just a few of the elements that will be affected by this answer. Will someone pick

users are in control. It makes no attempt to waste their time, push something by, or force anything on them. When the Podcast medium fails to provide this advantage, one of two negatives will happen: Consumption will either stop or the audience will adopt the fast-forward attempts they use with other media and traditional marketing will not take place. The medium as a message in Podcasting is continually growing in importance and must be grasped.

When Podcast Is Channel, But Not Medium

As mentioned multiple times in this book, the open channel of Podcasting will be heavily monetized as a channel for media that is not "traditional Podcast content." In the example touched on earlier of Teleseminar Secrets, some of the customers who paid $2,000 for the class have opted to receive the class as a Podcast. Certain guidelines are applicable to those situations when the Podcast channel is used to distribute media that is not a "true" Podcast (in media form at least):

Explain the exact stage for consumption during the first 30 seconds of each Podcast file. The introduction of a teleseminar could provide the exact place and

up and listen to the Podcast you created two months ago or just toss it in the trash? Evergreen content has no more inherent value than time-sensitive content; the two are simply produced differently. Few people are interested in watching video tapes of last month's evening news. Yet, episodes of blockbuster TV series like MASH or Marcus Welby, M.D. that are decades old still hold considerable appeal.

5. How much will production and distribution cost?

The use of video can considerably raise the price of a Podcast on both production and distribution sides. This is especially true for lengthy videos intended for a very large audience.

Once you have addressed the five basic issues, you are ready to deal with the specifics. Answering the media question of audio or video is simple. Now decide whether or not your media should be locked, which would require some form of digital-rights management. In theory, unlocked media provides equal access to all. However, the use of proprietary media can limit that access. Windows media files can only be played on a Windows machine, while MP3 is open to the world. Consider Audible formats and AAC Audio from Apple, Inc. Your media choice will dictate proprietary and open possibilities.

One more thing to consider when pondering the locking of content is the customer support issues related to such an approach. These can, and often are, the most expensive element to an electronic media distribution effort and, honestly, only a tiny percentage of Podcasts today are utilizing such technologies.

Quality is the last but certainly not the least to consider. Much less of an issue with audio, quality is critical to video production and demands much larger file sizes. An optimized video that looks good on a 1.5-inch Podcast screen is considerably different than an optimized video Podcast intended for a high-definition television set.

No Podcast should be produced without an end goal in mind. Before developing your message, decide whether it is marketing, supplemental, repurposed, or original. The monetization in-game for a marketing Podcast is new customers. For a stick Podcast, the monetization in-game would be the staying power of an existing company or product. Direct monetization plays are either premium paid Podcasts or sponsored Podcasts. The previous chapter offers additional information about the limitations and frustrations associated with sponsored Podcasts.

Delivery issues include hosting and bandwidth considerations. Large files that offer extremely high fidelity and are intended to reach a large audience are the most likely to pose potential problems. Tracking may or

date it took place with a note that the teleseminar is presented in its entirety without edits. Repeat that information in the traditional Podcast show notes. Give whatever consumption recommendations and rules it takes to set the stage for the medium. Perhaps you need to explain that the thin sound is a result of telephone production.

Teach the ideal consumption experience to your audience. Teaching your audience how to consume and making that consumption as easy as possible is paramount. Having that little media player is like carrying around the keys to the castle, and the power of the Internet remains in the palm of their hand wherever they go – but it is still your job as the communicator to teach them how to consume. For a movie, the statement might be: "This independent film was created for viewing on a large screen; consider burning a DVD of this video Podcast and watching it on your television.". For a 2 hour long teleseminar, you might want to warn them of the time frame at the beginning, or explain that you have chopped the event into 20 minute segments to make consumption easier. The consumption of a traditional event is not possible on multiple, simultaneous levels—a fact that we perceive at least subconsciously. Every sporting event has three levels of consumption, beginning with those who are in attendance. The sights, aromas, back noise, and energy of the playing field and the crowd all become part of the intensity. Those who listen to the same event on the radio can't see a thing but they have the

may not be important to you. Maybe you need to know how many downloads have been completed, how many were incomplete, and the various IP addresses involved.

The ideal consumption is another topic that is covered in greater detail in Chapter Two. Which one of the three basic consumption models—desktop, commuter, or leisure—best meets the needs of your aim goal? Your consumption scenario affects length, but length should also be determined by telling the audience exactly what they needed to hear and nothing else. People actively desire to consume the entirety of a topic with AffiliateGuyPodcast.com Podcasts. Offering a 40-minute product to a commuter who only drives for 20 minutes can almost be disrespectful.

The specifics of scheduling include choices like daily, weekly, monthly, or impulse Podcasts. Regardless of your scheduling preference, your Podcasts need to be consumed. Now tracking comes into play; from the number of downloads to the breakdown of podcatcher products. Is your audience listening via desktop? Are they using Microsoft® Internet Explorer or Firefox®? Are they using iTunes or Juice[6]? Beyond the various platforms and products in use, it is important to look closely at trends. How often is your Podcast downloaded after the first day?

---

6. A listing and explanation of Podcast aggregators (Podcatchers) can be found at the end of this book.

When do downloads end, if they stop at all. Utilizing systems like Premium Podcast or AudibleWordCast enables the tracking of users, which opens up additional opportunities for study and evaluation.

Length will always play a major issue in consumption strategies, particularly as length relates to audience consumption. Someone who listens to Podcasts for two hours while she walks the dog is a different consumer than the fellow who listens for 10 minutes on his bus ride to work. Nightingale-Conant has successfully delivered content in approximately 20-minute sound bites for decades. Our own experience has proven that 20 minutes is a good length. We could go to 10 minutes or even divide the Podcast into sections as long as the audience has some cue that a particular section is over.

One thing that has yet to appear in the world of Podcasting is the use of Part One and Part Two or To Be Continued. Podcasts at this time seem to stand alone, which separates them from most broadcast shows and the majority of entertainment or educational pieces. On the other hand, the Podcast consumption strategy differs from the model based on "every week at 7:00 PM on Channel 3." Podcasts are in the cue, waiting to be consumed whenever and wherever the audience decides.

The power of time-shifting diffuses much of the emphasis on scheduling that other forms of media rely so heavily upon.

advantage of professional (color) commentary. The television version of that same sporting event brings together visual images and commentary but also various camera angles, interesting stats, and other programming extras. The event is the same is all three cases, but the audience is consuming it differently. You can be very successful in using the Podcast channel for media that is not Podcast if you adhere to the model of setting the stage for consumption.

In the world of Podcast, downloading equates to *retrieval* and consumption equates to *listening*. Being able to track the time and frequency of downloads would provide some measure of predictability and enhance scheduling efforts. Still, only the consumer ultimately knows if, when, and where he or she listened. It's like buying groceries at the store and placing them on the shelf for later consumption. That broccoli might end up on the dinner table or just shrivel in the crisper until it's thrown away.

Podcast scheduling would be positively influenced by tracking that offers specific feedback on the audience's routines and habits. Are the download patterns within the business-to-business community dramatically different than those of business-to-consumer? That's why the future of Podcasting is likely to enable some new forms of reporting mechanisms. We have some Internet technology right now that can track how far down the sales page a reader scrolled, but that took a decade to innovate. The day may come when media files will have the capability to return information about the end user to the Podcaster. For now, let's not kid ourselves into believing that we know more than we actually do.

CONCLUSION

Podcasting is two things: it is a content medium and a channel for time (and place) shifted media delivery. The most successful business applications for Podcasting understand both of these elements – knowing how to leverage the specific value in both.

Developing a clear strategy, before launch, for your Podcast based on the consumption options described in chapter 2 combined with an understanding of your audience and the medium can produce results any business will be delighted with.

AT THE PRIVATE MEMBER SITE

A video walkthrough of the Podcast Monetization Roadmap discussed in this chapter is provided at this book's Private Member Website. The video explains the five steps past Strategy Casting, mentioned earlier. You can view the video (and additional content on the "What" of Business Podcasting) at http://www.TheBusinessPodcastingBible.com/what.

THE BUSINESS **PODCASTING BIBLE**

CHAPTER FOUR

"For those who like this kind of thing, this is the kind of thing they like."
—Abraham Lincoln

"We have to understand that people are different. I don't know, if we really understand who we're dealing with over there."
—Neil Young

U nderstanding the *who* of the Podcast process is absolutely critical. The audience for Podcast is not the same audience we have seen for traditional media. As a group, they are more technically adept and ready to assume a high level of control in the media process. This audience is in charge – and we can leverage that for our business benefit.

WHO IS THE AUDIENCE?

What else makes this group so unique? This is not a captive audience at your beck and call. The Podcast audience calls the shots, not the content producer. If anything, your listeners are at the top of the chain and you are at the bottom. If you can build to this new audience, a Podcast can be a phenomenal communication tool. If you try to build to an old audience with yesterday's paradigms and attitudes toward communication, you are missing the boat—the yacht, actually. You'll be missing no less than 99 percent of the power of Podcasting.

Another item of interest for early adopters who are reading this first version of the book goes like this: The excitement that surrounds Podcasting gives any potential communicator a unique chance to teach an audience to consume the Podcast. *You* can serve as the guide. Talk about the inside track in a new market. You could be the one who teaches them how to be in charge of their own learning process. You can teach them how to be technically adept. You can help them take command of what, when, and how they are learning. As their mentor along this path, you will be handing them the keys to the kingdom. Best of all, your enabled, empowered, strengthened audience will return that favor with a force that has never been seen in traditional forms of communication and media.

The Podcast audience—at least upon maturity—will be the hungriest, most permission based audience imaginable. They will welcome, with open arms, what you have to say and how you have to say it. Those who go through the trouble of acquiring a significant base of knowledge about Podcasting might be interested receivers, Podcast producers or both. Right now, we would venture a guess that most people who listen to our Podcasts have the intention of producing a Podcast of their own—particularly those in the business-to-business environment.

Once Podcasting passes through this early adoption phase, the audience will begin to resemble what we see today in a Tivo audience. They know what is important in their lives and they know what they want. They are not just randomly clicking through channels with the remote. Tivo consumers are serious. When the smoke of Podcast novelty clears, the focus will rest on *utility*. Time-shifting will become the norm, instead of the buzzword, and more of the audience will become serious listeners who are saying, "I want you in my ear. I want you in the palm of my hand. I want you to send me regular updates via audio or video."

We saw the same thing with the introduction of the Google search engine. Before Google, the Internet was mostly an experience of "surfing" – clicking around from site to site (not quite unlike today's channel surfing).

With the introduction of Google, people know what they want go to Google to get it and expect Google to deliver (which they do quite well).

This audience differs in important ways from the average listener or reader. Podcast consumers are very interested in permission based communication. They also tend to be more critical than any other group. Not only intelligent but educated, they are leading the pack (leaders have control).

The general public has yet to reach the point where downloading a Podcast is as commonly understood as sending an email. When it reaches that point, we have hit critical mass.

The complexities of accessing a Podcast during this early adoption phase still scares off a large number of potential consumers. Think back to the early days of the Internet when AOL came on board and hollered, "Hey! This stuff is a piece of cake. Come into our world and see for yourself!" That's when large numbers of people began to stick their big toes into the water. They made it easy. Those who make Podcasting easy can have the numbers (actually bigger) than AOL had. Doesn't that sound attractive?

The opportunity embraced by the *who* of Podcast reception is thrilling. We are not talking about the guy buried in the newspaper or the music-loving radio fan. Podcast consumers do not fall into the category of "unattached passive listeners." In fact, this audience is made up of incredibly *active, passionate, and serious listeners* (the ideal audience for any business). These people want to engage in a dialog in a time shifted manner; which means whenever it might be convenient for them to do so.

Although this test has yet to happen, we'd bet good money that a study comparing Podcast consumers with those who prefer other media types would easily show the Podcast audience to be more monetizable. At least from the perspective of a business environment, we believe it is much easier to create residual income through a Podcast audience than through book or magazine readers or radio station listeners.

Sure, someone could be a member of multiple audiences. Some very hungry consumers devour everything. They are avid readers who listen to valuable radio content and select specific television programs. Actually, that is the very person who would be likely to prefer Podcast above all the other forms of communication. Why? He or she is extremely busy with all that content and needs to take full advantage of every moment of the day. These busy, productive, educated people are wild about the concept of resurrecting dead time for learning or catching up on an update from the boss. They are thrilled about having the power to invite a guest into the palm of their hand.

Many Podcast consumers appreciate having a head start on those who are still gathering that content from traditional media. The Podcast audience is taking a stand and affirming the convenience of time-shifting in money and mindshare. They are also paying homage to the content of the Podcast—something they have discovered that many others have not.

The Podcast audience is in charge – or quickly on the way. If part of your presentation is an affirmation to your audience that they are in charge, the results will be a surprisingly loyal following ready to consume your message, *albeit on their terms.*

THE THREE PHASES OF PODCAST CONSUMPTION

Podcast consumers don't all start out as 60 gig iPod video owners who have made the conscious decision to consume all of their media on their own terms. They all go through the three phases of Podcast consumption:

1. Interested consumption

This group has heard about the opportunity to consume your digital content and is intrigued with the opportunity. They might have discovered the click-to-play option at your Podcast, or perhaps found you at Yahoo! and picked up a $30 player to tote their downloaded content. Maybe they purchased a $400 video iPod. Perhaps they think these items cost too much. Whatever the story, they know about your content and are interested in taking it for a trial run.

This is a great place to be with listeners. If you can convince them to subscribe to your content and take it with them over engaging in the click-to-play option, you can start delivering fresh content on a regular basis to their computers or PMPs (and they'll appreciate you for providing the service). Consumers who are interested can become subscribers if you can bring them to the next phase.

The logical tip for this interest-to-consumption level is to introduce the concept (and benefits) of subscription on every episode. This does not apply to a locked Premium Podcast that carries a price tag, as that audience has already passed through the interest-to-consumption phase. However, it does apply to general and open Podcasts that are available through iTunes

professional wants to move away from using his own money. In the second example, someone wants to move toward the right health professional. What matters the most to you? Not everyone in your audience will be able to answer that basic question with certainty, but many will.

And that information is worth millions.

Communicating in this way—discovering what your audience really needs from you—replicates the dynamics of a great marriage or any working relationship. First you court the prospect who becomes the client, who in turn becomes the evangelist. The regular conversation of the Podcast helps move the relationship to maturity.

Just keep asking that basic question and keep moving toward the target of "*what is most impor-tant*" to your audience.

Once you have established a good rapport with your listeners, you can begin to offer solutions. Whether they are moving toward a situation or away from one, the dialog between you remains the key. Go with them on the journey. Give your listeners permission to respond. Allowing people to know that they are being understood and engaging in respectful dialog is one of Stephen Covey's *Seven Habits of Highly Effective People*. This principal is also as old as civilization itself.

Marketing dialog raises marketing intimacy. Poor communication or the lack of communication can bring down a marriage. It can set off a flood of product returns. Books can remain unfinished, left to gather dust. Someone might thumb through the first 10

or Yahoo! or similar websites. Keep the concept of a subscription at the forefront. Give your audience the benefits of subscription and a few compelling reasons to subscribe.

2. Regular consumption

The jump from initial to regular consumption is simply defined as "They listened to a second show at a second time." Consuming two or three shows in a row still falls into the category of interest consumption. Maybe the person was just bored, sitting in front of the computer with nothing else to do and a lot of time to kill. That same person might move into regular consumption the next week when he sees that a new show is available and responds by downloading and listening.

Of course, *regular* consumption dictates that they realize there is content to consume on a *regular basis* and that you provide said content on a *regular basis*. Nothing will get them to *regular consumption* faster than encouragement (and ethical bribes) from you to do just that.

3. Habitual consumption

In this final and ultimate stage, consumption becomes a part of the daily routine. Your goal is to bring the other two groups of consumers into phase three, where they schedule a regular time for consumption—hopefully with an element of anticipation. This is accomplished on the

THE BUSINESS PODCASTING **BIBLE**

most basic of levels through content quality. Develop and present content that will draw interest and attract subscribers. Obviously, our previously described "best" consumption scenarios are ideal, if possible.

Some of your listeners will consume your Podcast on the commuter train or in the car. Others will take you along on their workout. Perhaps your employees will be listening to your morning update at their desks at the same time they are preparing for the day. The consumption scenario isn't important, the habit is.

Habitual consumption is the absolute golden hen of Podcasting that allows you to start gathering golden eggs. Habitual consumption is the key to monetization. Once you have a consumer on the level of habitual consumption, the connection is actually quite difficult to break. After hearing a fellow complain loudly about the NBC Evening News, I couldn't help but ask, "Why do you watch a broadcast you dislike?" He had been watching NBC Evening News for the last 30 years and he wasn't going to stop now. That is the definition of habitual consumption. Successful Podcasters don't have to wait for 30 years to see that brand of unflinching loyalty.

Howard Stern is a great example. Some people have always complained about his content. In fact, he has thousands of listeners who were warned not to listen to him but decided to listen anyway. Label it curiosity. Of

pages and then give up trying to understand the message. No one, including the author, is teaching that person how to consume the information.

Being able to dialog with your listeners is the aspect of Podcasting that separates it from other forms of media. No one dialogs with a billboard. Unless a magazine conducts a survey via direct mail, you are not likely to dialog with the editor or anyone else on staff. Dialoging via email has real drawbacks, although it certainly is possible. The Internet allows dialog through blogs and other means. However Podcast, if implemented correctly, is the crown jewel of dialog between the content producer and the consumers of that content.

The key to the value of dialog is response speed. How fast should you respond to each question? Respond as quickly as you can. Sometimes a simple "Thank you for your message" or "I understand what you are saying" in an auto-responded message can be effective. We sometimes offer a response on our next show. People who introduce excellent questions or issues that have a much wider appeal or interest to others are ideal for the show. The rest of the audience also benefits from that dialog. The rest of the audience knows that we are listening.

When we do acknowledge a question that we have received, we also give the name of our listener (and their geographic location if they give it). Being acknowledged is personally pleasing and fun to share with a few friends. Your continued response to your audience is a critical ingredient in developing

course, they were insulted and complained. Stern himself just keeps repeating the message that would seem to be counter to his own interests: "Don't listen to me if you don't like what you hear." For some strange reason, these people are in the habit of being insulted by Howard on a daily basis.

One of my personal truisms for teleseminars is the need to polarize the audience, and this is also true for Podcasting. The undecided listener is the biggest pain of all, particularly within the marketing and business arenas. "Do I like this or not? I'm not sure." If you can polarize your listening audience into those who love you and those who love to hate you, at least they have decided. They have cut off a set of circumstances. That's really the meaning behind making a decision: Cutting off or narrowing down. The best part is – those who hate you can simply unsubscribe and find a show of their own liking. Make sure your audience knows this.

Whether we are producing a teleseminar or a Podcast, we want to polarize our audience. We want our listeners to know exactly what we do and do not represent, which returns us again to the importance of content delivery. Polarizing the audience leads to just one decision: Your listeners will either turn up the volume or turn the channel. We hope this book carries that same power of polarization: Read and absorb and learn or come to the decision that Podcast is not the right tool for your goals.

Podcasting offers the unique opportunity of polarizing an audience between "I want more of it or none of it." Howard Stern and Larry King are adept at using polarization to their advantage. Oprah Winfrey uses that power in a different way. Even people who perceive her as a goody-goody who lacks a controversial edge will remain glued to her show just to see what she is going to do next. Great communicators tend to be naturals at the polarization game. *Being* that strong, decisive voice is the best way to elicit a strong and decisive response from your audience.

The ongoing dialog that Podcasting introduces between the content provider and the listener is fascinating. Your audience can be listening and complaining at the same time, just like that fellow who hates a news show that he has never missed in 30 years. Podcasting is an ideal vehicle for achieving habitual consumption and a rare depth of polarized loyalty. Your loyal audience heads for a certain place at a certain time of the day, perhaps moved by nothing more than a sense of morbid curiosity, and wonders, "What am I going to hear today?"

Today's rapid adoption of Podcasting and the near hysteria surrounding this new and sexy communication tool only serves to elevate the importance of these consumption phases. Many new Podcasters would be overjoyed to see 1,000 downloads of an episode.

true intimacy. Without it, the dialog is no longer valid for your listeners. When they no longer feel heard—whether or not that is true—they will drop you. Acknowledge them and bring them into the show in a very personal and intimate way.

One of the advantages you gain through this approach is a content-building system. Applying the Socratic method allows your listeners to identify their needs, but it also allows you to build content around those expressed needs. This is direct response at the deepest level. The first level of acknowledgement is an exciting one: Users are helping the producer write content and shape the show. On another less obvious level, the dialog continues whether or not it becomes part of the show. We read many notes that are not mentioned or become folded into a conversation that might begin: "Many people are concerned about..."

Our listeners know that the dialog is always taking place whether or not they hear their names called out. A husband who responds to most of his wife's points but not all of them can be very effective. His wife would certainly prefer that to having him say: "I wrote down a list of your top ten complaints and here are my written answers." An audience is the same.

Responding to your user base through your Podcast and via website through the boards and blogs is a sure-fire way to elicit respect. This deep level of communication is not available anywhere else. Communication has always been a part of good business, whether reading mail or placing the token phone call. One of

They translate that figure directly into a listening audience. From our perspective, they might have attracted 1,000 new listeners who decided, "This show is not for me." Download statistics say nothing about consumption. We would rather know that 50 of those 1,000 people also listened to the prior episode. That figure may not be as impressive but its value is exponentially higher.

As Podcast content developers, we want to continually introduce topics and opportunities that interest and intrigue our audience. We want them to hear us, to like our content, and to start consuming it on a regular basis. We want that consumption to be so regular that it becomes part of who they are and what they want out of life. We don't have a Podcast that everyone yells about or subscribes to just to see what crazy Alex and Paul will say next.

Most Podcasters—like the majority of entertainers, educators, and business professionals—are not driven by a need to create shock waves and controversy. That is only the extreme edge of the concept of polarization. Serious Business Podcasters want to provide valuable, worthwhile content that draws a loyal, habitual audience. And some of them want to explore and develop the outstanding monetization opportunities that powerful position makes possible.

The *who* in the Podcast process is very willing to learn and listen—particularly in the fiercely competitive world of business. The very psychological makeup of this audience is competitive. They want to consume information and are comfortable with the process, but they don't want boundaries. They want to consume on their own terms.

This audience is not likely to flop down on the couch and watch the news at a certain time each day. They would rather Tivo the news and listen a couple of hours later when it fits into their own schedule. Much like an email that sits in the inbox for a couple of hours (or days / or weeks), the show can wait. Nothing is going to change in the world if they listen to the broadcast 120 minutes later.

The *who* in Podcasting probably has a greater willingness to learn than any other group. During a T. Harv Ecker presentation, we have seen as many as 2,500 complete strangers giving each other hugs. We have been in rooms at The Big Seminar where people are jumping up and down like Tom Cruise on Oprah's couch. They are ecstatic about this new technique and new technology with the power to place their face on the Internet.

The habitual consumers of Podcasting are highly monetizable because of their humility and their hunger to learn. Even if they complain about the content, they are open to new ideas. The clay is still malleable and they are willing to change.

In fact, those who are unwilling to change will have the most problem with our content (and, honestly, Podcasting in general). Our

my least favorite greetings is the recording from a canned voicemail CD that says, "Your phone call is very important to us."

The brand of communication most of us have experienced in the business world in the past was vague and impersonal. Sometimes it was just acknowledgement that we were right about the discrepancy in the bill. "Here is a gift certificate and our apologies. Come back again." While that communication is more intimate than "Your phone call is very important to us," it pales in comparison to a show that mentions you by name and asks you what it is that you want.

Sure, some people write to us just hoping to hear their names mentioned in the cast. On the other hand, few of them really expect that recognition. The result is a stimulating anticipatory process for the audience. Our listeners might wonder if we are really reading their messages or if we really care about their input. Suddenly, they hear their name and the results are amazing.

The communication goes both ways. At the first Podcast Expo, a gentleman by the name of Dan Safkow introduced himself and his company, LogoYourAudio.com, that produces custom MP3 players with preloaded content. I told him it was a great idea and that we mentioned the dream many times on the show. Dan's response, "That's where I got the idea."

Make this dialogue part of your regular ritual and you will eventually develop a sense of what people expect in the form of a response. That ongoing dialog is extremely powerful, and the intimacy of that communication makes it a great business tool. In

content is flowing through a dynamic audience in the process of changing themselves. Our role as content provider is really that of a touchstone or a north star. Together, we are keeping pace with the lightning speed of change, identifying and qualifying opportunities and pitfalls.

The very openness of the channel is part of its tremendous power—openness that needs to be protected. Case in point: Based on user complaints, AOL introduced spam blocking as a positive feature. Unfortunately, that blocker caught up a few valid emails as well. In many cases, the senders just gave up. AOL customers had no idea that valid email was being blocked. They didn't know that they didn't know.

The potential for blockage is extremely relevant to this book. Without freedom of speech or open lines of communication, the Podcaster's hands are essentially tied. If any type of regulatory group steps into the middle, Podcast blockers could become a reality. However, we don't foresee that happening with a permission based medium where the only violation could occur after a subscription is already in place.

Once the listeners are habitual, very little can go wrong. Before they are habitual, everything can go wrong.

Today's Podcast listeners are the most willing of any audience to communicate, at least on their own terms. They want to control consumption but they are extremely willing to learn and reasonably willing to forgive. Tens of thousands of our own downloads have proven this profile.

Your (initial) Podcast audience will be technically savvy and often very busy. Podcast listeners are active and productive people. This medium allows them to shift some tasks from very busy times to dead time (a benefit only the busy find attractive). Consuming content via Podcast makes it possible for them to control when and where they listen, to take control of their busy lives (many times, a bigger benefit than the actual content you are offering them). The action of consumption becomes the habit, not the action of tuning in Thursday nights at 10pm.

Busy people need the freedom of time-shifting because they work around priorities. People who have nothing better to do on Wednesday night than sit in front of the TV and watch *Lost* are not the people who buy a Tivo. Those who enjoy watching *Lost* and have a teleseminar, church meeting, or business opportunity on Wednesday nights are the ones who will be shopping for that Tivo.

Habitual Podcast consumers are mobile and use that to their advantage. Aggressive and high-performing people are always on the go—the crème de la crème of an audience from the standpoint of monetization. These people are seldom going to be listening from the same place at the same time. They have a sizable disposable income, and most have invested in quality mobile equipment

today's hyper-linked 24/7 economy, the market itself has become a conversation—one that must be conducted with a human voice. That is the very theme of the very important *Clue Train Manifesto*—one of the recommended books you will find on the list at the end of this book.

These conversations have to be two-way conversations, not top-down monologues. The Internet first introduced the two-way approach that we see in Podcast development. The Internet allowed us to email a company and expect an immediate response. Before that time, we were sending type-written or hand-written letters through the postal service and waiting four to six weeks to receive a form letter in return. *Now we get an autoresponder, the electronic version of the form letter, in minutes.*

Companies today expect their employees to answer an email communication within 24 hours and give reasonably responsive telephone service. Dialog goes on in many different ways in the business world, some of them more effective and more intimate than others. Podcasting has introduced one very unique communication model: For the first time ever, dialog is part of the media and part of the medium.

Just like communication is the key to a great marriage, effective communication wields enough power to turn a good business into a great business. Socrates' model is as important today as it was 2400 years ago.

Podcasting expands that power to include an ongoing two-way conversation that becomes part of your marketing mix and part of your commu-

that allows them to time-shift and control their schedule. If they can spend $500 on a tool that enables consumption, they can spend money on valuable content, or as a result of it.

Teaching people to consume is the final area where Podcast is extremely applicable and capable of creating great success. The Big Seminar V gave away 500 MP3 players around the entire room with the message, "Start consuming Podcasts and portable, time shifted content." One of the case studies in our appendix is about a businessman who is teaching South American stock trading to an audience that doesn't speak English. This is a new approach for a group that is not typically mobile with its media or controlling of content consumption. "Teachers of consumption" will be reaching people who would not otherwise be attracted to this new media.

Notice that we highlighted a number of "big names" in our discussion of habitual consumption? This was on purpose. Habitual consumption produces big names – and vice versa.

THE PODCAST AUDIENCE OF THE IMMEDIATE FUTURE

We have already established that today's Podcast audience is techno-savvy, educated, hungry for knowledge, critical, and highly mobile. These are busy people who depend on time-shifting to make their personal and professional lives work. Another segment of today's audience is being brought into the fold through consumption teachers. Those who are being encouraged to try something new will be an interesting group to follow as the future of Podcasting unfolds.

Your co-authors are a perfect example of the audience mix you will often find. Without Paul, Alex would have no idea what a Podcast really is. Within their circle of Internet marketers, Alex is far down the list from a standpoint of techno-savvy. At the same time, he absolutely excels from the perspective of being willing to learn, needing time shifted control, being busy and productive, mobile, and having a high expendable income. From those important viewpoints, Alex is extremely open. That is why the partnership works so well.

Millions of very bright minds are still unaware of the power of Podcasting or even the nature of Podcasting as a communication tool. Part of our motive in writing this book is to touch people on the shoulder, put our show into their hands, and say, *"This is a Podcast—would you like to communicate this way?"*

You don't need to corner the market on every quality of a first-class Podcast audience. Opportunity in these early stages is your friend, even if your only strength is the ability to teach well. In the immediate

nication mix. Podcasting can provide immediate, relevant communication through a human voice that is genuine and persuasive. Now you are enjoying a level of communication that has no rival- and your audience will respond accordingly

Many content providers initiate communication in a cocoon. They might be sitting in their office or waiting around at a radio or television studio to tell us what it is that they think we need to know. Podcasting changes that scene as. From the beginning, the role of communication with the audience has been part of the plan.

Podcasting is communication delivery and production on the go. Not only can it be time and place shifted, but it can be produced and delivered from virtually anywhere. Travel time is not really conducive to writing; that usually requires supportive materials and books, let alone laptop power and desk space considerably bigger than what we get on the back of an airline seat. Podcasting is ideal for traveling because the content production mechanism can be so very portable. If done right, Podcasting gives us a combination of live coverage that captures the spirit of Publishers Clearing House and the reality of Survivor. These are exciting times.

Podcasting is so amazing because the information can be consumed from anywhere, but it can also be *delivered* from anywhere at any time. We Podcast any time we see a need to communicate with our listeners, instead of Tuesday at 10 taking 4 weeks off for vacation. The online availability of that Podcast remains predictable, not the delivery schedule. Our

future—something we will cover in future revisions of this book (and at the private member site for those who bought this first edition) —that Podcast audience will grow much larger. At times, the numbers will take a quantum leap. You want to be a part of this.

The Podcasting audience will exponentially grow, at times, overnight. Although Apple's iTunes now represents 88% of the audience for Marketing Online Live, we launched the show before Apple integrated Podcasting into iTunes. Our audience grew even more from that day until now than Apple's stock has – *but both represent amazing growth rates.*

The addition of four million new Tivo subscribers in the first two weeks of December 2005 is another great example of this principle of extreme growth. The (potential) Podcasting audience grew by four million almost overnight when Tivo turned on Podcasting functionality within their system and made it available to their subscribers. No one is going to stick a Tivo in his back pocket and hook it up to the FM receiver in his car – but millions more can consume this media with the simple flip of their corporate switch.

Exponential growth like this is to be expected in the coming years and enhances Podcast awareness and consumption within the general public. At the time of writing, Microsoft has yet to introduce their Podcatcher, Google has no search for

Podcasts and many multinational media companies have yet to announce what they'll be doing about the industry. Be on this wave and surf it into the future.

We happen to be privy to some upcoming large-scale marketing campaigns with an instant Podcasting element. In spite of all the hype and excitement over iTunes integration and Tivo, these marketing campaigns and the exposure they will bring to Podcasting will be bigger than anything we have seen at this point. Get ready.

Regardless of how you feel about Microsoft, the integration of RSS and Internet Explorer 7 (the latest version of its web browser) will have the potential to make a tremendous impact on the Podcasting community. When the default browser for the majority of the computers on the planet supports RSS—which is the backbone of Podcasting—this medium will be introduced to an entirely new market.

Apple and its iPod are both growing. If half of the rumors about things that will accommodate iPods come true, that market is going to continue to explode. One of the most exciting and overlooked portable media players is MP3 on the cell phone. The current examples are somewhat limited, but a few MP3 phones are available for less than $100. Name three serious business professionals who really care about taking silly photos with their cell phones or being able to download games instantly – now name a few

audience depends on that regularity (of availability), which in turn creates more consumption predictability.

The preparation of that Podcast is not dependent upon a certain time or specific day of the week. We can do three, four, or five shows in a single day. Unlike television or radio or motion pictures, Podcast production does not demand that people meet at a studio. We don't need on-site setups or a director. We can Podcast from anywhere with the content flowing from our own minds. What appears to be "stream of consciousness" is the refined culmination of our own expertise with insights gained through dialog with our audience. You can do the same.

The audience is the judge of Podcast content quality, not the Podcaster. Yahoo! is full of Podcasters who are simply babbling to hear the sound of their own voices. Does that mean every word of your content needs to be carefully chosen and every sentence highly crafted? Absolutely not. Authentic communication requires a certain level of spontaneity, the freedom to soar or flounder. The communication patterns in a marriage are not always smooth and on target. On the other hand, would your wife really want you to give her a prepared speech? Sometimes "I don't know" can be the most effective words in the English language.

Make Socrates proud and make your Podcast (and business great) — all at the same time.

who would listen to a Podcast through their Bluetooth headset if they had the chance.

The day is quickly coming when the average consumer will stroll into a Sprint or Verizon store for a show-and-tell of available models and features. The sales representative will say, "Have you heard of Podcasting? This phone sells for less than $100 and offers the ability to receive Podcasts." That is another point when we will see a phenomenal burst of Podcast consumption.

WHO IS IN ULTIMATE CONTROL OF THE PODCAST?

The vital issue of control must be understood—perhaps argued is a better term. In a very real sense, the consumer is in control of the Podcast. The audience decides if, when, and how to listen. Someone can decide to listen to only selected sections. With a few MP3 players, Podcast consumers can even speed up the feed. They could conceivably listen to a 30-minute Podcast in 20 minutes by selecting the right percentage of acceleration.

Once you grasp how fully the consumer controls Podcast consumption, you begin to understand that each element of the Podcast needs to stand alone. Any episodic series like reality TV or soap operas begin with a recap of "what happened last week" for those who missed the program. Podcast moves beyond this episode mentality into a realm where each episode or show must have stand-alone value. Each *segment* of that episode should ideally have stand-alone value, since consumers will be jumping back and forth at will. You can't assume that your listeners heard the first 10 minutes of your Podcast and base the rest of your development process on that assumption.

Each Podcast episode must encourage additional consumption. Your audience does not view you in the same way they see Howard Stern or Jay Leno or the NBC Evening News. Nor does your audience associate your Podcast with a single event like the latest movie or a new CD release. Encouraging consumption can be as simple as telling your audience what they can expect from the next episode. You might want to reiterate what they heard in the last episode. Mention of valuable content from the past encourages your audience to peruse your back catalog for topics of interest. Offer an ethical bribe for visiting your Podcast's website.

If you develop your Podcast with the reality that the consumer is in control, the consumer will sense and assume that control. They are going to know that *you* know they are in control. Until now, consumers have simply never experienced this level of respect and appreciation. As a result, they will return the favor and, many times, *give you back the control*. If your Podcast becomes a part of their daily lives, you have won.

With Podcasting, control is something your audience will always have and hold. However, on the level of habitual consumer they are not likely to fast-forward through much. These people are going to be listening to your Podcast from the very first word. They are going to consume the whole enchilada on a regular basis because you gave them the opportunity and the ability to do just that.

Sometimes, the dialog that we referred to earlier in this chapter is silence. Silence can sometimes indicate a level of trust and confidence that no longer needs to be verbalized or repeated. The audience may control consumption, but that is only one aspect of Podcasting. The Podcaster remains in control of production details like the Podcast topic, delivery, and other content issues. Hopefully, he has taken the time to strategize and ask his listeners what kind of content they want. If he has, the audience is indirectly exerting influence over the content.

Like a dance, both sides of control interrelate and exchange energies. Any successful marriage or partnership is based on this back-and-forth exchange of control. Sometimes my wife feels that she is in control during an argument and decides to bow out and give me the reins. At other times I will do the same thing. Both of us relinquish control at times because we sense that we hold the ultimate control in that particular situation. In a marriage, the ultimate control would probably be divorce. How does that relate to the world of Podcasting? The audience might threaten, "If I don't like the content, I'll stop downloading the show." The Podcaster might say, "If I am not pleased with your response to my content, I'm going to stop producing."

Voluntary control is part of the Podcast difference that makes it so powerful. Being able to bring together the perfect "message and market" marriage—having your content hit the mark—allows your audience to feel very much in control. They feel "in control" like any great prospect caught up in a successful sales dialog. And they will return your investment of time and trouble with loyalty and attentiveness—by joining your Podcast community. Every step of the way, the Podcast medium reinforces that feeling of being in control.

Mark Twain once said, "*Laws control the lesser man... Right conduct controls the greater one.*" Traditional "big media" can be likened to the "law" in Twain's statement: when you work en masse, you have no choice but to do things in big sweeping efforts that are effective from a numbers game only. But when it comes down to the individual, there are higher things that control them. Tap into this with your Podcast and you've tapped into the very element that makes us human.

In a very real sense, your audience *is* very much in control every step of the way. Consumption is the bottom line of Podcasting. Those Podcasts are just cluttering up cyberspace if no one is listening. At the same time, a successful Podcaster will discover a great power of influence over his audience once he has established a dialog with a mass of loyal listeners.

The Podcaster and the audience pass the ball of control to each other frequently—sometimes in subtle or indirect ways. At times, the balance might seem to shift because one of them jumped for a basket and made some critical points. In truth, they are constantly passing that ball back and forth. The Podcaster may be knocking everyone's socks off with riveting content and enjoying record audience growth. "I'm on top of the world." On the other hand, seemingly solid subscribers might respond to a change in Podcast time length or format by vanishing into thin air. "That doesn't work for me anymore."

Every episode, every chapter, and every moment of content must stand alone. Yes, build on what came before but give each element its own wings. Let's return to the metaphor of marriage, since it's so easily applied to relationships. As you build trust over the course of several years of marriage, your partner cuts more slack during occasional falls from grace—like that off-handed remark you made about her crazy aunt. Your track record has been so great up to this point, your partner is quick to trust your overall good intentions and chalk it up to misinterpretation or a moment of stress.

The early relationship between the Podcaster and the audience is ultimately in the hands of the consumer. The fate of content hangs on the whim and whimsy of the audience. "Do I really want this? Do I really like this? Should I listen to more? More importantly, do I like this person? Do I agree with this person? Do I want to hear more from this person?" The bud of this relationship is always vulnerable to damage or a sudden break. After all, no habitual consumption has been established. This is all new stuff and it may or may not be exciting.

The beginning of this relationship is extremely fragile. That is why we have such respect for someone like Howard Stern or Rush Limbaugh. They charge right out and start offending on the very first show. They might as well be asking the audience: "Can you stay with this? Sure, some of this stuff is so offensive that it takes your breath away. But you don't have to agree with everything and the rest of it is pretty darned entertaining."

Such personalities are accepted as completely authentic from the get go. Would Stern and Limbaugh waste time courting an audience? Never. These men have learned the fine art of polarizing their audiences with stellar (and often immediate) results. Both of them are at the top of their game in the category of "love them or hate them but never anywhere in the middle" kind of shock celebrities. They each have a wildly loyal following as well as a crowd of folks who would love to pitch rotten tomatoes their direction.

Podcasting says, "Here I am. Turn up the volume or turn the channel." In very real terms, the consumer or subscriber is now in complete control. "Forget you. I don't have to download your show. I can unsubscribe at any time and pop you like a soap bubble. You won't see it coming and you won't know it happened. Maybe I'll just download you and never listen."

The control held by the listener is truly daunting to the Podcast producer. Your audience ultimately turns up that volume button and physically makes that Podcast happen.

It is as if your life as a Podcaster will be hanging by the threat of this merciless and unpredictable group of hopeful subscribers. Some days, you may feel as if you are pulling petals off a daisy and chanting, "They love me. They love me not."

On the outside, the complete control of the listener seems undisputed. If you look more deeply into the layers that make up the inner Podcast world, you will see that the content provider can rise to a position of incredible influence with his habitual listeners. Like a puppeteer, he can begin to move the strings attached to his audience. What are those strings of influence? The ongoing dialog between Podcaster and audience that makes this medium so revolutionary. Hopefully, an audience who is well-matched to content will glide through the moves and find the dance incredibly enjoyable. Any relationship where only one side has all the control is doomed to disaster.

The Podcaster needs to capture that dialog like precious fireflies in a jar, and then examine it carefully as priceless input from this new and fragile audience. A successful Podcaster is going to use dialog with his audience to strategize, to launch, to improve, to change, to grow, to create new markets—and to *monetize*.

The strength of any relationship and its ability to continue to grow deeper is the speed with which you reconcile when things go wrong. An apology like the one Johnson & Johnson submitted after the Tylenol scandal of the '80s is a perfect example. Anyone who was around to watch that frenzy should be truly amazed that the brand name Tylenol ever survived, much less returned to market in record time. Tylenol still enjoys leading-product fame. But Johnson & Johnson stepped forward and placed its own financial loss below the safety and welfare of its customers. Consumers are going to give you big points for being willing to admit that something has gone wrong. With Podcasting, you can apologize and start a dialog about fixing the issue.

Apologizing is something that we do frequently when we blow things on our show. Sometimes we won't even realize what happened until the feedback arrives to clue us in to the hard facts. Strangely, our apology seems to return the control to us again. Audience trust in us is deepened, not damaged or broken. If we failed to take this humble route of honest dialog and admit our mistakes right away, the control would be entirely in the palm of the consumer. Once a Podcaster loses favor and influence with an audience, all control is lost as well.

Podcasters are definitely in control of production. The Podcaster is 100 percent in real time when he is producing, totally removed and isolated from the audience. At the same time, he is always mindful of what he is offering to his audience and how they might respond or react (now or later). The control between Podcaster and audience will always be an ebb and flow tidal movement. The reason that control is so fluid in this relationship is based on one fact: Dialog is the underlying controlling force in a Podcast, and dialog doesn't rest in anyone's palm for very long. Dialog, like the air we breathe, is constantly circulating.

Decisions made by the audience and the Podcaster can turn the tide of control. The consumer is the one who decides to listen and consume. The Podcaster is deciding which message will match his market at this precise time. How does he do that? By reaching into the water and swishing it around. If he's doing things incorrectly, he won't be getting any waves of feedback in return. If feedback begins to roll his way, he needs to stick with it and even intensify his attention on any hot buttons that emerge.

The right medium makes all the difference

Podcasting is introducing a dramatically more intimate medium to the world of communication than has been possible in the past. One of the best ways to deepen the understanding of this new medium is to make some appropriate comparisons to familiar Internet scenarios.

Podcast listeners share many similarities with the Google customer in search-engine marketing. Lots of people are surfing the web, going to search engines, and looking for content. Many other folks are consuming media—Podcast or otherwise. On the basis of statistics only, the traditional Google user is more likely to find just what she is seeking. In fact, Google has a reputation (deserved or other-

The constantly fluid motion of control between audience and Podcaster eventually leads to the sweet spot, which is what this book is also trying to find.

WHO BENEFITS THE MOST FROM A PODCAST?

Pocasters who leverage as many of the four Podcast consumer benefits (let's call them the PCBs) as possible are going to create some real excitement. Obviously, many different approaches and elements can make a Podcast exciting and captivating. We have narrowed down the four PCBs. We'll talk about each one of them and give examples.

1. time shifted access means they can listen *when* they want to.

2. Editorial control means they can listen to *what* they want to.

3. Portable consumption means they can listen *where* they want to.

4. Subscription content means that they can listen on a regular, consistent, and individual basis.

Any one of these elements taken alone would be exciting news, but the true power of Podcasting is the layering of these elements. The more you combine, the greater the benefit to your consumers. Let's take a look at a few examples of fine, good, better, and best.

An example of *fine* is the time shifted delivery of a corporate marketing message. This Podcast probably replaces a traditional message that required the audience to be physically present at some specific place and time in order to consume. Just the time-shifting advantage is exciting.

Good adds editorial control to time-shifting. Consumers develop a feeling of kinship with Podcasters who don't waste their time or force-feed them. I want to jump ahead if the first 30 minutes of an event will be spent bringing the audience up to speed with what I already know. I want to save 30 minutes of my busy day without losing one minute of valuable content.

Better adds the convenience of resurrecting down time to time-shifting and editorial control. Imagine receiving a corporate marketing Podcast and hearing, "Listen to the sections that interest you at your leisure." Unprecedented consumer control is one of the most exciting elements of Podcasting. Consumers not only control the content, they can listen on their own terms at the location of their choice.

Tivo has already given us a taste of power and control in consumption of content. Consider shows that begin with a recap of the previous week's episode. Sure, I enjoy watching my favorite show whenever I have the time and desire. Being able to fast-forward through last week's recap because I already saw it happen? Priceless.

wise) as the search engine for those who know what they are trying to find. Some of the other search engines tend to attract more newbie surfers. Since Google customers usually know what it is they are looking for, they are considerably more powerful when digging into their wallets.

We will pay good money on Google for a high priority on search terms for some of our other businesses. But we won't spend a dime in Yahoo! or MSN, because we know the Google user will convert.

This is all tracked and carefully examined. We are not making these decisions based on our gut feeling or gut reaction. I absolutely *know* that the Google user will convert in a way that the Yahoo! user simply will not (and I have the numbers to prove it). The devil is in the details, and these are the details you can't afford to overlook. It's possible that you might sell something to Yahoo! users that a Google user won't pick up. Test the waters and run checks and tallies. These are solid rules to play by if you really want to win.

Folks who prefer a Google search also like a clean page free of copy and advertising. The MSN person is just the opposite, especially if the person is a she. MSN fans love a ton of copy and click choices, some of them for Hollywood gossip or any number of other enticing information. Both of these people—the Google and the MSN—can buy the same amount of content or the same amount of consumer goods. They just want to be communicated to differently.

The paradox is this: once your listeners are consuming your content on their own terms, you

What if I only care to watch one of Letterman's interviews? I have that power – and I only take 10 minutes to do what took most people an hour.

The *best* example crowns all of the other layers with habitual consumption. *Best* would describe editorial control of a marketing Podcast on the morning commute. Here, the message becomes part of the consumer's schedule.

One of my personal favorites is the Daily Source Code Podcast by Adam Curry, who tries to weave countless elements of the "Podosphere" into a single show. I listen to his Podcast in my car, at the gym, and on the plane. When an element comes up that I don't care about, I fast-forward right through it. His 40-minute show often takes only about 15 minutes of my time, *but I do listen regularly—where and when I please.* The show is also broadcast on satellite radio. But if I had to catch that thing at 4:00 PM weekdays, it would never happen.

We can actually step through the fine, good, better, best layers in a single example: Transferring an informational teleseminar or event into a Podcast for later consumption. As anyone who visits Teleseminar SecretsPodcast.com will learn, the teleseminar is an extremely powerful medium—bigger than Podcasting at this point. However, the *power of Podcasting* enables us to time-shift that valuable teleseminar content.

Being able to listen to the content in your own time is *fine*. It would be *good* to have the editorial control to pick and choose the sections that interest you. Information-rich teleseminars can represent a tremendous commitment of time. Being able to catch that content later on an iPod and screen it for personal relevancy is extremely attractive. It would be even *better* if you could consume those selections on a portable media player during your down time.

The *best* option would be a subscription to a regular training program that you could consume at will. Now you have moved beyond the limitation of a course on Monday nights at 7:00 into an unlimited world. The course is waiting on your iPod for consumption—whenever and wherever you decide to listen and whatever you desire to absorb. Think of these PCBs as increments of power, and add as many of them as you possibly can to your Podcasting strategy. At this time, most people who consume Podcasts are not focused on the freedom it offers over time and space. They have been too blinded by the first flash of novelty and sex appeal to see the layers of benefits and opportunities this technology really opens up. Looking ahead a year or two, Podcasting will undoubtedly be consumed the way Tivo is today. You want to fast-forward through that commercial? I'll give you not just one, but three speeds for fast forward.

have them in a way no other media can have them. Once they have become the habitual consumer who is in control, they are going to return that control—or even more—right back to you again.

This chapter on the who of Podcasting is the reason why Podcasting or any type of communication medium is even in existence. We are attempting to define *who* we are speaking to, who our Podcast is addressing. Once the *who* is clear, the content begins to write itself. Knowing *who* means that you understand the listener's status and changing personal roles and know his fears and dreams.

Speaking to your audience at that point becomes easy and natural. It is certainly preferable to playing a game of "pin the tail on the donkey" with your dialog—the path most marketers

CHAPTER FOUR

take. Some people who would be knocked off the air in radio or television can enter the Podcast world, so be prepared for a glut of garbage. Even if the content has value, the Podcast might flounder because the message doesn't match the market. Consumers are going to become increasingly savvier over time about searching effectively through Podcast titles for the right match for their interests and needs.

Our very concentration on *who* in the writing of this book has driven us to take a closer look at *who* should be listening to Marketing Online Live. We stuck the post in the sand and said, "This is for business people who want to communicate internally and those who want to monetize their communication efforts." Podcasting is for business people, not just for entertainment and folly.

Even the early adopters are not really taking a close look at this time-shifting capability. Like everyone else, they are mesmerized by the sex appeal. Early adopters are fixated on being first in line, "Hey, I'm listening. Is this something I'm interested in? Can I do this too?" Those are the kinds of questions running around their heads. We *know* what they are thinking because we have talked to thousands of them.

Every serious Business Podcaster needs to understand the four Podcast consumer benefits inside out and upside down. You need to grasp the power of this highly leveraged communication tool that offers portable time-shifting and editorial control. At least in this early phase, you are going to have to teach your audience about these tremendous benefits.

W. Edwards Deming used to say that everything else besides leverage is a waste. In the world of Podcasting, leverage makes it possible to communicate on both the receiver's terms and the sender's terms. Podcasting technology increases the relevancy of communication by increasing *access*. Right now, we are creating content by working on this book. But if no one ever finds or consumes this content, everything has been a waste, no matter how good the content is.

Podcasting gives us greater access in more places—faster, better, and with less human effort. In fact, the portable time-shifting capability of Podcast makes it the most highly leveraged communication-based technology on today's market. Just keep in mind that your audience still needs to be led down that path of discovery.

The consumer is not aware of the four PCBs. That's why we invested additional money and gave away 500 MP3 players at Big Seminar V. Everyone received a downloadable file of the seminar recording as part of the package. We knew darn well that 99 percent would never listen to it on their computers, even though they paid $2,000 to attend the event. A few might think to burn it to CD and consume it during down time on a portable CD player. Giving this group of people a portable media player would allow them to drag and drop and take that seminar recording literally anywhere. We added the PCB of portability, and now we have an audience hooked on that possibility. The BigSeminarLive.com Podcast is now many times the size it once was, and we have monetized it accordingly.

Any business that could have a better dialog or provide a better service using as many of the four PCBs as possible could benefit from producing a Podcast. If you can't leverage *any* of the four PCBs, don't get into Podcasting. This differs dramatically from the image that is associated with Business Podcasting right now. Shooting something through the Podcast channel and ending up at iTunes might be a weak

When our readers grasp and internalize that this is *The Business Podcasting Bible* and not the *Podcasting Bible*, our back-and-forth dialog will flow more smoothly.

The *who* question seems to be the single-most important one of all. Considering this critical factor recently allowed me to coax more than 700 *who's* into paying $1,800 *what's*—translated as dollars. Understanding my *who* enabled me to produce a successful eight-module program entitled, "How to improve teleseminars."

The focal point for any Podcaster should be paring down "who is the listener" and then asking, "How can I find those people?" What questions should you be asking yourself about who your audience really is and what market would be a perfect match.

attempt at branding. Just seeing your name at iTunes carries some strength and leverage. We want you to really grasp the magnitude of the opportunity that opens up when you start leveraging the four PCBs. That approach to Podcasting is exponentially more powerful and would justify any expense related to your Podcasting strategy.

Let's get one thing straight: At the time of writing, *today's typical Podcast audience is not your ideal audience*. The ideal would be any media consumer who is looking for a better channel or could use a better channel but doesn't know it exists. Let's face it, most media consumers look at the available channels with disgust like the older fellow who yells at the NBC News. He could use a better channel. He just doesn't know it's available. You need to make it available and tell him about it.

Busy people are seldom excited about personally attending an event. They do it because that's the only way the information they want is being offered. People will love and appreciate you for handing them the option to consume on their own time, in their own place, *without airline travel*. The technology behind Podcasting should never get in the way of the message: "We have a better channel for you." Your strategies and your implementation must prevent technology from overshadowing this essential message.

We already know that technology will eventually make it much easier to consume Podcasts. It's already moving rapidly in that direction. Think about the place we were a year ago and where we are now. I'm blown away at the difference, and I can't wait to see where we are next year. If we could time travel back to 1995, we would say to the early adopters of the Internet, "Figure out your web play now, before the technology becomes so easy. When the ease comes, you'll be far ahead of the game."

The same thing is true of Podcasting right now. If the ideal audience for a Podcast is any media consumer who is looking for a better channel, the ideal audience for a Podcast is any media consumer. If you can figure out your strategy in time for the technology—which will continue to come very quickly—you can be in an incredibly powerful place.

Granted, it is difficult for *consumers* to beat technology to the punch. The masses always move slowly and need to be led. That's why the impact of Podcasting will depend largely upon early adopters, especially in business. They will be the ones to pass their ability along to others and teach them how to find and consume Podcasts.

We not only have to teach our listeners, we need to teach them to teach others. That educational approach is going to enhance the viral nature of the entire process. We saw this proliferation of technology with those who first adopted AOL Instant Messenger and taught others to do the same. It was IM that put AOL on the map. Sending an instant message is so much more intimate than sending email. The AOL IM network was closed, so you either joined the AOL game or you couldn't play. Access to AOL IM from the outside was not available in the beginning. AOL created a closed platform that forced people to buy its service if they wanted to communicate through instant messages.

In order to push this technology beyond the early adopters in the mainstream, we have to engage those early adopters in passing along the message. Sometimes that will mean delivering free content so that monetization becomes possible later. Sometimes, it will mean turning them into teachers the way we do with our affiliate partners. We train our resellers how to resell to others and train other resellers how to do the same thing.

In the early stages, consumption needs to remain firmly in the back our minds in every single Podcast message. How do we get this message out there? How can we tease? How can we goose the listener to spread the news on a tell-a-friend basis? Not only are these hooks going to be responsible for the acceleration of the Marketing Online Live show, they will allow any Podcast to succeed organically rather than through promotion and marketing.

In a word, they are the PCBs. You don't show them the fancy new video iPod unless they are a geeky tech-type. We actually did an entire call on this, which you can pick up at LearningSecretsRevealed.com. The first hour was all about the excitement of portable down-time content and learning—the excitement of capturing those hours in the day when nothing gets done and using them for education or self improvement. Only later did we explain that Podcasting was the tool that makes it all possible.

Socratic dialog versus marketing monologue

Having a monologue can be equated to having a billboard on the side of the freeway or the turnpike. Newscasters take this approach late at night. Over the years, Paul Harvey has always presented his show this way. Nearly every type of electronic and non-electronic communication has been a monologue. Once the marketer or communicator reaches a certain level of success and status, he or she begins to fall prey to the mindset that says, "I think I know it all."

That marketer feels that the burden of proof is completely resting on his shoulders. He feels as if he is imparting the truth and telling the story. He isn't going back to the principle-centered Socratic methodology and technology that is so

That's how you scatter the message. The first adopters didn't introduce IM to others by saying, "Check this out. AOL has a gigantic server that manages connections to millions of different users all at the same time." No, the message went more like this, "Do you have something brief to say, something very immediate? At the click of a button, we can make those tiny messages pop up on our screens." *That* was the message that made IM so huge.

The Podcasting message says, "We have a better media for you. Now you can stop yelling at NBC News. You can be in control of the delivery channel." The listeners can't believe their own ears. "How can I do that?" The answer is Podcasting.

Meet your audience. But now, for the first time in history, you can proudly say that you are, wherever they are, whenever they are.

TEACHING YOUR AUDIENCE TO CONSUME THE PODCAST

At the present time Podcasts are still very new, even for the technologically competent. Just recently, I attended an event and spoke with a fellow who is very well-known for his technical capabilities. This guy has programmed some truly amazing and forward-thinking Internet marketing technologies. During the bus ride on our way to dinner, he looked me straight in the eye and asked, "So what is this Podcasting thing all about?"

Even those who "understand" Podcasting are likely right now to see it as a world filled with iTunes and iPods. A friend said to me at lunch the other day, "Paul, I love to listen to these Podcasts but I don't want to buy an iPod." Like many other people, he has yet to tumble to the unique control this time shifted portability really offers. Another buddy has a car stereo that plays CDs and he has a lengthy commute. He's also the kind of guy who loves to buy CDs on 100-pack spindles for free after rebate. I told him to burn those Podcasts to CD and listen to them during his downtime. I bet him good money that he would want to buy an iPod within five days of CD burning. Once he realizes that he is in total control of consumption, he will be hungry for the benefits of this medium, and will purchase whatever made it as easy as possible. I won the bet for providing the benefits before introducing the technology

We are teaching our audience how to listen. We are teaching them about the value of what they are holding in their hands—portability, editorial control, time-shifting, and subscription options. Click-to-listen might be an excellent first step. Many people will not take the time to transfer until they know the content is worthwhile. Both of us appreciate what Yahoo! is offering. However, you need

simple even a child can handle it. That childhood mechanism shuts down at the point when they have asked "Why?" about 50 times in five minutes and hear the words, "Because I said so."

"Why does the sun come up? Why does the sun go down?" That child assumes the form of the audience, and the Socratic dialog is allowing that audience to interact. They can now ask questions and receive responses—not necessarily favorable responses. Many times the dialog is much more important than the nature of the response. The comparison of monolog to dialog is a simple recognition that two-way communication is enormously more powerful than one-way communication.

Bowling is a great example. I don't bowl but I know what bowling is.

The goal is knocking down the pins by rolling a heavy ball down a narrow lane and avoiding the gutters on either side. If you can send your ball in a fairly straight line through the marked arrows in the middle of the alley, you'll hit a few pins. Now imagine having a bed sheet in front of those bowling pins that keeps you from seeing the results. I can still hear the pins fall, but I can't be sure enough of anything or keep an accurate score. The sheet has blocked my feedback. That's a monologue. Who would want to keep playing that way?

You are the bowler with the sheet in front of you. Lift the sheet or part the curtain and we are able to keep score. Change the monologue where the sheet covers the pins into a dialog that reveals how many pins fell. These pins are not animate. They are

to encourage portable time-shifting and subscriptions on every episode.

Every episode of Marketing Online Live ends with an encouragement to subscribe to our show. The audience members who have already subscribed know this part by memory and usually turn off the show before they hear it. Those who aren't subscribers, consume our subscription directions and often take the very action we encourage in it.

Consider purchasing the portable media players for the right audience. The previously mentioned Alex Nano and the Big Seminar are two examples. Obviously, you need a paying audience. If you are going to deliver a $200 piece of hardware to every listener, the monetization options for your Podcast have to be in place. Once your audience really understands the benefits of this medium, they will be willing to learn the technology. Coming to them with the technology first will never work.

For an example of this live in action, visit BigSeminarLive.com, the Big Seminar Live Podcast. Sign up for the email series and see how we walk you through the process of understanding the benefits of a Podcast. We don't take you into the consumer side of it. We have many people who have subscribed to the Big Seminar Live Podcast email list who are not necessarily listeners. Nevertheless, slowly but surely they are being trained to consume. With every show, we are teaching them other ways to consume that are more convenient to accelerate that process.

Our hidden agenda—or not so hidden—is teaching them to teach others to consume. In the business-to-business environment, everyone is a Podcaster. In fact, every business is a Podcasting business. We could make that the subtitle for this book or an interesting title for another book: Why Every Business is a Podcasting Business and How Yours Can Benefit, Too.

Every business is a Podcasting business just like every business is a marketing business. Podcasting only enhances the communication between you and the customer or you and your colleagues in a business environment. Every Podcast needs to be teaching consumption in the tip or the tail or the middle—somewhere, so people can pass this knowledge along. Every show is a "passing along" opportunity like magazines are passed around a doctor's office.

METHODS AND TECHNOLOGIES FOR INITIATING THE DIALOG

1. Grab emails at your website and encourage users in every episode to visit your website. Ask them for their email address. Email addresses are easy to get once they know, like,

not shouting out, "Look, I'm down. Score me." In this case, the dialog is happening in the mind of the bowler. That dialog does not happen with broadcast today—or with most forms of communication now—because things change when people reach a certain level of status.

We need to have a sense of humility to dialog and communicate effectively. Let's say that someone approaches me and asks, "What is Podcast?" I could bend her ear with a three-hour monologue. But the right answer—the most authentic and economical answer—would be another question: "What does Podcasting mean to you right now?" Like a well-versed Google search, that dialog will easily steer the conversation toward the hot buttons for that person. We search Google to find something relevant to our personal search, not to see how many thousands of websites are in the Google database.

The person might reply, "I've heard that Podcasting is time shifted communication." That answer would bring me to another question, "What exactly does time-shifting mean to you?" After whatever answer she might give, I would ask yet another question, "Why is that important to you?" By asking just a few questions, I will be able to find out everything I need to know about her. I can then show them the benefits of time shifted communication considerably better than by handing them a book on the topic.

This approach is not new. Great sales representatives and persuasive leaders often engage others in dialog. Unfortunately, the great-

and trust you. Just don't betray that trust.

2. Don't be afraid to offer some sort of ethical bribe. Many times that will simply be premium content. They might find you through a traditional channel at the most open of shows, but you can use an ethical bribe to bring them into premium content tracked through a system like Premium Podcasting. At that point, things start to become very interesting.

3. Your website will be another technological tool for initiating dialog. Go out to MarketingOnlineLive.com and you can see we fully open comments for every episode. Look around the site and you'll realize that here again, the focus remains on capturing email addresses.[1]

Understanding the *who* in Podcasting requires a clear understanding of the six major differences between the Podcast consumer and everyone else.

1. The Podcast consumer has tasted both options and has chosen the

---

1. There are those who would say that email marketing is dead and that nobody gives away their email addresses any more. We've touched on the topic a few times in our show and believe we've said it all there. If anyone tells you that email marketing is dead, pray that they are your competitor.

Podcast. Not everyone will embrace Podcast and see it as worthwhile. This is very important.

The average consumer of traditional media has not tasted both options and feels stuck. The Podcast listener already knows about and appreciates the power of this medium. If you embrace and validate that power, you will have a consumer who has chosen you after seeing all the available options.

2. The Podcast consumer will decide *when* to listen. Obviously, be careful with time-sensitive content. Having an offer that closes on a Friday is probably not a good idea. The consumer decides when to listen, and many of them take advantage of weekend down time. Expecting a certain window of closure is fine. Just build your content accordingly.

3. The Podcast consumer decides *which part* of the content he or she will consume. We saw this first with CNN Headline News telling us that 19 minutes after the hour is sports. People would tune in at a specific time to catch the traffic report or the weather. With the consumer deciding what part and when they will consume, you must develop stand-alone content. Unless you are extremely focused, people may not want to take in all that you are offering.

est broadcasters do not. They might think that's what they are doing, but it is not. Some are able to tap into a conversation that is going on in the mind of the listener. Barbara Walters is a master of this level of perception. She might ask a celebrity, "Why are you so angry at your father?" Then we see that celebrity burst into tears. Walters has done her research and she is engaging in dialog by proxy. Maybe she didn't speak to everyone, but she has taken the pulse of her audience. Larry King and Oprah Winfrey operate in much the same way.

We have found that Podcasting is largely misunderstood as a communication medium. Too many Podcasters are under the false impression that they have to engage in a different dialog because it is being delivered via Podcast.

The opposite is true: The dialog is really the same; only the delivery differs. Podcasters believe they have to change their level of communication or the way they communicate. No, they can do the same thing in a more dialog-based manner. They just need to take a Socratic approach and ask the right questions at the right time. Engage your audience and they are going to be more open and willing to share.

This is why the *who* in Podcasting is so important. When we learn to ask the right questions, the *who* finds us. We don't have to find them – but we begin to understand who they are and what they need from us. The marriage is made when the listener finds us. We aren't going to be seeking them out through a newspaper ad or a cold call or an email message or a direct mail postcard.

4. The Podcast consumer expects the opportunity for dialog. Dialog is part of the discourse, part of the game, part of the process. First, provide the communication and the opportunity for dialog—then validate the user.

Embracing dialog is truly a competitive advantage. Those who fail to do this will lose. The dialog provides a clear advantage by being higher in the chain of communication. Dialog is a more elegant form of communication because it allows the other party to have their say and feel understood. We need more dialoging in our own Podcast. We need more surveys and more dialog to make the show more engaging and to encourage our audience to use the mouse more often—not just the portable media player.

5. The Podcast consumer starts and ends the dialog at will. We are not talking about traditional office hours or a limited directive like: "If you want to call in to my show, start phoning 30 minutes early when everyone else does." Because these consumers hold the dialog start and stop whistle, each episode must be self-contained. Each method for dialog must be open 24 hours a day, seven days a week. So far, we have yet to see a Podcast that offers a 1-800 number to call for live

dialog. However, hundreds of Podcasts offer a 1-800 line for comment messages (and integrate them into every part of their message).

6. The Podcast consumer utilizes multiple environments, so don't assume anything. We have heard a lot of talk about the future of Podcast commerce as a click-and-buy environment. What a silly idea. That avid consumer listening to your show on the bike at the gym or on the airplane is not going to be able to open up the web browser and follow through on the click-to-action that you recommended.

Memorize these six major differences between the Podcast consumer and the traditional consumer. Understand the differences, build your plan around them, and you will be in a great place.

THE POWER OF A GENUINE MESSAGE IN A TYPICALLY DISTRUSTED MEDIA

If you want to see the power that this medium provides, sit and watch a few cars at the McDonald's drive-through. Invariably, you will see some mom with a van filled with screaming kids for whom this fast-food restaurant has become a god-send. McDonalds answers multiple questions for

We want to connect with those people who are going online and *looking* for something like our show. Once they find us, they will stay with us if we can give them what they want. That is exactly what has unfolded for us in a relatively short period of time. Dialog is really the driving force behind this book. Without that background of dialogs, we would lack the stream of consciousness to write the book.

Being dialog-centered and not monologue-centered was the reason that we even responded to the publisher's inquiry. In the middle of a dialog that asked the audience for participation, he emailed in and said, "Hey, let's make this a book!" What could be more participatory or dialog-centered than that?

that mom. She can get the kids fed and give them what they want at the time they are clamoring for it. She can even do this in a way the kids love.

By the way, the real power of McDonalds for many Mom's is that 347pm afternoon realization that kids haven't had lunch yet and there is nothing at home for them to grab. McDonald's being there, for them, on their terms is what forms the emotional attachment.

The same should be true for your listeners. Be there for your listeners. Give them what they want at the time they are clamoring for it. Show them that you trust them and prove yourself worthy of their trust. Once you acknowledge that *they* are in control, your audience is going to respond in amazing ways.

Here are five things that you can do with a Podcast audience that are not usually possible with a traditional audience.

1. Eliminate all real excuses for consumption. Time, location, and availability are all moot with Podcasting. Think about the litany of excuses: I can't make your event. I just can't listen to the whole thing right now. I'm home sick today. I can't fly that week because something else is happening at the other end of the country.

2. Increase and intensify the frequency of your message as needed. If you think that you need to raise the bar, you can. Calm things down if you feel that is necessary. Your audience will respect you. If you don't need to give out the message this week, they will respect that.

3. Deliver the mountain if your audience can't reach it. When traditional consumption models are limiting or impossible, the power of Podcast soars in value. You don't have to chop an event; make a Podcast of it. Go ahead and give that call to action as long as you have a reasonable chance for a response.

4. Place your consumers in control. After all, they are invested in this delivery (and they're in control anyway). These are not average consumers. They have subscribed and chosen to listen—or

not to listen. If the dialog is valid and makes sense, you are in a good place.

5. Eliminate traditional delivery norms and expectations. The evening news is 30 minutes. The TV movie of the week is two hours. The reality show is an hour. The film at the theater is 90 minutes. The radio show—if it happens to be Rush—runs for three hours every weekday.

Traditional delivery norms can end up with useless padding. If you are attentive, you can hear a radio personality or TV hosts stalling to fill the empty space. Worse yet, he might have too much content toward the end and start to speed through, losing critical points. Maybe some annoying member of the audience took too much time with a question and now the host is scrambling to beat the clock. Podcasting gives you a chance to break free of those frustrations.

CONCLUSION

There are only two kinds of Podcast consumers: those who understand the power of medium and embrace it completely and those waiting for you to teach them how to do just that. The first audience is ripe for business communication and the second is ready for you to teach them how to join the ranks of the first.

An audience in charge understands that they are different and, in fact, resent any communication methodology that tells them otherwise. Communicate with them (in word and deed) that you understand their position and you'll have a hungry audience. If you audience isn't yet plugged in, teach them how to be in charge of their media consumption and you have an audience for life.

A customer in charge expects dialogue with you. Your Podcast can only be better from this kind of dialogue. Make it a regular part of your Podcast and you'll quickly rise to the top.

AT THE PRIVATE MEMBER SITE

At time of publication, Microsoft had yet to introduce a Podcatching client. Realize it is inevitable and it will increase the audience of consumers exponentially overnight as did Apple's and Tivo's play. We track this (and additional content on the "Who" of Business Podcasting) at http://www.TheBusinessPodcastingBible.com/who.

CHAPTER FIVE

"I rob banks because that's where the money is."

—Willy Sutton

"Opportunities can be obstacles."

—T. Harv Eker

We know many of you will jump strait to this chapter. We don't mind, but do suggest that the question of "where" is better answered if you understand the "Why," "How," "What" and "Who?"

For the Business Podcaster, it ain't worth doing if there isn't any money in it. In this chapter, we show you exactly where the money is.

WHERE IS THE MONEY?

In previous chapters we discussed the duality of Podcasting and that it was in fact two things: a new medium and a new media delivery channel.

Although there will be stories of Podcasts that didn't exist before 2004, the history of Podcasting will also tell of extremely profitable companies that embraced Podcasting as an additional content delivery channel—not a new one. Many people today only see Podcasting as an entirely different medium or format like the sitcom, a docudrama, or the American musical.

They want to segment Podcasting within that limited space. They are missing out. A recent article in the *The Wall Street Journal* stated that the concept of charging money to consume a Podcast proves the power of Podcast content. That's absolutely wrong. You can certainly explore the Podcasting medium, but it is the strong belief of your authors that the real power and real source of monetization lies in Podcast *as a content delivery channel*.

The 8-track cassette that seems comical today was an exciting innovation in the early '70s. Podcasting, as a means of content delivery may seem equally silly in a world that one day relies on telepathic communication. Right now, Podcasting is new and sexy—just like the 8-tracks, cassette tapes, CDs, laser discs, DVDs, and MP3s that were once all new and sexy. It might be the latest thing, but it isn't *the* thing—it's simply the "next" *delivery methodology*.

And, the money is in the delivery methodology.

Content is the real value of iPods, Nano's, Zens or any other type of MP3 player. Without content, the player has no value as no one will pay hundreds of dollars to listen to, or watch silence.In that same way, the Podcast is like the player—just another form of delivery (like satellite radio or cable television). Keeping that in mind enables us to keep Podcast in its true context from a business and monetization perspective.

No one seems to be discussing iPod monetization, but many people are looking to monetize the Podcast. Why? At the time of writing, considerably more money has been made supporting the "iPod" industry (think cases, speakers, battery packs or the FM transmitters we're such big fans of) that has been made from Podcasting.

The speed, mobility, and time shifted convenience of Podcasting set it apart as a communication methodology. What are we really dealing with here? We are essentially talking about the lightning exchange of ones and zeros, not something that we can see or touch. The word is *efficiency*.

Media delivery, finally, is efficient. The days of transmitters, FCC licenses and the broadcast are as "yesterday" as the eight track cassette and record player. Something, suddenly, changes everything.

And that, our loyal readers, is where the money is. Let's return to the example of calling Dell Computer and hearing, "What can I build for you today?" If you were launching a Podcast and you called the Dell of Podcasting, the question might be, "What Podcast show can I deliver for you today?" Podcast as a delivery channel is the only lens through which we can accurately view monetization. Any other approach leaves us at the mercy of the next great innovation. "Better" will inevitably trump whatever "best" you have right now. And when that new brand comes along, the rejection is devastating.

Part of the power of Podcasting is the fact that this communication model is nothing new. The laws of obsolescence that govern innovation cannot be applied to a conglomeration of existing technologies. The launch of Alex's Audiogenerator.com is a good example of this collaborative convergence. Rather than offer something new, the service brought together flash audio, a good web hosting system, phone-to-computer recording, flash distribution, and a membership website. The integration of these existing features, although nothing new, has made Audio Generator what it is today. Their advent of "audio postcards" is nothing more than a Web file in .html format that opens and automatically plays an audio message, yet it changed the face of email marketing at it's introduction.

Podcasting follows the same. Podcasting, *made up of not a single new technology*, draws together technologies and arranges them under a single idea that is suddenly being embraced for its power, convenience, and cost-effective value. In fact, it launches an industry. Substituting ones and zeros for air waves, the Podcaster is in business the same way that a major broadcasting station is in business. Selling *a Podcast* is just one tiny piece of the 10,000-piece puzzle of *Podcast monetization*.

Any author could have a literary circle of subscribers who received Podcasts of his content. After the subscribers vote on the content, the author can go back and write the book. Podcasting does not always have to remain at the bottom of the arc or at the end of the marketing continuum. As long as we understand Podcasting as a delivery methodology, we can use it effectively at the top or the beginning of the arc. Whether you use it for fact-finding surveys or monetize from it directly, Podcasting is still another delivery mechanism.

CHAPTER FIVE   137

So, where is the money? Anyone who is keenly interested in Business Podcasting might have just jumped right to this chapter and skipped everything that went before it. We understand the extreme importance of this concept. At the same time, we suggest that "Where is the money?" is not the first question to ask when approaching Podcast as a communication tool. The history of technology has been fascinating because technology itself is so distracting. People always look for revenue streams before they understand the nature of the power in their command. Our goal is two-fold:

1. Give you a clear understanding of all that this technology makes available to you.

2. Guide you toward revenue streams that are closely aligned with those technological advantages.

If anything, we want to encourage you to go back and *reread* every chapter that came before this one. We want you to have a deep and clear understanding of everything that led us to the point of asking "Where is the money?" The issue of profit and gain is so critical that we have written every word of the book in a purposeful order. Instead of being distracted by technology, make sure that the communication options provided by Podcasting remain at the forefront of any discussion of monetization.

THE DANGERS OF FIRE, AIM, READY

Too many people are shooting out Podcasts and approaching their monetization efforts with a *fire, aim, ready* mentality. They slap a cover on their Podcast, place it on iTunes, and wait for whatever happens (and wonder where the checks are). The worst case scenario for this shotgun launch is a complete disaster. Even those who meet with a degree of popularity and success will find it difficult to shift from giving away content to requesting paid subscriptions. That loyal audience suddenly feels betrayed and stung.

Setting your standard length at 10 minutes will make it tough for you to go beyond that time limit later—even if the quality and volume of your content dictates the change. We know many Podcasters who are unable to break free of a launch format that keeps their wheels spinning. This frequently happens to those who were seduced by the sexiness of video Podcasting. The tremendous commitment of time and effort required by video production reduces the content output to $1/100^{th}$ of what could have been possible with pure audio.

Podcast monetization demands a *ready, aim, fire* approach that we refer to as *Strategy Casting*™. What do we mean by that? Strategy casting quite simply states that you will not launch your Podcast until you have a clear plan for monetization. Content is king. Content determines the nature of your Podcast and its ultimate value. Without content, your so-called Podcast is nothing more than a mass of material moving through the airwaves or along the Podcast superhighway – and one that wastes your time at that.

Let's go one step beyond *ready, aim, fire* and paraphrase the philosophy of Ross Perot, one of the world's wealthiest entrepreneurs: *Ready, aim, fire, fire, fire, fire, fire.* That is exactly what we want you to do with your content. Be ready, aim in the right direction to the perfect target market, and then keep firing once you have matched that market with your message. As you'll see in this chapter, we take this approach every single week with our Marketing Online Live show.

In the early evolution of Podcasting, the very opposite has been true. Many have taken a *fire, fire, fire, fire, fire, ready, aim* approach, slapping Podcasts like wet noodles against the wall to see if anything sticks. What ends up on that wall is a loud statement that you, as a Podcaster, have absolutely no idea what you are doing. What other reason would you have for launching all those different Podcasts in such varied formats? Why should I listen to, or watch, you?

Once you have your arms firmly wrapped around a workable strategy, you can start to play with it. The importance of *Strategy Casting prior to Podcast launch* cannot be overstated. If you don't know where it is that you are headed, how can you possibly find the way? At this very moment, the iTunes directory is filled with literally thousands of Podcasts that lack worthwhile content[1]. Many of these would be in a much better place had their process begun with a little strategy.

---

1. At the time of writing, iTunes was filled with thousands of Podcasts that haven't been updated in months because they, obviously, have died on the vine. When you read this, the graveyard might be cleared out – but if it isn't, take a look around as it is a wonderful, but grim reminder of your need to plan.

WHOTHEMEDIA.COM?

Multiple options in "the media game" have long been available for building revenue, generating profit, monetization—whatever label you want to use. The "real money" in media production falls into three major categories:

1. Media Producers

Those who produce the media are the obvious first step in this game. Be they the rock star or the hot new director, media has to be produced for any revenue to be seen. Simply said: no product, no money.

But, of course, the rock stars play guitars, they don't run record companies. The generation of revenue needs to be handed over to someone who knows how to generate revenue from the rock star's efforts.

2. Media Distributors

More commonly recognized under the name of "the middle man," these people find and recognize great content and send it to the "right people." As a result, a great deal of cash is often generated in the process. These are the visionary folks who head out each year to the Sundance Film Festival, looking for an unpolished gem or emerging talent. These are the talent scouts who head to the clubs to find the hot new sound. Media production people have a keen sense of art—not of distribution and marketing techniques. It is up to the media distributors to catch the ball, match the art with a distribution channel, and generate the revenues in some sort of head-hunter anology. Successful middle men can reap great financial rewards without having a lick of talent.

But they do "hand it off" to someone because they need someone to push that new found talent.

3. Media Pushers

The pushers are the machines. These are the ones who have the system in place to squeeze every last dime out of the media that they picked up from their distributors. The sale and placement of advertising is component of revenue generation on this level if that option makes sense. If not, they sell the content direct, without anything getting in the way of the purity of it all.

Media producers, distributors, and pushers are the three legs of the media game tripod—all of them viable, important and best of all, profitable. Countless numbers of companies or individuals fall under more than one of these three categories.

Yes, occasionally, you'll find the artist who sells their own CDs or the film studio that owns the distribution company. But, let's admit it   more often than not, the artist would love to have a "big record deal" and the studio would give anything to have a major player distribute their content. Television rights for the latest Hollywood blockbuster anyone?

Podcasting enters the picture and writes a new page in media history. Now all three media game participants can be encompassed within the same company. In fact, Podcasting makes it possible for an *individual* to function as all three. If you understand the focus of the media game and can leverage this knowledge to your benefit, the distinctive value of Podcast becomes very clear.In the past, companies who wanted to place the CEO in front of a microphone for a special announcement or for weekly staff updates had to rely on media distributors . They might have turned to Ma Bell, Fed Ex, or Disc on Demand CD Duplication Services. They had to deal with others for the production and/or distribution of the message and pay the associated costs plus professional fees. While these expenses can be extremely worthwhile in terms of profitability, Podcasting has introduced a new paradigm. Now, the *media producer* for that company can be that very same CEO in front of a microphone. The company also assumes the (now obvious) role of distributor and pusher and the loop is closed.

The media distribution could be the IT department who places the MP3 file behind the infrastructure. The media pushers might be high-level managers who say, "If you want to keep your job, listen to the weekly update every day on the way to work."

Now let's move beyond the business application example into our Marketing Online Live show. Many of our distributors have taken our previous content and printed it, duplicated it, burned it to CD, and put it on portable media players. Many people get a piece of the action in this vast network. We have no problem with that and have seen profits from it. But, now, for Marketing Online Live, we are the producer, the distributor and the pusher of our content. The benefit of being all three far outweighs any offers for a "radio show of our own" or other options to give a piece of our pie away.

For the first time ever, Marketing Online Live is complete and total media. We are the producer, distributor and pusher.

WhotheMedia.com? YouTheMedia.com.

By embracing the WhoTheMedia.com concept, a Podcaster embraces the roles of producer, distributor, and pusher. That doesn't mean you have to go it alone just because *you are the media*. Bringing other people into the fold can be extremely helpful, but is simply, no longer, a necessity. Anyone who offers services that provide value and ease to the process would not be classified as business partners—they are now vendors. You own it all. You are the media.

Find a content producer and show him a pie chart of what he is producing and what he is selling. This piece belongs to the affiliates. This much goes to the distribution company. This much has to cover the delivery system. Now awaken that content provider to the radical concept that he can have all of that back—in terms of control and profit – and dish it out as he pleases.

Let's go back to the Hollywood analogy. No one would produce a million-dollar movie that would require $5 million to market and distribute when box office receipts are expected to top at $3 million. That same $3 million box office profit takes on an entirely different meaning when you can make that million-dollar movie without any distribution costs. Now you are seeing a *three-time return on investment*.

The same concept applies to Podcasting. *When you are the media*[2], a new world of possibilities opens up. Name one Hollywood producer who would not salivate at the thought of a three-time return on his media pro-

---

2. And, dear reader, you are the media.

THE BUSINESS **PODCASTING BIBLE**

duction. Podcasting requires minimal out-of-pocket expenses. You can enter the world of Business Podcasting for less than a $100 fare. That means that you could potentially monetize your Podcast for less than $100 without the purchase or use of expensive equipment. Less than $100 broadcasts your message to the world. How could you not monetize that?.

Podcast really means *access* The more we talk about access and the easier it becomes for us to access others, the more valuable the Podcasting channel will grow. Today's Podcast is fractured and decentralized, much like 500 cable stations that have no shared satellite or centralized station. These channels might be coming from homes, office buildings—from virtually anywhere. This will clean up quickly.

Being the media means being the media in Novato, California as well as Tigard, Oregon, or anywhere else you happen to find yourself and your microphone. It also means that you are the media *and* the medium between Novato and Tigard. This new "moving media" is both efficient and inexpensive. Being able to review ROI against a high degree of production flexibility and low cost moves the weight of pressure to the message—which can be all about finding the right match.

If I am terminally ill and you have a magic pill that will cure me, your message is going to resonate loudly. My interest depends on my own needs, regardless of how magical and wonderful that pill of yours might be. Right now, I'm perfectly fit and well. I don't care what your pill does or how expensive or inexpensive it is. I'm just not in the market right now.

Podcasting places more pressure on the audience and the sender. For the first time, the media is also the sender. The receiver is the person who is "catching" or receiving the Podcast. No other medium (or person) stands between. The sender is the media because the sender is the Podcast. The distance between sender and receiver has collapsed because the cost of this message is a percentage of a penny, along with the line of space and time that once divided them. The result is a message that can be instantly received and consumed or saved and played later.

It is ironic that access and content are usually far more valuable than the media that delivers them. I am willing to pay thirty dollars for an audio recording of Stephen Covey lecturing in front of an audience of 5,000 people. Shelling out that money is not a problem – it is well worth it. The audio version of his books are well-produced products distributed by a national media company and run around thirty dollars. I, of course, purchase them electronically for far less, but that is another topic altogether.

Now, I am a big fan of Covey and "blame" his teachings on a lot of my success. I imagine Stephen Covey spending about 30 minutes each week on his cell phone, perhaps while driving to his next event or flying to the next city. Covey could also conceivably record into a portable digital recorder and then allow me to access that material. How much would that be worth to me? Now I have a candid and spontaneous new way to grasp insights into Covey's teachings and philosophy. I can hear his reactions to what is happening in business news. Covey has used his down time to develop a Podcast that I can consume during my own down time and that content would be worth 10 to 100 times as much as any of his fancy produced audio books. I'm sure you have business leaders of which you could say the same.

Producers can also reap benefits from the time-shifting element of Podcasting. Give me access to 30 minutes a week of someone's mindshare. Guarantee me that access, and I don't care if the sound is studio quality or even stereo-separated audio. Media production often tries to toss glitter or heavy dramatics over weak content. I smile every time I hear that a movie has been made from a short story. The same thought always runs through my head, "Why did they feel the need to stretch it?" The answer is a Hollywood standard formula: If the audience doesn't get at least 90 minutes out that movie, it isn't worth the trouble. I want exactly as long as it takes, and not a minute more and I bet my reader feels the same way.

The content is the value. The access to the content producer is the value. The opportunity is the value – not the iPod or Podcast format. You may have the opportunity to enhance your production with dazzling video or compelling audio, but focus on access all the more. Media production has to create and deliver the content that people want and need before the focus on quality production can really begin. That approach is far superior than making a great sound that hopefully will catch on someday with millions of adoring fans. The distribution channel is destined to become increasingly sophisticated, opening more doors for high-fidelity Podcasting – but worry on the content first. You can only cram so much fidelity into a .4-ounce, battery-operated ear piece or on a video screen a few inches in diameter.

Going out to iTunes and typing in my topic of interest suddenly plugs me into the thoughts of some of the world's leading authorities on that subject. When I head for the Yahoo! Podcasts directory, I might find a dozen experts in that industry. I can take those messages with me on my Zen or my Muvo to any place of my choosing.

Media has already changed. The answer to the WhoTheMedia.com question from production to marketing and distribution can now be "one and the same." We are already at an amazing place, headed for a world of sight and sound that is limited only by the imagination—not time and space.

DIRECT AND INDIRECT MODELS OF PODCAST MONETIZATION

We might have the first book on Podcast monetization in the industry but ours will not be the last. The topic is wildly popular because people love to discuss it – but so few people really understand it. We'll admit, the idea of quitting your day job on nothing more than a microphone purchased at Radio Shack is an attractive one, but not really a strategy based on reality. Podcasting is nothing more than a technology that can be monetized if you integrate it into your existing business efforts. If you have no existing business efforts to integrate your content into, launching the perfect Podcast shouldn't be your first step.

If you were to walk into a Barnes & Noble today, you are unlikely to find any books on the monetization of telephones. You'll find no "Copier Money Secrets" online or *Fax Machine Path to Riches* tapes at Nightingdale Conant[3]. Why? Because any company with a monetization schedule has integrated telephones, copiers, and fax machines into its business plan. In and of themselves, these items are not a business – they are part of doing business. The Podcast should be part of your business along side these other tools.

---

3. We understand that this analogy might be lost on a number of our readers. Coming from the information publishing industry, catchy titles like these often sell very well despite their ability to deliver. We're having a little fun here at the expense of our industry. Thanks for playing along.

Podcasting and the customer acquisition process

The customer acquisition process is whatever you have to do to attract business—the acquisition of customers. As information marketers, your authors rely heavily on the world of Internet leads through informational email marketing opportunities. If you haven't tried this method of customer acquisition, we can't recommend it highly enough.

As viable as the method is, it isn't always easy. We live in a world glutted with noisy, intrusive messages that are all vying for our attention. Do I want one more email newsletter in my inbox? Regardless of how many of my peers might recommend it, I am going to think long and hard before subscribing to anything. If

It's true that some businesses could never be operated successfully without a telephone. The same should be true with Podcasting. The issue is not the way you monetize but the way you *utilize Podcasting in your monetization efforts.* Some people are focused on the direct models, which are fine and good. We will be discussing these models in further depth in this chapter, but they only tell part of the story. Producing content in your home studio and then selling that content is definitely a monetization option. However, this very direct option represents only a small piece of the grand-scale Podcast monetization pie. As you read this chapter, keep your attention focused on the direct *and indirect* models for monetization.

DIRECT MONETIZATION MODELS

Direct Podcast monetization models can be distilled into three major categories, each with many different subdivisions.

1. Advertiser supported monetization

2. Listener supported monetization

3. Premium Podcasting models

ADVERTISER SUPPORTED MODELS

The best model for advertiser support monetization is the advertorial, where *ads are content* and not separate messages integrated into content. Presenting an advertisement in the form of content is one way to achieve what we call *Tivo Proofing*. Even as part of a Podcast piece, your ad is likely to end up on fast forward if your audience has that option. Remember that the user is in control, especially if he or she knows ahead of time that the commercial time slot is 30 seconds. A simple spin of the iPod wheel will take them right past that 30-second spot. Chapter-enhanced Podcasting allows listeners to click right through that section of the Podcast. If you must embrace the advertiser supported model, at the very least get creative in the process.

Some excellent examples of presenting ads as content, or *Tivo Proofing*, have emerged through the genre of reality television. Entire episodes of The Apprentice usually revolve around the best way to market Brand X, whatever it might be. The focal point of the prize-winning episode attached to the Survivor television series is the episode where someone wins a Chevy Tahoe. Somehow integrate the product you are advertising into the content and you have some chance of success with this approach[4].Advertorial supported Podcasts have a clear form of monetization.

this "newsletter" comes in the form of a Podcast with the cache of marketing intimacy and something that I can catch during my down time, I am infinitesimally more likely to subscribe. Bottom line: Gaining consumer trust through Podcasting is a relatively inexpensive process and is proving in our experience to be quite viable.

The frosting on the cake? The return on a call-to-action will be exponentially more successful because of the intimacy involved.

Consider a customer acquisition strategy through Podcasting. Direct or indirect method of Podcast monetization? Hard to define — but impossible to ignore.

---

4. As your authors we need to be entirely truthful – there are some who will gladly pay you for a traditional ad insertion into your Podcast and while this era of "silly money" is still strong, you might want to go for this low hanging fruit. When we speak of the "best" options in Podcast advertising, we speak of the best option for the product being advertised, and not always the content producer.

However, the second, more traditional approach is the insertion of ads into content. These insertions could be made directly in the Podcast but can also include other options more friendly to ad insertions, such as the the Podcast's support website. The second approach could also take the form of ads in newsletters or other communication media from the company. For that matter, everything could be bundled together in one neat package and sold accordingly. The trend in today's Podcast commercials is more and more ad-insertion options across the media properties involved. Your Podcast advertisement might also buy you a banner on the website and ad space in the newsletter.

The third and last model for advertiser supported content is called *Podcast patronage*, defined as a sponsorship model that contains a direct advertising piece as part of the show's structure. Instead of being a completely and totally independent (and inserted) clip, the sponsor becomes integrated into the message and sometimes even defines the Podcast name. A great example of this concept is called Download with Heather & Janelle, sponsored by Acuvue, a leading contact lens manufacture. The show never fails to mention: "The Heather and Janelle Podcast brought to you by Acuvue." This is a textbook example of the Podcast patronage paradigm. These two teenage girls don't spend 45 minutes talking about different models of contact lenses. Their chosen topics and guest stars demonstrate a real understanding of the teen-girl mindset. A significant number of girls will be much happier buying Acuvue because of the bond they feel with Heather and Janelle. The same concept rules the infomercial world. People will sit transfixed for 30 full minutes, watching such a totally entertaining sales pitch that it could only be called advertainment. And don't worry, Johnson and Johnson gets plenty of bang for their advertising dollar. The site constantly encourages the listeners to visit the product website which reads more like a brochure for Acuvue than anything else.

T. Harv Eker's video Podcast is a living, breathing, and extremely compelling direct marketing piece for T. Harv Eker and Peak Potentials. The official show of the Podcast and Portable Media Expo is the Podcast Brothers show, where Tim and Emile Bourquin host a weekly program on the business side of Podcasting and portable audio and video. As they plan each episode filled with valuable content and great entertainment, the end game is always to draw more attendees to the annual expo.

Podcasting through the advertainment model can become a powerful lead-generation program. Take some time to sift through our case studies at the end of the book (and private member site) for more ideas and details. If you decide to use advertainment and are extremely clear about your product, the audience—the segment you are seeking through this process or the opt-in piece you hope to snag—will already be presold. They will click through and sign up immediately to receive your marketing messages. That very unique advantage of advertainment is really not duplicated anywhere else.

People are already familiar with the idea of ad-supported models. That's been crammed down our throats in virtually every medium for as long as we can remember: Commercial breaks or a word from our sponsor – you know the drill. Because of this familiarity, this model is easy to explain and sell and present through an exciting new medium. At the same time, the enigmatic powers associated with Podcasting may be difficult for the average person to visualize or grasp.

That's one of the reasons why we wrote this book. We are looking at a new economy or a new technology. We not only have a medium that is easy for most of us to use,

Podcast networks

Podcast networks seem to be popping up everywhere. Cross-promotion is the conceptual idea for a Podcast network, and the world of Podcasting is filled with countless independent shows that need promotion badly. They also provide the opportunity for large ad-buys across a smaller batch of shows. You could easily have an extremely popular show—within its specialized and relatively small niche—perhaps 200 listeners. Finding advertisers who are willing to spend big money to reach out to an audience of 200 is nearly impossible. Crunch the numbers and look at the ROI. Now combine 200 or 300 Podcast shows that *each* have 200 listeners and you have a marketplace. Now the stage is set to attract big-name advertisers and rival the power of a much larger network.

Only a few of these Podcast networks have sprung up so far, but the Podshow.com network brought up by Adam Curry offers an intriguing example. The network is enhanced by impressive financial backing from key players in the Internet space. Curry has brought together a very eclectic and fascinating group of content producers and is attempting to bring in advertisers on a large scale. He has already successfully brought in GoDaddy.com and EarthLink with predictions of catching more big fish in the future.

Another Podcast network brought up by Todd Cochrane is not on the large scale of Pod Show.com and lacks an equal financial backing. Still, Cochrane has managed to integrate a great

but one that collapses space and time into the moment we are ready to listen. You could lose hours trying to explain this incredible medium to someone. We know because we have tried.

If you can wrap ad-supported content around a model that people understand, you are going to have buy-ins and support and sign-ups much sooner than you ever dreamed possible.

The question is, will it last for the long run?

Key point number one: Many advertiser-supported models require significant numbers to produce the financial results or heightened brand recognition that a sponsor expects. Coca Cola buys prime or exclusive advertising time on a major network show because it reaches millions of people in a single shot. The long-standing companies who remain at the top of the game have mastered the art of reinvention. Coca Cola has to find ways to remain the preferred refreshment in a changing world. Staying on top is a game of its own.

Many ad-supported models require significant numbers on both sides. Unfortunately, the return is not equally impressive. In regard to ad buys: Just because you can reach 1/1,000 of your audience does not mean that you are going to get 1/1,000 of the price. Big-name advertisers love the big numbers. They're kind of lazy that way.

In our opinion, the advertiser-supported model has a tendency to negate and ignore the real power of Podcasting. We think it would be a mistake for anyone to dive into the ad-supported model without taking the time to explore and work with the tremendous freedoms Podcasting offers when not regulated to that format. Jumping right into an advertiser-supported approach ties you to all of the traditional models that Podcasting no longer requires you to embrace.

The final con about this model is the limitation of your power. You can no longer be the media. You could have had three legs, but you chopped one off just to look like everyone else on the block.

ADVERTISING SALES IN PODCASTING

Consider bringing in a traditional ad sales person to manage important pieces like selling traditional Podcast ads or supportive projects like websites or newsletters. Ad people are everywhere. Many of them lost their jobs when the last bubble burst and are very experienced and successful at what they do. They can bring in the higher rates, understand the language of the industry, and speak the language of the traditional ad-buy rates. They can bring in higher dollars and often pay for themselves—perhaps many times over.

variety of attractive features in Podcaster News.com. Focusing more on news than content, he has signed contracts with people such as those playing on the HBO® series *Big Love*.

We know that countless Podcast networks are operative, and we'll probably receive website posts or emails that say, "Why didn't you mention mine?" Are they the best move for the Podcaster? At this point we say no.

If you want to produce a standard, traditional show—acting only as content producer—and you want someone else to handle distribution and marketing, the power of a Podcast network begins to make a lot of sense. On the other hand, the idea of being the producer, the distributor, and the marketer might thrill and excite you. If so, the options provided by a

Podcast network begin to look less attractive.

That's the grand scale. On the limited scale, you need sufficient numbers associated with your network. Otherwise, you are basically looking at too many players and not enough soup. Someone might be able to double your ad rate, but if they take two-thirds of the revenue to make that happen—you are down. It will be very interesting to see how these Podcast networks will pan out.

Many compare them to the Internet malls of the mid '90s. People said, "Online stores aren't going to work unless people can cross promote them." The online malls were brought together, and history has shown the wildly positive direction that took. Will Podcast networks go the same way? We say yes—but we have been wrong about some things

Once you have identified someone who has inspired your confidence and trust, have your sales manager study what is happening in the industry. To assist him or her in becoming well-versed in the language of Podcast-world negotiations, have your sales manager read this book.

Matching the terms of your advertising contracts to your business strategy will be a changing landscape. If your show is new, it makes sense to gather a sizable number of short-term contracts. The initial investment is lower, which makes this untried medium more attractive to potential advertisers. Should you happen to start growing by leaps and bounds, you will be more free to negotiate new terms—terms that reflect your numbers growth and marketplace success. When we are standing on the edge of major media attention, we don't want anyone to place an ad-buy based on last quarter's numbers.

For those who feel a sense of excitement about securing a few short-term contracts and launching a Podcast, the weekly Podcast Brothers (http://www.podcastbrothers.com) show manages to keep a tight grip on the industry. By entering that space, you will be able to keep a pulse on the latest news and business developments.

Podcasting is an excellent medium for direct-response marketing. Advertisements that include a call to action take on an entirely new dimension in this medium.

These responses are going to gather the type of demographics that advertisers crave, and pay money for. Boasting that you have 10,000 downloads means nothing. Compare that statement with the fact that one out of every five downloads is resulting in a fresh website visit and you've got the attention of the direct response marketer.

You can create a calling card and offer it to potential advertisers who are anxious to compare cost versus exposure or tap into just the right market. Now they can make some viable comparisons between Podcast advertising and other buy-ins like AdWords, email insertions, or traditional banner buys.

Take advantage of your role as the Podcast producer and media person by testing several different types of ads to see what clicks and what falls flat. Which placements seem to be the most noticed or memorable? Is the ad at the beginning of your Podcast so compelling that people pause immediately and jump to that website while it's still on their mind? Are they going to glance right over that first ad? Would it be better placed at the end of the Podcast once you have earned their trust? What about placing that ad right in the middle? Should this be a call to action or a giveaway? How are you going to get their contact information?

Test a wide variety of approaches and options in your Podcast advertising. This is one area where a little risk-taking in the

in the past, so we'll wait for truth to tell.

In many ways the Podcast network is like any other network, only simplified. The Podcast network is easier to assign and pull together; It's relatively inexpensive and most people will be able to do it. These networks make it possible for anyone with an intention and initiative to play in the game without a large bundle of money. Now, that can be boon or bane.

Our motivation to make anything work is directly proportional to our investment—capital or otherwise. It would be easy to collect a bunch of lazy Podcasters or egocentric babblers in one of these networks. The selective screening and commitment to excellence that you see in traditional network broadcasting is based on the financial skin that is always at stake. Are big-network folks motivated to produce the biggest and best? Absolutely. It's all about return.

The other side of this Podcasting freedom coin is the guy who really has something to say—business-minded people like the authors of this book or our readers. For us, the low cost of Podcasting is the very thing that makes it so appealing.

early stages when reinvention is relatively easy may pour the foundation for incredible financial success a little further down the road. Try something and find out what happens, then go from there.

Part of the testing is tracking, of course. Direct tracking via referral to a URL is always preferable to indirect tracking that only reveals statistics and trends. Being able to ask, "How did you hear about us?" helps you to gather invaluable information about the hot spots in your market. Having that intimate knowledge of your own market makes it so much easier to attract advertisers who want to reach specific demographics. Sellers are always seeking willing buyers. They just need to know exactly how advertising dollars spent with you will make that happen.

A parting note on investment versus return: How often have you been able to test the effectiveness of a chosen media for $6.25? With very little in your checking account, you could conceivably launch a beta Podcast that would go out to thousands of listeners. These listeners, in turn, would hopefully reply with hundreds of requests for ad space.

Like anything else in business, advertising requires management. After all, someone else is giving you money with expectations of an acceptable return. This point brings you to the need for an advertising division, because someone needs to remain focused on and attentively manage this vital activity. You can't be everything. Great companies are always set up with a division of expertise and the power that comes from integrating those layers. It would be absurd for a newspaper to have the same person roving as a reporter, writing the stories, handling the advertising and marketing, and keeping the books.

Consider yourself a newspaper. Consider yourself as some form of media, because you are. As you build your business and track results, your managers' performance will have a tremendous impact. Choose your managers carefully but do acknowledge how many doors the right person can open. I have an affiliate manager. Without him, the sales figures for one of my products last year would have been down by one third. Having him in my corner will lower the hurdle for next year, since that many people have already moved through my funnel. He is worth many times the money I spend on him.

One of the first and hardest lessons of Podcast advertising is "Find an advertising manager." If you can't seem to come up with one, don't sell advertising. Go back to that Podcasting strategy and start envisioning other avenues of building revenue. It may sound obvious, but is sadly all too often overlooked: You need an advertising director and you need to compensate that individual very well. The cost of that function has to be included in the equation.

LISTENER SUPPORTED MODELS

Listener-supported models for Podcast monetization are also becoming very popular. The first model is classified as "donation" or tip jar. It's likely that you have visited a Podcast or a blog that has a "donate here" or "click here to donate" option or something similar. There are even scripts available (no charge, just leave a donation) to automate the process. In short, if you like the show, you're asked to leave a few bucks in the coffer. Yes, begging has a "cyber" version.

With a passionate audience and great content, this approach will generate a bit of a revenue stream. If the tip-jar or donation model seems to be your path, you will score more touchdowns at the end of the day if you give details and specifics about your request (don't just have a tip-jar, tell them to donate $5 to the cause). Play the emotional cards right and make your audience or customers feel as good as you possibly can about digging into their pockets for you or your cause.

Known for inventing the unique selling proposition (USP), Rosser Reeves was supposedly in Central Park when he noticed a panhandler with the sign, "Anything will help." When Reeves added a few descriptive words to the message, more money began falling into the cup. Oddly, something very similar happened to me before I ever heard about the Reeves story. I noticed the sign of a panhandler standing on the divider of a busy Los Angeles intersection: "Could you spare change?" My gut reaction was to change the wording to: "It's winter, I'm hungry…can you spare a dollar?" He did, and his revenues went up dramatically.

These examples really deal with two messages. First, we are bringing the attention of passers by to the present with the image of winter. This is an undeniable truth. We convey the truth in any number of ways, from announcing the current time to today's date or our own name. Thank you for visiting this website, and that's the truth. We employ these mechanisms in marketing to achieve a consensus and agreement from people.

Everyone knows how miserable the winter can be, especially without warm clothing or a roof over your head. But why suggest giving a dollar instead of loose change? Well, that fellow needed to pull in more than nickels and dimes. When we changed the wording on his sign, dollar bills began to appear. By the end of the day, his tally was about ten times the money that he usually collected. Reeves and I aren't magicians. We just enhanced the message with an image that might capture more attention and evoke a positive response.

Some might be offended that we compare a Podcast tip jar to a homeless beggar, but let's be honest, it is the same thing.

Using a Podcast to bring someone to the present might look something like this: "I have no idea *when* you might be listening to this Podcast." That is absolute truth. That's a great statement. Nobody can challenge or deny what you just said. "I have no idea *where* you are listening to this Podcast." Again, we have a very truthful statement. We are bringing people to the threshold of a truth that could be denied through the vehicle of the undeniable truth. Pairing the two or anchoring the one with the other is an excellent strategy.

You can apply simple suggestions the way the panhandler's signs were slightly altered to motivate the receiver into action. *Lead your audience* at the same time that you are learning from them. Be willing to change and grow.

Using a tip jar model, you might say, "I don't know when you are listening to this. You must be somewhat enjoying this because you are reading deeply into the website." Both of these are true statements. Recommending a donation can actually be helpful because many times people want to contribute but aren't sure what to give. Giving them a recommendation is a direct response mechanism. Tell them how much you want. Give them a low, medium, and high and then expect the medium to come through. We are not suggesting the donation model—at least for anyone with the gusto to be a self-content production designer who can find monetization streams that will pay better.

Membership is the next option for a listener-supported model. The membership process differs from "traditional" Premium Podcasting (discussed later) by offering listeners a membership opportunity but not requiring it. Marketing makes all the difference. The more people who join as members, the better your options become. Some successful membership options are no more than paying several dollars each month for enhanced access to content.

The merchandising approach may have you giving away valuable content, but it opens the door to the sale of additional products that will be coming down the pike. The original merchandising king in media delivery was probably The Grateful Dead. This popular rock band never did much about the transference of content back and forth. They almost seemed to encourage the bootlegging of concert recordings. Why? Because the band made its big money on the stage, adding up ticket prices plus t-shirts and every other sort of memorabilia. Perpetuating the loyal "Deadhead" fan base made great sense in light of the band's strongest revenue streams.

This might be the model for you. Get a few bucks for your content if you can, but work the back end and the options having an audience can bring you.

Merchandising through a listener-supported model could easily take the form of archived CDs or DVDs of your Podcast. Content that was chopped up for the Podcast can now be integrated back into a valuable whole, a marketable and real product. Those weekly 10-minute Podcasts, minus the extra intro and exit minute at the very beginning and end, could be strung together like pearls or songs on a CD. Someone who doesn't want to subscribe or listen to your Podcast can enjoy and subscribe to the archived version of your shows.

The pros behind the listener-supported model can be summed up in one truism: This model respects the "Podcast culture" of *free access*. Whether the perception of the Podcast culture as open and free is the smartest one to adopt is a moot point. This aspect of the Podcast culture needs to be identified and recognized, and the listener-supported model of donation makes it happen. What could be easier and less expensive to install and integrate? You can obtain a PayPal® account in a couple of minutes and a PayPal donation button in literally a couple of seconds.

The cons of the listener-supported model rest largely in its perceived value. Many business people may not perceive the content as edifying or dynamic and feel it has no value if no one has assigned a value to it. Once again, your content will always be worth something if you own all three legs of the media stool. At the very least, it is worth a price tag.

Extra considerations for the listener-supported model include a request for donations with varied options and amounts. Don't be afraid to tell them how much of a donation you would like to see. Just keep in mind that some people see PayPal as the devil, and we have an entire culture of folks who believe that Podcasts should always be free. Donation options could include acquiring a post office box or a similar mail-box service for a nominal monthly fee. You might request the blank CDs or blank iPods or some other option.

Finally, consider offering content for free but with an option for those who prefer to accelerate or enhance consumption. You will see this approach at Revision3.com. Listener support can be as simple as a Podcast fundraiser, which mimics more traditional and older forms of media. National Public Radio and the Public Broadcasting Service both produce excellent content, and this model pays for and subsidizes some truly exceptional content.

Of course, both of your authors would pull *more* money out of their own pockets if PBS ever offers to spare us the distraction and interruption of all that fundraising.

PREMIUM PODCASTING MODELS

Plenty of models for Premium Podcasting are available. Premium content separates the amateurs from the professional and focuses on content that is worth the price of consumption. Hopefully, *many people* will be willing to pay. After all, no one denounces the fact that more than one billion three-minute musical segments were sold at a cost of 99 cents each. People pay for content.

"So what?" is the attitude of many. What's a buck worth anyway? Now apply the value of 33 cents per minute to a Podcast that runs an hour. Even at that low rate, the time would be worth $20. Take a look at Audible.com - an electronic book on tape at their site retails for $20 to as high as $60. How serious is that relationship? Audible and Apple just signed a contract to keep Audible as their key provider in the same music store that sold 1 billion songs.

Suddenly the numbers get very interesting.

People are willing to pay for valuable content. Having that premium content and distributing it through the Podcast channel is truly the easiest, cleanest, and fastest model for Podcast monetization. No need to worry about reporting listeners, keeping ad people on staff, negotiating, drawing up contracts, or any number of related activities and responsibilities. The systems are all in place to track and manage everything. If the content is good, and people are willing to pay for it, everything else works out in the wash.

Consider the following options for Premium Podcasting:

• Podcasted Events

Premium Podcasts are ideal for physical events, particularly for one that come out on a set schedule like the biannual Big Seminar (http://www.bigseminarnow.com) from Armand Morin. People have already set aside time and money from their lives to pay for attending the event. If people are willing to spend thousands to attend the event, wouldn't many more be willing to get the content, and not have to travel? Others may have missed the event but would be happy to pay for that content to be delivered to their iPod or to their desktop via the Podcast channel the Monday following the event. The possibilities are endless.

• Podcast Micro Payments

The concept behind Podcast micro payments would require something like an iTunes-type interface for Podcast content. As a listener, I might not want to pay much money for Podcasts. However, I might be willing to pay a buck or two for a wacky radio DJ or a weekly news commentary – much as I would the latest song from Brittany Spears. A massive audience would be needed for this to pay the bills – but it is a conceivable and viable option. We aren't bullish on this approach, since it requires an efficient middle man who doesn't take much and the focus is quality over quantity.

Right now, players like iTunes and PayPal do not have the infrastructure that would be required to make something like this easy. That could change by the printing of this book. At this point, Podcast micro payments are interesting to discuss but are not a viable option.

• Podcast Pay-Per-View (PPV)

People may wonder about pay-per-view working for content delivery – but the model is clearly there. It already works well in cable television and for the book model. Scores of people who visit Audible.com and visit the iTunes Music Store are willing to pay a one-time fee of $20 to download the new Brian Tracy book or to listen to *The Business Podcasting Bible*. Pay-per-view as a content distribution scheme is obviously a part of the equation and should be examined.

• Podcast Series

Running a series in a Premium Podcasting channel is another option. Some Podcasts should not go on forever. Teaching a new skill or covering a research topic are good examples of defined topics with a beginning, middle, and end. One of the interesting features of a Premium Podcast series is the freedom of consumption time and place. It's possible that not everyone will begin consuming the series at the same time.

Remember that the power of Podcasting is all about the concept of time and place shifting. Products that encourage time shifting should be delivered via a time-shifting channel. Why would you have to start the training session during the same week and on the same day as everyone else does? These Premium Podcast series could almost function like autoresponders, where people start in their own time and receive input sequentially on their own path.

• Coaching By Podcast

Another milestone in the monetization process is the coaching model. The biggest expense and time investment is delivering content to the participants. Many business coaches spend a great deal of time shooting their content back up to teleseminar replays on private membership websites and similar tactics. That would not be happening if coaches could record their content, click the save, and shoot that program out to their audience through a Premium Podcast model.

Audible is another player in today's Podcasting space. We have already talked about the Audible model and its infrastructure in several places, but it also merits discussion in this area of the book. The Access to Leaders Podcast from co-author Alex Mandossian is handled through the Audible channel, and was the first Podcast ever purchased in their Wordcast system. At the time of this publication, the Wordcast system makes it difficult to "comp" a recording or charge different prices but we expect that to change soon, and will track their progress in the private member website for this book.

Premium Podcasting must come in an engine that allows complete control—like the three-legged stool of being the media. Distribution for multiple prices must be part of the engine. You are able to control who has access to what and the price entry. It also allows listeners to enjoy something like Premium Podcasting in the form of bonus content for other products or media providers. We truly believe that the model demonstrated by this book of Premium Podcast content for anyone who bought our tome will be copied by many book authors – and we encourage them to do it.

The overriding pro for Premium Podcasting is the fact that it makes the most sense for those who want to monetize Podcast media in and of itself. The theme is a simple one and a concept that we both wholeheartedly embrace: People are willing to pay for content that they perceive as valuable, either educational or entertaining. Making the consumption process quick and easy makes even more sense. The philosophy of paying for worthwhile content is already firmly established in the world of business. Introducing that age-old theme in a new channel is fresh, but we believe that it will evolve quickly.

The cons of Premium Podcasting are just the flip side of the pros. This new paradigm is still in the formative stages of its evolution. It might be tough to convince some people to take the plunge, but the shift will happen quickly once it has some momentum. The virtual nature of content that doesn't come in a home study package or a cd case is sometimes "hard" to pay for. We hope that this book, and the concepts associated with it, will play a leading role in that dawning.

As bullish as we are on this approach, one simple fact is vital: As you are planning to move your content out to an audience, remember that charging for it will limit the number of listeners. Advertorial content through a Premium Podcast will be quite limited. Every content producer needs to review the options for paid and premium content as part of the strategy casting process.

Any additional considerations for Premium Podcasts? Make sure that your audience understands the value of the content before you ask for payment (and not vice versa). Producers often discover that the audience is not as excited as they are about their content. Help the audience to understand the value of what you have placed before them before you ask them to pay for it. Explain the beauty of time shifting, which needs to be part of any sales process utilizing this technology. Premium Podcasting also opens the door to physically manifesting the content through other media later, so make sure they understand the value of getting that content right now..

CDs can be viable teaching tools, especially when they cover class material and are delivered at the end of a specified timeframe with transcripts attached. The physical nature of such a deliverable, makes it easier to consume as you have to rip open the shrinkwrap and place the disk in your drive. This is very important to examine within the Premium Podcast monetization model. One option to visualize the power of this program is by providing an MP3 player as part of the purchase. The Alex Nano is really not physically different from one called the Paul Colligan Nano or the Marc Victor Hansen Nano or the Brian Tracy Nano. These are simply preloaded products. We have made a retail purchase of the iPod Nano, and then loaded it full of our own content. But now, the virtual becomes physical, and the purchase is a bit easier to consume.

The covers to these courses, just like album covers, are also loaded into the iPod. I would rather not have the iPod offer prompts like "play list" or "artist" because I am not an artist—I am a teacher, a trainer and a business professional. But for now, that is just the way iPod is structured. The challenge is a small one considering that the iPod is such a powerful and sexy little instrument. Some minor shortcomings can be overlooked.

This simple process bears repeating: We buy the iPod Nano, preload our content, place the iPod back into its original box, and wrap another box over that. Now we are ready to market our own content-rich iPod. At this point, our investment is about $100 to $150 per iPod. However, we are selling our iPod with its 101 hours of preloaded content for $2,997—the early bird cost for those who take advantage of pre-reservation, pre-distribution release pricing. After that, the price goes up to $3,997. And, yes, people are already paying that much for the "right" content. The Nano is simply the attractive packaging we slip around the content.

People want to know how we can possibly sell our iPods for that much money. For one thing, the price is a steal. Those iPods may be selling for slightly under $4,000 but they hold as much as $20,000 worth of valuable content. Secondly, the price includes lifetime upgrades, delivered through a Premium Podcasting channel. Anyone who purchases my Alex Nano has also purchased a lifetime of audio content updates from my "Best of Alex" online play list. Not only is that offer profound, it immediately accelerates the lifetime value of every client and continues to raise my value in the "information space." Furthermore, the stick strategy instantly associated with the Alex Nano will pay for itself in lack of returns.

Some people are going to have trouble wrapping their arms around the lack of physical manifestation for that $3,000 entry price. Others will embrace this concept in a heartbeat and consider it a bargain. Many of our direct peers would be in that second group. And remember, I am not wasting time on the Alex Nano with some basement factory operation. Hiring out the production helps to keep my focus on content development – the same focus we hope every one of our readers has.

Whether we are talking about a $3,000 iPod Nano with lifetime upgrade capabilities or simply a once-a-month CD with transcripts attached, the details are not important. Both approaches are very viable and they help prove that people are willing to pay for content. Being able to shoot the same content down both channels is a great way to cast a much wider net and pull in more consumers.

Back in the early days of Internet marketing, one very successful fellow proudly described raiding the backyard shack that served as his inventory of products. He took all the tape sets and books to the dump and swore that he would no longer bother with physical media. The thought of doing everything electronically—of living in the "e" world— sounded so easy and exciting. Five years later, he realized that a certain segment of his audience would never fully embrace "e" so he returned to a shed filled with personal content. People are interested in consuming through different channels.

Especially in the genre of Premium Podcasting, give them as many channels and mediums as possible.

MULTI-MONETIZATION MODALITY MODELS

One top-notch copywriter admits to a considerable revenue stream from the tip button attached to his blog. Approximately $600 to $700 a month in additional income flows his way through that little tip button. Would taking that button away add value to his other existing channels? The answer is most likely no, because this fellow is such an avid tester that he would not have left that question unanswered. We aren't advocating a donation button on your Podcast, but we do want to push the envelope of your ideas about using various monetization models.

One popular Podcast is free to download, until the next episode "airs." At that point, you have to pay to listen to the first episode and a surprising amount of people do. Always having a single Podcast available in iTunes and Yahoo generates visitors and good content and sales close them in the back. AffiliateGuyPodcast.com gives the first 20 minutes away for free and then charges for the rest. These models work well.

Consider mixing your monetization models in new and different ways. Take a curious but intelligent approach and blend as it makes good sense. Test and track and keep what works, tossing out the rest. Keep in mind that *you are the media* as you go through this process. Why not insert advertorial content into a Premium Podcast? What about a member-supported premium content interface that offers additional or bonus material to subscribers for a free show? Have you considered letting your audience purchase CDs or DVDs of your content? That would never work you say? Does the cable station offer a DVD or The Wizard of Oz right after they aired it for kicks?

INDIRECT MONETIZATION MODELS

Sometimes Podcast monetization is achieved through simple cost reduction. They may not want to admit it, but companies spend a great deal of money on the distribution of internal content. During the time when I worked for a biomedical firm in quality assurance, my colleagues and I decided to run a few numbers. Although this was a small firm in the biomedical field—maybe 200 employees—we were going through more than a ton of paper each month just for tracking and other internal issues. Would an electronic version of some of these documents saved the company some good change?

Twelve tons of paper at the end of the year is a sizable bill, regardless of wholesale contracts. Paper costs money. Cutting that monthly ton of paper in half by using an internal electronic distribution mechanism could create a substantial savings. Quite possibly, you would save some significant dollars and still have enough left over to hand out free iPod Nanos to everyone in the organization. Now your employees are seeing that cost reduction program as a personal benefit, they're participating in the process, and they get a cool iPod as well – life is good.

Imagine the smile on the face of the employees standing in the back of the room who have just received their iPod Nano and a $10 iTunes gift certificate. What a great company! The bookkeeper knows full well that this shift in communication media has just saved the company more than a half-million dollars a year. Yet the naysayers wonder how they could be so frivolous with their spending.

Monetization by cost reduction is just as viable as a Podcast monetization model as anything we have discussed. In some ways, it is more viable because it deals with the known. You aren't changing the top line; you are just fattening the bottom line. We cannot understate the critical comparison of production and distribution costs of audio and/or multimedia content versus that of written content. These efficiencies and savings play an important role in any Podcast monetization model.

I remember clearly a time when I needed to make changes to an affiliate program called the Colligan Web Store. These changes were specific and detailed—the type of information that would require my affiliates to pay close attention and take a few notes. After spending nearly an hour trying to compose a letter, I saw the advantage of having my affiliate audience right in front of me. My finest communication moments happen with a PowerPoint slide deck and a lapel microphone.

Using Camtasia Studio and the screen cast model, I created the slide deck and presentation as if my affiliates *were* sitting there right in front of me. I suddenly recaptured about half of my own day, since it would have taken me at least that long to compose the letter—and my message was more personal. My affiliates could actually *hear* the inflection of my voice and *feel* my excitement. They would have a chance to hear, first-hand, about the changes that were coming our way.

No, I didn't realize any cost reduction in terms of hard goods. My message would have been sent via email, not printed and sent via snail mail. However, I did realize the cost reduction of freeing up my own valuable time. My effectiveness and the quality of my presentation improved considerably. Without a doubt, monetization through cost reduction was part of my equation.

One of the calling cards of co-author Alex Mandossian is the concept of "writing with your mouth," which is reflected in the Teleseminar Secrets program. After all, your mouth has a voice and that voice forms words. We may be able to write at an impressive rate, but our thought processes are much faster. If the pen could keep up with the spoken word, we might have 70 pages of content at the end of a one-hour session. In reality, an hour of labor is more likely to produce three or perhaps four well-written pages. Writing with your voice can be 20 times more effective, and Podcasts provide that level of efficiency. If you want to see what it looks like to write with your voice, start transcribing a Podcast filled with quality content.

Just repurposing content and presenting it in a different way can raise its value. People absorb information in different ways (modalities of learning). We learn in many different ways and reading is certainly one of them. Listening is another. If we had been forced to author this book through a traditional "write down every word" process, the time required for that task would have been out of the question. Being able to write the book using our voices and follow with fine edits made it possible for us to push content to market that will result in faster monetization. Now, we can cash in on book revenues and any additional sales that might come down the same funnel.

Anyone who is part of an organization of any size that internally distributes content should consider reducing that production time. Forget about Premium Podcasting or ad revenue or any of the other obvious advantages. Just by grabbing the bull by the horns, you could reduce content production time by a fifth and slash distribution costs to basically zero without making any other changes. Indirect monetization through internal content distribution is tremendous.

ADDITIONAL CHANNELS FOR EXISTING CONTENT MODEL

Passing out existing content through different channels is a model with internal and external applications. We have already discussed the external version, so let's review the benefit of time shifted consumption from an internal standpoint. Any option that coaxes your employees to consume job-related content during their down time is to your advantage and that of the company. Maybe it's a training manual that you want them to review. Your employees might be listening on the airplane, at the gym, or during lunch time on a stroll. They are filling down time with valuable content, which frees their at-work attention for the more pressing business at hand.

Some companies don't invite every employee to an important briefing simply because they need to keep phone coverage or an open customer service line. Now the people who had to miss that meeting can listen to a recording of the meeting on their drive home. Everyone stays connected and on the same page with all bases covered.

In the case of the BigSeminarLive.com channel, the revenue stream from ticket sales already exists. The revenue and channel stream from the sale of CDs and DVDs are already in place. You would probably see an entirely new audience emerge if Big Seminar was distributed as a Premium Podcast event. Many people would perceive the delay of a month or two as too long and would prefer immediate content, not something that feels somehow out of date. Would one channel cannibalize the other? In some areas, possibly, but when the books were done at the end of the year, the "traditional" CD and DVD channel plus the Premium Podcast channel would result in more sales and profits.

Some events will lend themselves easily to Podcast production. The content is already developed, polished, and being presented. The people who are recording the event from the back of the room already have the necessary video and audio streams, so the cost of distribution through the Podcast channel is basically zero[5].

We talked about the Premium Podcast and the production of a physical manifestation of it through a preloaded model like Alex Nano. Let's take the flip side of that situation – digital content delivered down another channel. What would the end author gain by selling his audio eBook through Audible for $20? How much of that price is the author's take? What about the "AudibleListener" program that currently lets you grab any two books in their library for less than $23 a month? Does Audible have more customers than I do? Yes. Can they sell my book in the iTunes Music Store – an arena I can't touch yet? Yes. Is the spread worth it? You have to decide that for yourselves.

This isn't a critique of Audible, mind you. They are there and doing it well, and we'll continue to work with them. This is a reminder of how much more power you have when you control the content yourself. Case in point: currently, Audible's Wordcast program let's you set the price with them only taking 20% for their service – compare that to a traditional publishing house model and you can see the power of this channel in action.

Don't hesitate to begin with existing content and stir in the new modality of Podcasting to discover entirely new channels. That same author could take his audio book and read it one chapter at a time with commentary. This compilation of chapters could be distributed as a Podcast series. If the author doesn't have the time for Podcast production, he can hire a professional voice. Scott Sigler's excellent novel "Earthcore,"

---

5. As a matter of fact, the recordings for the event side of the Big Seminar Live Podcast are taken from the same recordings as the CDs and DVDs are eventually sold from. I take my iPod to the back of the room at the end of each day and have them transfer the content directly to me. They don't even spend the penny to burn it to CD as I usually hand them a portable hard drive (many times my iPod) to place the content on.

currently on sale at Amazon for $19.95, was initially released as an audio Podcast. The contract, and audience, for the book came from the Podcast. Expect that model to be repeated frequently.

One of the most exciting things this past year has been our discovery of people with hundreds of hours of fabulous content sitting on a shelf (or hard drive) somewhere. They simply need a new distribution channel. The entire concept of additional channels for existing content is an amazing model for indirect monetization.

Another viable model is the Podcast as stick strategy. Stick strategies are the conventions that motivate customers to stick with your product or service. You want them to stick with their decision to call you or make an appointment. Whatever type of commitment they have made, the stick strategy seals the deal. Now why is that so important? Because prospects who cancel or fail to show up are a waste of your time and energy. People who unsubscribe are lost from your sphere of influence. Customers who fail to unwrap the product packaging are not likely to reorder. A stick strategy is designed to prevent that from happening as often as possible. Millions of dollars have been added to a company's bottom line, overnight, with the implementation of a solid stick strategy.

A good example of a stick strategy is to follow the purchase of a product with an invitation to call a 24-hour phone line for an important message. The product packaging clearly invites the call. Even if a week or two has lapsed, that phone message can take your customer back to the mindset of excitement and enthusiasm that he or she first felt. The technique is utilized in the home study version of Alex's Teleseminar Secrets as has prevented an estimated six-figure amount in early returns. Stick strategies can be as simple as the words "rinse, lather, and repeat" on the back of a shampoo bottle. We could reduce it even further to the six letters that make up the word "repeat." Those six letters are making sure the user knows to shampoo over and over and over again. That's a stick strategy.

You can develop any number of stick strategies that will ensure listeners for your Podcast. Many of these strategies may seem obvious but not all. The key is to bring as many of these different strategies into your marketing arsenal as possible. Without them, you may lose out on substantial business or have to deal with refund requests from people who just failed to consume your product. Be sure to throw Podcasting into that arsenal of stick strategies.

Imagine holding up a diet protein shake drink and reading a message printed right on the can that says: "Need a personal coach to walk beside you every step of the way on your diet?" As the consumer of this nutritional shake, you are likely to own an iPod, based on demographic feedback about disposable income. Having regular access to professional nutritional advice that incorporates your diet product is stick strategy at its finest. Your product loyalty could be tremendous.

Now imagine buying a product and being able to subscribe to a video Podcast series that would walk you through its proper use (and upgrades or changes). Anything that keeps people associated with a product—anything that keeps them involved and aware of the product—can be a viable stick strategy. Any content that you can produce can be sent down the powerful Podcasting channel.

Perhaps your audio content already exists in some form. Maybe it needs to be created. Take an afternoon and make it happen. Either way, you could provide a bonus with each one of your products that would almost serve as a time shifted instruction manual. The sticker on the front of your box might read: "We know that you are ready to start using this, so please visit our Podcast and receive our daily audio updates."

Your busy customer might have placed that shrink-wrapped product on the shelf where it sits unopened several weeks later. Finally, he's picking up the package and reading the sticker. When he listens to the Podcast, your voice is suddenly plugged right into his ear. This is instant intimacy. Within the space of this tremendous marketing intimacy, your customer hears the enthusiastic words, "Okay, if you haven't opened that thing up yet, open it up right now!" How much more likely would your customer be to start consuming the product? You would be capturing that single consumption just by *writing with your voice*. You don't have to run through 18 levels with a professional copywriter to create a successful message.

Perhaps your customer has purchased something from you like a new software program or some innovative device. Use Podcasting to train them how to use (and benefit from) the product they just purchased. Your new customer will be able to listen to an explanation of the product and how to use it to his full advantage – at the time and place of his choosing. The message comes directly from you via one of the most intimate of all communication models with time shifted convenience. What more could you ask for?

Branding and training represent the final models for indirect monetization. Using a Podcast to achieve these goals is a much different process than that of advertiser support. Instead of coaxing your target audience into buying your product, you are convincing them to consume it. The approach is not the same and the end-game stakes are considerably higher. We have already seen Podcasts that support product sales – how about supporting them after the sale? A consumer could conceivably buy your product and you could send them training updates by Podcast.

Let's take the options for updating with Podcast one step further. Wouldn't it be fascinating if my favorite software tool vendor were to say: "Each time we come up with a new product, we'll shoot a little video to your Podcast channel that explains all the advantages and new features. We'll even include an instant click-to-buy option for your convenience." Not only would I sign up in a heartbeat, I would be much more likely to consume that content over a printed newsletter or even an email message.

Our main Podcast, MarketingOnlineLive.com, is truly a branding monetization model. We have yet to sell anything directly from the site (minus some third-party products sold through banner ads at the site). Indirectly, the results have been amazing. The show is a great advertising medium for a number of our programs and has drawn an impressive number of attendees to $1000-per-ticket events. We now have valuable business partnerships and will sell many more copies of this book because of the show—all through indirect monetization.

CONCLUSION

Using broad brushstrokes, let's review the new world that Podcasting has revealed. First, you can be the media (and own the profits associated with all elements of such). You can do the things that once required the assistance of others. This simple fact transforms the content and media production game plan in ways that need to be examined and thoroughly understood.

Podcast monetization is not only found in the sales of ads on a Podcast, or the sale of Podcast content. It can be found in the savings associated with communicating electronically or the new found revenue stream in repurposing existing content for this channel.

Companies and organizations have traditionally paid for reams of paper or spindles of blank CDs and professional distribution by folks like UPS or FedEx. Expenses and service charges that were once unavoidable are no longer necessary.

Monetization should not be the immediate focus. Placing the cart before the horse will limit and minimize the magnitude of the power standing right in front of you. The utility that Podcasting provides should remain the focus of every monetization discussion within your organization or firm—or in the white-boarding sessions you have with yourself. It is not how Podcasting can make you money, it is what the Podcast technology can do directly and indirectly for your business.

The direct sale of Podcast content should be examined in comparison to additional delivery costs for media like film, radio, CDs, and others. Truly integrating the utility of the Podcasting channel and the associated media into your business and monetization strategies will enable you to do extremely well. Go back into this chapter and select the elements that seem best suited to your goals. Just keep in mind all that is encompassed within the concept of "you are the media."

How is that reality going to impact your monetization and communication efforts?

AT THE PRIVATE MEMBER SITE

We track all of the Podcast monetization models, the Podcast networks and the money in this industry at http://www.TheBusinessPodcastingBible.com/where. Join us for the conversation and download our chart of the different models for use with your Podcast monetization strategies.

 # CHAPTER SIX

"Eighty percent of success is showing up."

—Woody Allen

"Don't tell me about the labor pains, just show me the baby."

—Michael Lee Austin

We saved the big question of "When?" for the last chapter of the book because it is the last question to ask yourself in the launch process. Everything else needs to be in place first.

Of course, that won't happen if you are just sitting around waiting for things to fall into place – but you already know that if you've gotten this far in the book. You have important work to do if you are going to launch. When all of your ducks are lined up, you can now answer the final question …"When do *I* start Podcasting?"

Remember that *"when"* is the very cornerstone of the whole time-shifting process that we have been discussing and encouraging throughout this book. The world of *"when I say so"* has been replaced with *"when I want to"* and your Podcast launch must reflect this new reality.

WHEN DO I START PODCASTING?

The answer to the question, "When should I launch?" is, honestly, a simple one: *"Right before your audience is ready to consume."* One of the interesting things about the time-shifting of content consumption is the transference of that same freedom to the content producer. Yesterday's rigid schedules go away. People no longer have to meet at the studio every Thursday at 3:00 PM or be on the phone every Monday at 8:00 PM. *You have the freedom to launch when you want (or need) to.*

Many of you are incredibly excited about everything you have read in this book and want to move forward quickly. But if you launch before your audience is ready to consume, you are going to end up with a mess (that no one listens to). Moving quickly is fine—just move quickly through all of the steps that you need to complete before you can prepare your audience to consume your content.

Believe it or not, you could surprise your audience with content they're not ready for yet. The result would be a "deer in the headlights" type response that prevents anyone from moving forward. You don't want your audience to be surprised anymore by the introduction of such content than you would want to surprise someone that you are firing.

If you have to fire an employee and they were surprised at the firing, be honest, *you have failed in your communication responsibilities*. They should have seen the firing coming from a million miles away. Whether that person is a wage earner or a vendor or a member of your team, he or she should have been well aware of any serious issues and the implications accordingly. Developing a dialog and communicating with your market every step of the way is essential. Through this dialog, your listeners will tell you—perhaps even beg you—to launch. They will tell you what to launch with and what will make the best impact. Launch dates should be based on their input. Podcasts should never be sprung on consumers the way many people spring a book on an audience. Even this book was written solely because the market was ready for it.[1] The book stores at the mall outlets are filled with 99 cent books of great content launched before the audience was ready.

---

1. But, of course, this book had a blog following the launch process almost a year before publication. In the interest of our short little history, we keep up the entire thing at http://www.thebusinesspodcastingbible.com.

THE BUSINESS **PODCASTING BIBLE**

On the flip side, the question of *"when?"* can also be a stumbling block if you over-analyze and procrastinate. Without a specific time or reason to launch, you never will. Here again, the element of time-shifting plays an important role. Until now, content has always been developed around a schedule of someone else's choosing. For example, even the launch of this book required us to meet a publisher's deadline. The embracing of time-shifting turns that schedule into something of a moving target. At some point, you have to pin down a reason to Podcast and a specific time to launch. If you don't believe us, try this simple test.

Open up your email program and head for that folder that we know you have: Email newsletters that you intended to read or e-books you were going to check out someday. You might have quite a stack of them. Why? You had no specific reason or timeframe for consumption. Without that definitive point, it is extremely unlikely that "someday" will ever arrive.

Don't get caught on a track to nowhere. You will find a printable PDF worksheet in the private member site for this book with all of the questions you need to answer before you will be ready to launch. The rest of this chapter is simply commentary on the worksheet.

But first, we highly recommend that you physically write your launch date on the calendar (in pencil). You can always move it or change it. When you do launch, you can expect a few universal things to happen. They happen to everyone who has launched up to this point. They are going to happen again and again and again. We are going to cover those issues toward the end of the chapter so no one is surprised by the process. Hopefully, we can keep you from being surprised by the things that will come your way and help you move through them with greater ease.

THE PODCAST LAUNCH CHECKLIST

1. Is your audience ready for a launch?

You can't answer *yes* to that question unless you have communicated with your audience and they have said *yes* first. If your audience isn't ready for a launch, launching your Podcast for your audience is moot and will cause, in the beginning, more damage than good. This *yes* can't come from your own head; it has to come from your audience.

When will they know they're ready? They'll know when they hunger for the kind of communication that Podcast content, or existing content show down the Podcast channel can bring. When they want more, and are ready to take action to receive it, they are ready.

2. What is your reason for launching?

Once you have a green light from your audience, are *you* truly ready to launch? While much is made of the financial ease of launching a Podcast, other important investments of time and mind share are required. You need to have a compelling reason to take on the time involvement, mind share, and commitment associated with producing a Podcast. That dialog with your audience will also help you to become very clear on your reason—clear on whether a Podcast is the right medium for your intended message and audience.

Perhaps, honestly, the best communication vehicle might be an email newsletter or a printed faxed media piece delivered on a predictable basis.

3. Is your audience ready to consume?

Your audience might be ready for a launch, and you might completely understand your reason for launching. Still, your audience has to be ready to listen, to consume your Podcast. Otherwise, those downloaded Podcasts (if they get that far) will be as effective as the email newsletters and e-books sitting around in that folder we spoke of earlier. You might have the most technically savvy audience in the world, but they must also desire to consume your Podcast on some regular basis. The audience has to be hungry enough to consume your content and have the means to do so.

I know numerous "geeks" who have yet to consume their first Podcast. It is not an issue of capability; it is an issue of desire.

4. Do your listeners know how to consume your content?

Your audience might *say* they would be thrilled with the concept of three hours of Podcast content from you every day of the week. However, some people really can't take in that much content. We have seen people return great products to us solely *because they were not ready to consume the content.* As mentioned earlier, you must check that they are willing to consume.

It is also not enough to just convince someone to purchase something from you[2]. Implementation translates into starting something, not doing something—and consumption is the beginning of that process. Coaxing someone to consume means getting them started. Your aim should be to provide some type of tutorial that will help them do just that. It might be an online video tutorial, as we have done, or perhaps just text. Use whatever tool you feel is best but *teach your audience to consume*

Podcasts can be consumed on the subway or in a bus. They can be consumed while riding a bicycle or riding a John Deere mower or sitting in front of a computer. Your challenge as a Business Podcaster who is interested in monetization is to teach your audience how to consume in the most strategic way possible to you. Open their eyes to the possibilities. Give them mental imagery on how to consume and give them directions: Read this first document. Listen to this first audio file. View this first video file.

Starting the consumption process is critical. Even in the sales copy that you develop to encourage the Podcast purchase, provide mental imagery that shows them how to consume the product—in this case, the content of your Podcast.

LAUNCHING WHEN IT MAKES SENSE TO LAUNCH

Look to your target audience and ask aloud, "*Is my audience iPod savvy? Are they willing to wear ear buds and consume my content?*" If you don't know these answers – you need to stop right now.

First, the audience needs to be ready for this vehicle, *your vehicle*. Otherwise, it won't matter how ready you are or how excited you feel (or even how great this book made you feel about the topic). If your audience

---

2. And an audience who consumes your free content is paying with their very valuable time.

is not ready for this vehicle, you are in absolutely no position to launch. Don't launch until launch makes sense.

Being able to convince them to consume your content on a regular basis is really more important than the content. We constantly talk about the many airplane trips where we see dozens of men in suits with little white ear buds. Every Podcaster should be asking: "How many of those people are listening to music? How many are listening to entertainment audio books, and how many are consuming Podcasts? Are any of them listening to my show? Why not? What could I do to get them to listen? They're all consuming content – *they just aren't consuming your content.*

Prepare your audience for the consumption process, first conceptually and then technically. time shifted content is the world's greatest tool for anyone who consumes it. Time shifted-content is also the world's best excuse for anyone who does not (*I can always get to it eventually*). Remember the early days of music-file trading when teenagers had near terabytes of "stolen music" that they were going to listen to "one day." They were never going to listen to all that music. It was just the pack rat mentality of having all those tunes in one place and knowing that they *could be accessed sometime—anytime.*

By the way, tens of thousands of Podcasts a day are downloaded in that same packrat mentality. Your download numbers are meaningless – *your consumption rate is all that matters.*

As information marketers, we know all to well of information junkies who will purchase anything or download anything. That doesn't mean they are going to consume any of it. They are never going to take action. Time-shifting just offers one more reason to avoid personal responsibility, to avoid taking the decisive action of consuming the content. With a sold information product, we can track our success in communicating the need for consumption in our return rates. When a product comes back, we can ask the customer, "*What went wrong?*" We can make our content and our sales process better as a result of that dialogue. The same isn't true for the downloaded but unconsumed Podcast.

Why does the NBC "Must See TV" campaign work so well? Because many people feel comfortable with having someone else tell them what to do, whether or not they admit that. NBC says, "Thursday night, you are going to sit down in front of your television and consume." That's exactly what many folks do. Sure, some people are excited about Tivo and the idea of choosing the time and the night of the week that they consume their favorite shows, but millions of people still like to be told exactly what to do—and those folks are going to be around for quite some time.

The greatest advance in Web based banner advertising was the person who added "Click Here" to the first banner ad. Click through rates doubled as a result of this simple direction. The addition of the word "Now" did even better and then, finally, the flashing "Click Here Now" was developed and the power of the banner ad was suddenly very real.

Instead of launching a campaign like the banner advertisers, hoping for action, launch your Podcast with an understanding of what will get your audience to listen, and perform that important "click" of their own.

If you can't convince your user base to consume your content on a regular basis on their own initiative, you might want to consider shifting away from Podcasting toward something specific like a *moment in time* teleseminar or a *physical* event. These are, honestly, easier to consume and provide a reason to do so in the specific timing of the delivery.

We have actually seen a definable decline in active teleseminar participation because of the trend that makes the teleseminar information available later through audio generator links, Podcasting, listener lines, replay lines, web transcripts, and other means of consumption. Many say they are going to return and consume the content later, in another form, but often they never come back. The message "Please bookmark this page" on a Web page has, literally, no definable effect at all . But, when you give people a *reason*[3] to come back, they will do so. When you give people a reason to attend a teleseminar live, you'll be surprised with the results. If your Podcast audience knows, and desires, what's "in it for them" if they consume your Podcast, you'll have a smashing success on your hands.

---

3. Remember, it needs to be a reason important to them.

And don't launch your Podcast until you have, at the very least, an idea of what that process is.

Unfortunately, some people feel forced to exponentially increase their content because of the opportunities made available to them via Podcasting (and the Internet in general). That's the trap that many people fall into, and one that this book will hopefully eliminate for many. We can't over-emphasize enough that you need a *reason* to Podcast and your audience needs a *reason* to listen much more than any of us need *more content*

Here's a fun challenge. Put the book down for a minute and jump over to iTunes and grab a few Podcasts that interest you—business, entertainment, or education. Consume a few and see if you can figure out what the Podcaster had in mind. With some Podcasts, the reason will be very clear. But all too often, you will have a tough time grasping why the Podcast producer is offering this content. Finally, ask yourself how many of these Podcasts do you honestly see yourself listening to on a regular basis. Pretty low number, isn't it?

We are constantly talking to Podcasters and asking them, "What are your plans? What are your goals? Why *this* Podcast?" Sadly, the answer is usually, "I don't know … *because I can?*" Take a piece of paper out right now and make two columns: Label the first column "those who know why they are Podcasting" and label the second one, "those who don't." Now head out to iTunes, pick out a few more titles out at random and give them a quick listen. Place each one of those Podcasts beneath the column it seems to fit. You'll know within the first few minutes of each cast, trust me. Now circle the titles in both columns that you believe have the best chance of succeeding. Are your circles clustered in just one column?

Our human nature is drawn toward purpose. We are attracted to goals. We look for meaning. If we can find that on a Podcast, we are certainly going to be attracted to that content – and will come back if there is more to be had. Having a reason for producing this Podcast is the net you cast that will bring in your listeners.

Now, let's go deeper into the big picture. This final chapter is the underlying reason why *The Business Podcasting Bible* is in your hands right now.

Chapter One offered five main opportunities under, "Why Business Podcast?"

1. Maximization of business intimacy.

2. Acceleration of communication.

3. Ability to boost bottom lines.

4. Time-shifting of information content.

5. Place the power of the Internet in the palm of a hand.

The rest of this book, up to this point, has elaborated on those five elements. If your Podcast is not closely tied to one of these five reasons, you might want to go back and read the book again and find your reason before you speak your first word into a microphone. You must be very sure that your strategy aligns itself with one of these five opportunities. If it doesn't, your Podcast will end up in another reader's "those who don't" category and you'll find that you have wasted a great deal of time on "the latest fad.""Because everybody else is doing it" will never be a valid reason to Podcast – even if "everyone else" is your biggest competitor.

Go out to Google right now and search on any term on the planet you might know. You are going to find hundreds and thousands of pages in cyberspace that deal with that content, that topic. The amazing thing about Google is the way a search brings the very best stuff right to the top a remarkable percentage of the time. In a sense, Google is a computerized aggregator. The Podcast listener is the human aggregator and the stuff they deem important will rise to the top. Everything else below the first few have a terrible chance of ever being consumed.

Visitors to Google or iTunes are going to see dozens of different Podcasts about their industry, about their passion, and then listen to the ones that rise to the top. If yours is not one that is regularly viewed, that rises to the top, you are in a bad place. You never have a second chance to make a good first impression, especially in Podcasting.

The press has been pretty noisy about a concept called *podfading*. Essentially, this is the "trend" of Podcasters who have simply given up and who leave their information (and Podcasts) live as a reminder or what once was, but have no reason to be anymore. Podfading occurs when the audience (or the producer) loses all interest in the Podcast and the producer ceases production. Will your show end up on some list of Podfaders? If so, save yourself the heartache.

You have to have a solid reason for doing this. How else can you develop a sustainable approach that includes a long-term strategy? You are essentially clueless if you can't describe in one or two sentences exactly why you are Podcasting. Without knowing the *why*, there is no *when*.

Your purpose should be obvious. Your publishing cycle—how often the show should be released—should be understood from the very beginning. And by the way, here is a hint. If you expect your audience to consume on a regular basis, you must publish on a regular basis. The publishing cycle dictates a *production* cycle, which means that you will need to know exact production and editing schedules far in advance. If you aren't compelled to produce on a regular basis, what message are you sending to your audience, the very people you expect to consume on a regular basis?

Marketing is education and teaching—educating your market to consume and to respond. Marketing through direct response calls them to action. It entices them into calling a phone number or visiting a website or some other suggested response. None of this happens without consumption. The Podcaster can intensify the message frequency and the intimacy of the messages, but the listener retains the ability to say yes or no. If your audience wants to hear from you on Mondays, you might go to your listeners and ask if they would like to hear from you every weekday. That dramatic increase in frequency and intimacy—hearing someone's voice five days a week instead of one—elicits a different response – and you won't be able to predict what that response will ever be

Look for that on the evening news with celebrity anchors. Think of Johnny Carson, David Letterman, and Jay Leno—the talk show hosts who are in our faces five days a week. The perceived intimacy is considerably higher than it would be for a guest speaker who occasionally reinforced those personal appearances with content in a book or on a CD. Frequency and intimacy: Be careful if you turn up the volume button – but consider the strategic implications.

The Podcast audience is so permission based that they can remove themselves at any given time. They can vanish into thin air. Just because they have stopped listening does not mean they will take the time to unsubscribe (and give you numbers that accurately reflect reality). Your numbers may not reflect what is really happening – they only reflect what once was. If you are using Podcast as a communication tool and intensify anything in the process, dialog with your audience to be sure that what you are doing is effective, don't read you stats and assume a thing.

One of the underlying reasons for this book is to lead you to a place where you thoroughly understand how Podcasting integrates into your overall business strategy. If you take that time to prepare and strategize, you are already miles ahead of a large chunk of Podcasters – even if you launch a "little later" than everyone else.

SUCCESSFUL PODCASTING REQUIRES TIME AND PREPARATION

The sexy new technology of Podcasting and its low cost tend to draw a great deal of interest and attention. People adore the fact that a microphone that sells for less than $100 and an old laptop computer can become a recording studio. Hosting packages sell for as little as $10 a month. Even a decent HD video camera can be yours for less than a thousand dollars. For those looking to utilize the Podcast channel for already existing content can start for even less.

These considerations are at the bottom of the equation when you are deciding when to launch. If anything, they drive people to launch without adequate strategy casting and preparation. *Time* is the real currency of Podcasting—business-oriented or otherwise. The production, the raw content production, requires time.

"Winging it" is seldom a good idea unless you are producing a spontaneous show format and are ready for the most rapid of response to what you find from your efforts. Take this approach and a 30 minute Podcasting session might require hours of follow up. Even so, prior planning and preparation tend to pave the road to success in whatever you do, Podcast or otherwise. At the very least, you will find that you will be investing time in the actual production of your "winging it" show. Post production, chopping, editing, removing, and arranging takes time. Promoting your Podcast takes time—just announcing to your potential audience that your show is available takes time. Attracting listeners, finding your way into the search engines and indexes, and achieving results from your Podcast all take time.

Make sure that you are ready to make the investment of your own valuable time before you launch. Ask yourself a simple question: "Do I have any idea how much time this venture is really going to take?" You can't produce an effective Podcast just by sitting in front of a microphone and rattling off a 15-minute monologue—not unless you also know how to repurpose and repackage that content as an effective Podcast – or, at the very least, know how to hand it off to someone to do just that. Grasping how much time Podcasting requires is a critical point because *time is money* (for both you and the listener). We know lots of people who are attracted to the technology and low cost until they understand the magnitude of the undertaking. At that point, they just laugh and walk away. We applaud the response.

Once you run all the numbers and know what Podcasting will demand, you can start to review the various ways it can be approached. Perhaps outsourcing the production or even outsourcing content development might alter the picture and make the time investment more worthwhile.

There is even something to be said for not launching a Podcast of your own and, simply, advertising or working with an already existing entity to leverage what they already have in place.

Sometimes the answer to "when" is, simply "*not yet.*"

WHEN WILL YOUR AUDIENCE BE READY?

Before you can launch successfully, your audience must be ready on multiple levels. Most people only focus on one specific level and ignore the rest. We want you to recognize and concentrate on all three of these major qualifications because they are of equal importance.

1. The audience must be sufficiently capable from a technological standpoint to consume your content. The modern misconception is that everyone and his mother has iPod on the brain. That is simply not the case.

2. The audience must desire to consume your content (at the frequency you shoot it out). This simple truth must be faced. As fabulous and wonderful as you judge your Podcast to be, the audience may not feel the same way. They also might want you monthly, despite the fact that you scheduled a Podcast for every Tuesday this year.

3. The audience must be willing to take the personal responsibility involved in Podcast consumption. With no set start and stop time and personal choice comes the personal responsibility to consume. Don't be afraid to educate your audience and train your listeners to consume a Podcast. Don't have a Podcast distributed to thousands that ends up in the same as the email newsletters we discussed earlier.

Teaching your audience through video, audio, text, or any other convention is important both technically and mentally. Explaining the technology gives them the mechanics of consumption. Reaching them on a mental level might mean reminders, prompts, and suggestions. As important as training your audience can be, don't waste time reinventing the wheel. Leverage some of the great books, courses, articles, and online guides about receiving Podcasts that are already in place.[4]

The other day at the airport, I was surprised to see three small iPod-type guidebooks that seemed to be very well written. Each one explained how to synch and how to subscribe to Podcasts. Is it a bad idea to send your audience elsewhere to learn how to receive Podcasts? Absolutely not. Teaming up with top technology can be a great idea (and leveraging strategy). Send that new iPod owner on a field trip to the Apple store. After all,

---

4. Also reference some of the examples we link to in the private member site.

 CHAPTER SIX

he will only return his new toy if he never learns how to use it. Recommend a visit to the shopping mall where an experienced Apple user can teach your audience how to download and listen to Podcasts. Recommend a book or a video. Recommend anything that will capture interest and generate real excitement. If someone else is teaching consumption, encourage that process.

Acquaint yourself with the resources that are available on the market to educate your customer, but be prepared to develop your own. Some of the subtle nuances associated with the iPod may be frustrating for consumers and new users. At the same time, no Podcaster on the planet can deny the power and impact of Steve Jobs' charisma and the iPod's multi-million-dollar ad campaign. Have you been to an Apple store in the last few years? They make computing exciting, fun and approach it in ways that only a multi multi multi million dollar investment can. But, let's be honest, the local Apple store is going to teach people how to consume its own Podcasts, *not yours*. They might in fact introduce your customer to competitive Podcasts.

Consider how to leverage Apple's ease of use and market dominance. In some cases where a profit stream has been established, you might want to physically give away iPods to each member of your audience to leverage the market dominance of Apple. Some real advantages can be derived when everyone is using the same player (it sure makes tech support and consumption directions easier). If you can't furnish an iPod, consider giving away a less expensive MP3 player instead.

Never let the questions be about the technology. Direct the conversation to a dialogue about benefits. The number one question that invariably comes up when we are traveling and speaking about Podcasts is, "Should I purchase a flash player or should I go for the latest hard drive model? Our answer is always the same, "Do you want to bring along a lot of information or all of your information?" The iPod Nano holds a tremendous amount of content. Do you really need more?

Piggybacking on the technology that has already been established is the fastest way to move forward. Take the time to register in the back of this book so that you can tap into the wealth of information on our private members' website. You'll see options for vendors that will give you a chance to mix and match your capabilities around your own strengths and weaknesses. You may see a vendor who is adept at keeping everyone up to speed on the technology side, freeing you to develop quality content.

Teleseminars are not wildly successful because they are the most dynamic or thrilling way to communicate. Their appeal has a great deal to do with the telephone itself. People constantly use their phones and feel completely comfortable with them as a familiar technology. Many of our teleseminar consumers have 30 years experience in our content delivery technology and it just doesn't get any easier than that. Without trying to sound too comical here, consider the amount of tech support problems we have with people who can't figure out their phones and understand how easy it is for us to focus on content. We have already discussed that Podcasting is nothing new, but rather a convergence of existing technologies that have been infused with a new sense of power. The public is already enthusiastic about embracing this unique medium, so piggyback on that power surge and harness some of the excitement (and existing training) about Podcasting to your advantage.

In short, let someone else do the tech support.

Podcasting is going to reach an entirely new comfort level with consumers based on two very important advantages: Speed of access and convenience[5]. As human beings, we are interested in immediate gratification. We want immediate and easy access to content. At the same time, we want the freedom to consume that content whenever and however we please. We want that chocolate-chip cookie while it's fresh, even if we decide to save it until after dinner. Taken together, these two basic elements of Podcasting manage to cater to our seemingly contradictory impulses of instant gratification and procrastination.

Right now, I'm looking at a SAMSUNG sports camcorder. My first introduction to this model was a time when I had the opportunity to try one out before delivering it from one friend to another. I decided to buy the same model for myself, since I was already familiar with its features. The

---

5. And the devices are going to get easier to use (and Podcasts will get easier to receive) as time goes on.

funny thing about this story is that I'm actually looking at the *unopened box* for my SAMSUNG camcorder. I feel good about the fact that I own this piece of equipment, even though I'm not ready to use it yet. Much like content on an iPod, that unveiling will have to wait for another more opportune time. My schedule revolves around priorities, and taking time to play around with my new camcorder is way down the list. Samsung is fine with this because they've already received my money and my chances for returns are low. However, as a Podcaster, my show on your hard drive is pointless until you listen.

As you work with your audience, give them a taste of the incredible power associated with Podcast consumption. Then just allow their natural needs and desires to kick in: The need to be in control, the desire for instant access, and the tendency to "pack rat" for later consumption. Speak of the power to make yourself better through this technology. Empower your listeners and you will be in a far better place than other marketers. Never create; always improve.

Sometimes we are not aware of what we want until someone lights a fire. I just returned from an event where the great T. Harv Acker presented and I truly appreciated having both Millionaire Mind Intensive and Guerilla Business School on my iPod for consumption and review on my way home. I wouldn't have had the space for this content if I had only brought a Nano with me. The hard drive of all of the information products I own was akin to a trailer that holds my entire library with me that I take wherever I go. Tell stories like these to your audience and they'll realize the power of taking *you* with *them*. Once they've done that, you've won.

Podcasts offer instant download capability and add the convenience of allowing you to listen whenever and however you desire. CDs don't offer that same luxury of instant gratification. You either have to run out and buy the CD of your choice or wait for it to arrive in the mail. Podcasts cater to the pleasure associated with impulse, which could be defined as "consumption based on desire and convenience." Teach this fact.

You have to be number one to win in your client's mind when the context is a physical, single, timed event. That's what makes Super Bowl advertising so astronomically expensive: Millions of people are fixating their full attention on this single event. When my favorite TV show on Wednesday night conflicts with a teleseminar scheduled for the same time, I am forced to choose one or the other. Time-shifting changes all that. Having a Tivo or even a simple VCR gives me the chance to save the television show for later consumption and listen to the teleseminar. The teleseminar that also offers a Podcast option does even better because I can subscribe at the moment I hear about the event, and then listen later when I am ready.

Being number one in the client's mind is no longer necessary when you realize that your audience can grab your content and consume it at will. Granted, certain times of the day will be at an absolute premium. As professionals who work out of our homes, we have special times when our kids are up and in that play mode. We wouldn't give up that time for anything. Time-shifting allows us to prioritize around our own needs, desires, and values—not around other people's arbitrary schedules. Gaining such far-reaching control over *time* is revolutionary in its ramifications.

Your audience needs to be technically capable and keenly aware of what that Podcast technology enables them to do. We highly recommend that you embrace and leverage every sensible evangelist of technology to help bring your audience into the fold. Why waste time trying to teach someone to use an iPod when Apple has done such an exemplary job of that instruction?

Beyond being technically capable of consuming a Podcast, your audience must *want* to consume it. Triggering their desire is a key element. Many content producers make the big mistake of presenting an exaggerated egoistic view of themselves. Does your audience really want to listen to you for an hour each week now that you have the capability to deliver that much content? Just looking at the Podcasts at iTunes makes you wonder, "Who on earth would ever want to listen to that?" The answer is "No one at all." Someone, somewhere just got excited about the sound of his own voice.

Brevity in the consumption of the content can sometimes be the very answer you need. A five-minute Podcast that delivers what others take an hour to convey could be worth a great deal of money. At the success of the iTunes television shows and Rush Limbaugh Premium Podcasting, I would bet big money that people are not putting *Lost* on their iPods just because it's a novel capability. They know that *Lost* lasts an hour on television. If they watch it on their iPods, they can claim about 15 minutes of their lives back again and still enjoy the show. For many of us, 15 minutes of our life is worth much more than a buck ninety-nine.

The same is true for the audience of the Rush Limbaugh show. His listeners are investing three hours a day, five days a week. Nevertheless, they are getting back hours and hours of their lives by being able to listen to him during their down time—and all for just $25 a month.

In addition to having the desire to consume and being technically ready to consume, your listeners need to understand the personal responsibility involved with consuming content. We can't stress this point strongly enough. Your audience has to pull (and listen to) your content on a regular basis. iPods and other Podcast aggregation tools make the pulling incredibly easy, but consumption is still their job. But as more and more content goes down this channel, those iPods are going to look like that bulging email folder filled with unread e-newsletters. You have to teach your listeners about their personal responsibility as consumers of the content.

Encourage them to consume, but realize that they have to go the last 15 feet. You can have all the bandwidth in the world, but someone has to come out to your house and walk the last 15 feet to connect the wires from your house to those heading out to the street. You can deliver tremendous content to the iPod. You can deliver quickly, fast, amazing, wonderful, gorgeous, life-altering content to the iPod. But the consumer is the last 15 feet. Your audience makes the final connection.

Don't launch until they understand this simple fact.

PODCAST CONSUMPTION STRATEGIES

We've discussed Podcast consumption issues throughout this book but we summarize the three most important issues here.

1. Multiple vehicles for Podcast consumption.

Anyone with a Podcast strategy should utilize each and every vehicle for Podcast consumption.

The first is the computer. Computers are still the first option for many people when they have the opportunity to consume content. As exciting and beautiful and sexy as an iPod player might be to some of us, many people still want to log onto a web page and click the play button. That doesn't mean that you can't be instrumental in helping them to be more comfortable with portable consumption and time-shifting. Some will respond to this instruction and coaching over time because the rewards of time-shifting are so fantastic.

Just be sure to include the computer as you develop your Podcast delivery channel. Some people will want to consume that way, period. Even iPods owners are often computer users who spend considerable time on or off the Internet. Knowing that an impressive percentage of your audience is frequently sitting in front of a computer gives you some real marketing opportunities. Remind them to click-and-play, send an email, or ask for comments on a blog. Use any convention that you can to encourage, coach, or engage your audience in dialog.

The second vehicle is the Portable Media Player (PMP). As mentioned earlier, this can be an iPod, or any other portable device that provides for the downloading and playback of digital music. People with portable media players are very like to take your Podcast along with them when they step away from the computer. These people should definitely be included in your strategy. Too many folks think they are Podcasting just because they added a play button to their website. That is not the case.

The third vehicle is the home. Home entertainment options are small at the moment but continue to grow. Tivo makes it possible to consume a Podcast on your television set. Right now, the capability is audio but video will be here soon. The Microsoft media center platform is coming into play as well. When Microsoft announces a Podcasting client consumable by the general public[6], it should become part of every strategy of Podcast consumption.

Teaching your audience to consume is not limited to saying, "Go buy an iPod." The last thing you want to do is restrict your audience's consumption

---

6. Although nothing was announced at the writing of this book, know that we will cover this event, when it happens, in depth at the private member site.

options. Listen on your computer. Listen on a portable media player or in front of your television set. It's all good *as long as you listen*.

Be aware of these multiple direct vehicles, because a successful Podcast strategy should utilize them all. Any Podcast strategy should train people for all of them and make them all available. Indirect vehicles for Podcast delivery should also be in place. Some people will not mind, and perhaps even prefer, if you deliver content by CD or DVD in the physical mail. Delivery on a preloaded portable media player is another viable option and completely doable if your monetization strategy is in place.

2. Podcast consumption tracking.

At this point, no portable player on the planet will report back to you on consumption of Podcast content. That is a very important fact as we must, from the very beginning, understand that we will probably never have an automatic reporting of who has consumed our Podcasts. We'll need to figure that out for ourselves. Now, obviously, the technology is continuingly upgraded and updates on the latest tracking options and other important trends are just two of the many elements of the industry that we will track at the private member site. Please register and start reaping the additional value of membership.

But between now and then, let's examine this issue:

It's true that you can track *downloads* of your Podcast, and any strategy should include an examination of those statistics. Just remember that *downloads* do not equate to *listens* anymore than email sends equate to reads. Downloads represent people who grabbed the content and put it on their hard drive; people who were, at the very least, *at one time interested in what you had to say*. Maybe they moved it to portable player or burned it to CD or did whatever. On the other hand, maybe that content is still sitting right there on the hard drive with little chance of a listen. Someone may have started to listen and stopped at some point during the piece.

What does it mean that you can't track consumption? Two things: 1) *a considerable amount of money* has been made in other media options where tracking options were even less decisive and 2) you are going to have to find some intelligent ways to track consumption.

We first introduced the term, PLA, or *Post Listen Action*, at the first Corporate Podcasting Summit. We hope this metric term will enter into the general dialogue but, regardless of that, we explain the term here as well. In short, if you can get them to do something after they listen, if you can get them to take action after consumption has been completed, *you can track that*. Using established statistical practices, we can extrapolate numbers considerably better than *assuming* a percentage of downloads are consumed.

Post Listen Actions (PLAs), include visits to a specific (tracked) website, a call to a toll free phone number, an email sent or any other action you can use to track that a user not only consumed your Podcast, but took action accordingly.

This is not just an issue of general open Podcasting. Keep in mind that none of the Premium Podcasting options discussed in this book can track consumption on portable media players. They can only track downloads (sometimes to the specific user). If the audience is not downloading, the audience is definitely not listening, but there is still more to determine. Downloads are the first thing that a Podcaster should be checking. Premium Podcasting allows a Podcaster to monitor on a user-by-user basis who is downloading content; but again, consumption can't be automatically recorded (yet).

3. Audience consumption education.

Teaching your audience to consume is tremendously important. Take myself as an example. The name Alex Mandossian may be well known in information marketing circles, but I, on only rare occasions grab my Podcasts from iTunes. Sure, it's not that difficult, but there are easier options for me. Why bother when Yahoo! allows me to listen immediately without any extra steps? Why go the iTunes route when many Podcasts have immediate click to listen buttons on their sites. Further, the iTunes search mechanism is still lousy and I find Google or Podcasts.Yahoo.com to still be easier for a technophobe like me. We'll bet your audience is much more like Alex than they are like Paul.

Even a term like "podcatchers" is a technological problem for a guy like me, because I only know about content. I know how to learn and listen and read. I still don't know how to download a Podcast, and I consider myself on the upper echelon of techno-dummy. I can FTP and email. Over the past year, I've made three million dollars just putting up websites. I know how to do all of these things, but I still don't know how to get my Podcast. I need Paul for that. Not everyone has a Paul, so what can we do?

Ease of use of consumption will have to be the key. We need a simple online platform to download Podcasts and make Podcasts available to the public. People like me are ashamed of our inability to download a Podcast, and there are so many of us still out there. We are highly successful, educated people who just haven't taken the time to learn the few simple steps that would dissolve all the mystery about Podcasts and iPods.

AOL addressed this simplicity issue with email and with an online platform. The initiative was so successful in attracting technophobes that AOL has been the curse of the online community as it relates to email and marketing ever since. Podcasting is a distance from email for ease of use in the areas of consumption feasibility, usability, and integration. We know of folks who still have problems cutting and pasting. Podcasts? Forget it.Those same people can turn on a radio and find a cable station. They know how to work a remote control, but the universal remote control is beyond their grasp. With that universal remote, they could integrate every element of their electronic equipment, but simply won't, until they get easier to use. These "smart techno-dummies" need to learn more about Podcasting. They need to learn about the beauty of receiving a Podcast and perhaps the right way to produce one.

There are companies forming and launching that are attempting to make it easier. Podshow.com and Melodeo.com are two of the outstanding players today but their audiences are currently very small and their impact, at this point, insignificant. Time will tell who will be the "AOL" of Podcasting.[7]

Keeping our focus on the receiving end enables us to create a market, not launch a technology company. This market must be taught how to consume. They aren't lazy; they just need to be shown from the point of view

---

7. We'll obviously be tracking this in the private member site.

of the mechanism. Let's just part the curtain on the "techno-dummy business community" and realize that they are not going into the second level of anything yet. They might have a user name and password, but they don't know how to go in and manipulate those settings.

Although I have referred to myself as a techno-dummy, I think a more apt description would be technophobic. I'm afraid that technology is going to steal my time and money away from the activities that really generate revenue. I'm not really a dummy when it comes to technology. On the other hand, I don't dive into it wholeheartedly because, honestly, I don't need or want to. When finding a Podcast becomes as easy as finding a frequency on a radio station, we have arrived. One of the goals of this book is to illustrate how far from that point we are right now.

Consumption and access are two different things. Access means receiving the Podcast and being in the position to consume. Consumption is listening to a Podcast you already have. When you can provide the access and the audience can consume accordingly, you have "won" the game. Many people already know how to utilize an iPod or an MP3 player. Countless others do not. We need a Google or some de facto standard that makes sense—something that makes it easy for everyone to utilize this technology, not just those who are more technically astute. We need a standard so simple that Alex would no longer need Paul as a crutch. Nothing is really difficult, including preloading. Handing out preloaded iPods is certainly one way to hurdle the obstacle of people who don't know how to receive Podcasts.

We need to teach our listeners about *access*. If you look at The Podcast Brothers website at PortableMediaExpo.com, you will find a brilliantly designed website. Brothers Tim and Emile Bourquin are the ones who do the Podcast and Portable Media Expo and other great shows for this industry. Each episode on their website offers a subscription button for the techno-savvy and a Real Audio button or Windows Media Player button for those who "understand" that approach. The important issue is that the audience is listening, not that the latest and greatest technology is being used to enable them to listen.

Real Audio for most purposes is dead, but for the people who are still running around the Internet with Windows 98 machines. In about 4.5 seconds, you can tweak your service and be able to a Real Audio button for those who simply won't upgrade. Now you can upload each episode, so you go out to iTunes, Real Media, Windows Player, download and click-to-play. With a flash button and all the options make it as easy as humanly possible to consume.

Some people at the top of their field consider themselves to be competitors. What they have really done is focus on the technical side of the world, using geek speak and techno mumbo jumbo to impress people. The Podcast Brothers website is extremely popular and a stellar example. You can click on a button that matches what you know, and the music and content starts playing. Always deliver your content in a way that as many people as possible can grab it. Follow this with excellent training about consumption, and you will have a competitive advantage over everyone.

What other vehicles are out there besides iTunes, which has 80 percent of the market at this time? Bringing in these other pieces could take you to a very interesting place. On the portable side of the picture, 80 percent of your Podcast content is reportedly being consumed on the client side through the web browser. Interesting statistics, aren't they? Consumption and access are definitely two of the most important concepts that you can teach.

REWARDING CONSUMPTION

Consumption is easier to deal with than access, because access has nothing to do with laziness. Access is limited by your knowledge and causes frustration. Consumption is in our own hands. We don't have to worry about limitations. What a great episode for Marketing Online Live: What is the difference between consumption and access as it relates to Podcasting?

Openly remind your audience to consume. The download can become automatic once they have figured the process out, but don't stop there. From day one, your strategy should include the use of email, voice broadcast, fax, even physical postcards as reminders to your audience to consume. Vendors in this space will always change, so we won't list them in this book. Please take a moment to register at the back of the book and visit the private member's site. We'll update with some of our favorite vendors as we are introduced to them.

The last thing is the simple rewarding of consumption. Once something becomes habitual, it just continues to repeat. Reward your audience for consumption of the first three months of your service and you'll have them for much longer. Once you have your audience in the regular habit of consuming your content, you can stop leaning on them as firmly. The key is bringing them into that place where consumption is a regular habit. The more we repeat a habit, the more deeply ingrained it becomes. Habit is one of the strongest forces in our lives because the behavior becomes automatic. We no longer have inner debates about whether to do something or not. We just do it.

When will you be ready to Podcast? First, complete the Podcast launch check list that we have provided at the private member site. In the previous chapter we discussed fire, aim, ready. We discussed the danger of that approach, just as we stressed in this chapter that "When?" is the very last question. Answer everything that leads up to that last question in a full and complete way and you'll be good to go.

WHAT CAN YOU EXPECT WHEN YOU LAUNCH?

In the spirit of planning and to save you from being startled later, we want to share

Is Podcasting for everyone?

Is Podcasting for everyone? Of course not; some people have no need for a Podcast. On the other hand, those people would probably not have picked up this book and certainly would not have read it this far. But, let's be honest, for some audiences, Podcasting will never work (and shouldn't be tried). And some businesses that are considering Podcasting and examining their Podcasting strategy should have those items far down on their completion list after the reworking of their mission statement and other basic business principles far more important than the publishing of their online media content.

Figure out what your Podcast message is *first*. Then you can wonder about the way your Podcast is going to be placed on iTunes or other important details. The question should be actually restated, "When will Podcasting be right for whatever it is that you are doing with your audience?"

That question is a big underlying rock at the foundation of this chapter. When you answer all six of the Podcast launch readiness questions, you may discover that you have an 18-month trail to walk toward your goal. You may identify some internal issues that require your attention. If this book only brought you that far down the road, it has succeeded beyond our wildest dreams.

Podcasting is not for everyone. Podcasting is for those who embrace it *right now*. For some, Podcasting remains way down a to do list that

some of the things that will happen when you launch.

1. Media attention that you should take advantage of.

Harness the power of the press as you launch, particularly if you launch relatively early in the game before too many other players glut the Podcast highway. Spreading the news that you have embraced this additional communication vehicle is going to be a press-worthy event for at least the next year. Any company should ride that wave and use it to promote their company, or Podcast, or whatever it might be. At launch, make sure that your contact information like phone numbers and email addresses are readily accessible on everything you produce.

Media coverage of your launch is great – and can bring you new listeners and customers for free. Issuing a press release in conjunction with the launch will make it extremely easy for the press to follow up and helps explain this new media in an "old" medium that they understand, and are programmed to respond to.

2. The earliest tech support will be the toughest.

Believe us or not, *you are going to be accused of making someone lose all of his iTunes music*. A successful Podcast will result in accusations of spyware if you've penetrated the market far enough. I guarantee such things will come. The moment that you introduce a new technology into their world, you are suddenly responsible—from the viewpoint of certain minds—for anything that goes wrong. Early tech support is always interesting. Be ready for it, and be ready to respond quickly to what you've learned.

Our good friend Armand Morin started to get a lot of returns when he first launched a tape series for his Internet training (he's been in the industry that long). People were returning cassette tapes saying that they were "*broken*." They were only half-way through the content when it just stopped. Morin went in and added a few words at the end of the tape: "This is the end of side one. Flip it over, hit rewind, and listen to side two."

That simple instruction reduced his returns tremendously and cut his complaints in half. For those of us who are familiar with both sides of a cassette tape, something like this is hard to imagine. Trust us when we say that an entire user base is "out there" who has no idea about flipping a tape to the other side. Your earliest tech support is going to be the hardest. Be prepared to have a few strange people crossing over.

From the standpoint of valuable input and feedback, take full advantage of every question you receive in tech support and every answer you give. Develop some frequently asked questions. Your tech support people should only write a single response to any one question. Encourage them to

seems to get longer every day (with Podcasting racing down the list, not up). Others need to only fix a few things before they even consider Podcasting. You are the only one who can judge if either one of these descriptions matches your own situation.

answer clearly and accurately the first time and use that content to create a guide that will help others. Post that content on your site.

3. Excitement will fizzle.

The early excitement that will invariably come through your Podcast will not be sustainable. If you are looking for that early buzz, just get over it. Podcasting at its finest is not a media sensation. Podcasting at its finest is an incredible communication vehicle. Sure, it can be a buzz to see your picture in iTunes. Realizing that you have reached a thousandth download of a certain episode is a buzz. Getting viewer email from somebody on the other side of the planet who consumed your content and loved it—all these things are an absolute kick in the pants. Best of all, they just continue to arrive. And your picture is not going to disappear from iTunes.

The early excitement surrounding the launch of a Podcast is going to diminish very quickly. You have to have a strong foundation and a sure strategy to grow, and hopefully to continue growing and growing. You are going to jump from your thousandth download to your two thousandth download of any particular show, and the viewer email will continue to flow. But early excitement will never carry you all the way through to a solid success. Knowing that adrenalin is not sustainable is something you absolutely need to expect at launch.

4. Gaping holes will be revealed.

Something else is going to happen when you launch: A lightning flash will reveal some elements that you missed. Maybe these problems were hidden from view, like the audience who didn't know about flipping over cassette tapes. Some people have launched on a certain file format that others can't play or use a speed that sounds bad in the flash players. Whatever minor or major detail it might be that you missed will come to light in short order when you launch. Ask any reputable, experienced person about beta products and listen to the stories.

When the holes are revealed, respond accordingly and, if at all possible, respond to them in your Podcast. This let's your users know that you are listening to then and that the dialogue of the Podcast is, in fact, very real. In the Podcasting "space," covering a gaping hole can do more for your reputation than your initial launch ever did.

Email advice is one of the most frustrating parts of this career and one that you must accept as part of the game. Identify it, utilize it if you want to, but take it for what it is. Some emails will say your show is too fast. Others will complain that it's too slow. You will hear emphatically that your show is too long or too short and some will tell you that it has too much information. The opinions of your audience are like email addresses. Many have more than they should and are way too eager to share them. You are the one who has to make hay. You have to make sense of the conflicting feedback and then respond accordingly.

But do respond accordingly.

You will also receive a great deal of so-called expert advice when you launch a Podcast. These people are not the ones who are actually consuming your content, your actual audience base. You should pay close attention to anything your audience says. These experts are offering advice about the steps you need to take or what you need to do. Once in a while, an idea may cross the board that has real merit. For the most part, unsolicited advice is only worth so much. Some will give you technical advice. Others will tell you how to fix your content or your business plan. You will also find that most of them have day jobs and most have never launched a successful Podcast in their lives—so be careful.

Give the lion's share of your attention to our audience. You can glance over the bulk of advice that comes in, but pay more attention to your audience than anything else. We guarantee that the things we have covered here will all happen when you launch. If you expect them and know how to respond to them, your launch will be successful. Your Podcast doesn't have to be another one that became lost in the hype and was never seen again.

5. You will question your own timing.

Is it possible to launch too early? Absolutely. You launched too early if you had little or no clear understanding about what you were trying to accomplish. It was too early if your audience wasn't ready or any of the other warning factors that we discussed in this chapter (or others). At this point you have two choices: Fix your Podcast and bring it into that fold or start over. Let's talk about both options.

But first, let's spell out the truth of a "broken" Podcast, *nobody is listening*. It's not like you've opened a store on Broadway that thousands have shunned – you launched, and it was pretty much a fizzle. Use that to your advantage and when you relaunch, relaunch well.

If you decide to fix your Podcast, do it quietly. Work slowly and quietly behind the scenes and make the necessary improvements and changes. Don't jump from a two-minute update to an hour dialog just because your show was too short. If the hour dialog is the right answer, make the move in smaller increments. The less your audience notices the changes you are making, the better. You don't have to tell them that you are fixing anything, just make a good plan and implement it.

Many people have launched a video Podcast with the best of intentions and realized that video doesn't make sense for what they are trying to accomplish. All video portable players play audio, and all computers that play video play audio. All television sets that play video play audio, so down-grading your Podcast from video to audio is very doable. A few people have come to us for whom launching with audio was a mistake. They needed to move up to video. If that is the case for you, be prepared to face the additional issues.

The *loud fix* refers to making an announcement to your audience: "We weren't doing this properly. We've done our research and homework and are making XYZ changes. Please join us along this new path." The loud fix is an intimate dialog with the audience. There is nothing more intimate than confessing that you were wrong. Intimacy should be an element of either solution. Your focus on audience response will be very keen during the time when you are quietly introducing incremental changes to your show. That depth of intimacy will be an invaluable saving grace in any attempt you might make to start over again.

Use intimacy to your advantage. Come to your audience and voice your honest opinion of things that need to change. Tell them about any perceived mistakes you have been making. Tell them that you have heard them and are responding. Give them the names of the people who emailed you—the authors of the very information that awakened you. Now continue that dialog with your audience. Tell them you are going to make changes, but you need to hear from your base. Issue out an "ask campaign" or a similar ploy to keep the dialogue going. The intimacy of this communication is extremely viable. Use it.

Don't toss out your original efforts unless your new Podcast is completely different in every single way, shape, and form. With your infrastructure already in place, you could redirect the old feed to your new feed very quietly. We understand from a technology standpoint, most people who are reading this book won't know what that means. Simply hand this section over to your tech guy and let him set everything up. The Podcasting infrastructure allows you to quietly change the title of your Podcast, the image, the format, and the location in iTunes or something similar.

Your tech guru needs to review the rules at technologies like Apple or Feedburner. You can slowly move your audience from website A to website B and from name A to name B. The change from iTunes to Feedburner will go right along with you. If the old feed location is in some of the old directories and the inbound links and everything associated with that are still viable to you, some will catch up. In fact, most of the best ones will catch up.

It is possible to arrange some type of feed redirect from your old feed to the new feed. In fact, this is not complicated. That way, the need for a do-over won't necessarily kill your existing audience base. Some of the most revered Podcasters never went down this path in the do-over phase. Essentially, thousands of listeners are waiting to get the next episode of X. That episode is never going to arrive because they did not transition using the existing technology.

Don't be afraid to change or start over. Just bring your audience gently along. You may find that they are much more willing to come along than you might have thought.

Of course, your questioning of timing might just be the butterflies anyone gets when they present to an audience. If you planned right and launched well and have the tracking elements in place to make sure you stay true to your vision, stay true to your vision and change only when it makes sense.

GESTATION IS THE KEY

"When?" is the last question of this book because it is the very last question you should ask yourself. Podcasting is not a *fire, aim or ready* type situation. We want you to take the approach of *ready, aim, fire, fire, fire, fire*. Everything that has come before this final chapter has been devoted to *ready, aim*.

The metaphor for a great Podcast is bamboo. It takes two to three years for bamboo to gestate beneath the ground. Once it reaches the sunlight, it grows anywhere from three to six inches a day. What does that mean? When your Podcast is exposed to the light of your audience, it can grow rapidly like bamboo. First, it must be allowed to gestate. The rest of the world only sees the growth of bamboo. No one cares about the years spent nurturing this growth beneath the surface. That's why bamboo is such a richly appropriate symbol for the world of Podcasting. "When?" has to be the final question. When you are truly ready, you can take off like a bat out of hell.

Do you need years? Some of you will. Others can launch in a few weeks. By now you should know what will work best for you. If you don't, please don't launch until you do.

When relates to time shifting. Beyond being the last question, *when* is the cornerstone of the communication breakthroughs of Podcasting. Just keep in mind that one of the answers to "When?" is "Never." Just because I have a Podcast on my iPod doesn't mean that I will take the step to listen and consume. Podcasters must guide their efforts with a clear and solid strategy. Otherwise, the audience may never listen and everything else will be in vain.

The green light for launching is the ability to answer the sixth question to your satisfaction. Is your audience ready for launch? Do you know your reason for launching? Are you ready for launching? Is your audience ready for consumption? Does your audience have a desire for consumption? Are your listeners aware of their personal responsibility in this conversation?

Answer the full six questions and answer the *when* question last. Complete the worksheet and know what to expect when you launch. If you follow these guidelines, the launch process should be more predictable and run more smoothly. And like the bamboo, after some months of gestation beneath the surface, your growth above the surface will be phenomenal and the world will be watching.

CONCLUSION

As excited about Podcasting as we are, as bullish as we can be about this technology (heck, we did sit down and write a book about it!), the call is simple: *don't launch until you are ready to do so.*

The first five chapters of the book lead up to this point. We believe that a basic understanding of the technologies and elements at play are required to launch a successful venture. Yes, you could *fire, aim, ready*, but your chances of success are considerably better if you follow our path.

Unless you met our requirements for a company that shouldn't launch a Podcast, *please do, and soon.* The thrill of meeting your audience's needs on their time at their convenience provides a thrill of service like no other.

We're here to help. The private member site for this book will continue to grow and be a powerful resource for you. We'll also link to the sites and services that pop up, as the industry matures, and let you know what works best.

Finally, when you do launch, *let us know.* We'll have a special area of the member site to list the Podcasts launched as a result of this tome. We hope to listen to your Podcast soon and perhaps consume it on our own iPods *at the time and location of our own choosing, of course.*

AT THE PRIVATE MEMBER SITE

Among other things, an extended (and printable) version of this chapter's *"Podcast Launch Checklist"* is available at the private member site for this book. You can grab this worksheet for use in your launch efforts (as well as additional launch training support material) at http://www.thebusinesspodcastingbible.com/when/. We'll also use the site to keep you informed on any changes to any technologies or tracking paradigms discussed so far. Make sure you sign up today!

Appendices

About the Free Bonuses and the Business Podcasting Bible Member Site:

———————

Claim your free bonuses, exclusive Premium Podcast content, additional chapters, video tutorials, content errata, PDF worksheets and more today!

Special Bonus – Your book registration enters you into our "1 iPod a Month (Until Podcasting Doesn't Matter) Giveaway." Simply register at the private member site for information on how to win your own pre-loaded iPod.

Register your copy of this book at the Business Podcasting Bible Private Member Site today at http://www.TheBusinessPodcastingBible.com/members/.

No additional purchase is required.

THE BUSINESS **PODCASTING BIBLE**

Time Tested Strategies to Monetize Your Podcast, Even If You're Starting From Scratch.

Launches Q4 2006.

Claim Your Free Podcast Secrets Preview at
http://www.PodcastSecrets.com

THE BUSINESS **PODCASTING BIBLE**

Charging for Podcasts – a Primer

A t time of publication, the market for paid (Premium) Podcasts is very small. It is the strong belief of your authors that this will change quickly and dramatically as the general market embraces the power of this technology and medium.

The technology that enables Premium Podcasting is also in its infancy. At this point, there are only two technologies we believe are worth mentioning:

The first can be found at http://www.PremiumPodcasting.com. *In full disclosure, the company is partially owned by your authors and was designed to meet the requirements we saw in the industry.* The company's Web service technology manages the Premium Podcast content you get as a customer of this book, so you'll be able to see it in action.

The current pricing structure / model for Premium Podcasting is a single monthly fee that enables you to serve Premium Content to up to 10,000 listeners. At time of publication, the monthly fee was less than a dollar a day.

The second player/technology is the Wordcast division of the publicly traded Audible.com. Their site is at http://Wordcast.Audible.com. Their Wordcast services enable Podcasters the opportunity to leverage the Audible technology and hosting platform to provide numerous Premium

Podcasting options. Pricing is varied based on the services required. Please visit their site for more information.

We will track this trend carefully in the private member site (please see the first page in the appendix for registration information) and update our readers as the industry changes and matures.

The Ten Commandments of Business Podcasting

Thou Shalt Ask Thy Audience

Thou Shalt Know Thy Audience

Thou Shalt Match Message to Market

Thou Shalt Repurpose When Possible

Thou Shalt Separate Channel from Medium

Thou Shalt Go In With a Strategy

Thou Shalt Teach Consumption

Thou Shalt Have a Monetization Strategy

Thou Shalt Consume the Best

Thou Shalt Live the Freedom Lifestyle

Top Podcatchers and Podcast Directories

P odcatchers are software programs (Web or desktop based) that allow users to subscribe to Podcasts. Podcatchers traditionally facilitate syncing of Podcast content to a PMP (Portable Media Player). Podcast directories are places where consumers can search for Podcasts the same way they might search for Web content in a traditional Web directory such as Google or Yahoo.

Putting this appendix element together and sending it to print almost guarantees obsolescence before it reaches your hand. This element of the Podcasting industry continues to change on an almost daily basis. For example, at time of publication, Microsoft had yet to release any Podcatching software. Your authors promise to keep this list up to date in the private member site.

iTunes Podcatching Client and Directory

With the success of the iPod portable media player (reports place the iPod at a market penetration of greater than 80%), Apple is the 800 "pound gorilla" of the industry for both Podcatching and Podcast Directory.

In the case of iTunes, the two are tied together brilliantly. The only way to (legally) put content on your iPod is with iTunes (there are versions for both the Apple and PC platforms), so every customer of the iPod is required to use iTunes to manage their Podcast collection. *At time of publication, 86.8% of the Marketing Online Live audience downloaded the show through the iTunes software.*

iTunes is a free download. iTunes currently integrates a Podcast directory into the iTunes Podcatching software. As almost every single iPod user uses the iTunes software, the impact of the directory is obvious.

Currently, Apple makes it very easy to submit a Podcast to their directory. A "Submit a Podcast" option in the iTunes directory leads to a simple form that usually sees an approved Podcast in the directory in less than 48 hours.

More information about iTunes can be found at http://www.iTunes.com

The Yahoo Podcast Directory and the Podcast Plug-in for the \Yahoo Music Engine

At time of publication, the Yahoo Podcast Directory was the only major directory for Podcasting from a 'traditional' search engine and was still in beta. At this point, there is no tight integration with the Yahoo search engine, but its impact and role in the Podcasting space is still very important.

Currently located at http://Podcasts.Yahoo.com, the Yahoo Podcast directory offers a Podcast directory that enables user reviews and ratings, click to play, tagging, and more. No software is required other than a Web browser. In a very strategic move, there is even an option to subscribe to a Podcast found in the directory in iTunes.

Yahoo runs an online music service to compete with iTunes. Access to this service is through a free software package called "The Yahoo Music Engine." Unlike iTunes, which only syncs with the iPod, the Yahoo Music engine can sync with almost every player on the market. Currently, there is no version of the software for the Apple platform.

Yahoo offers a plug-in for their Music Engine that allows Podcast subscription and aggregation similar to the iTunes offering (although not nearly as intuitive, etc.). Once installed, users can subscribe to Podcasts directly through the Web interface.

It is rumored that when the Yahoo Podcast Directory goes out of beta, it will be tightly integrated with the regular Yahoo Directory. At that point, the impact of the project could surpass Apple's iTunes.

It is the opinion of your authors that the future of Podcast directories and Podcatching software will, in the end, be more like Yahoo's approach than Apple's "walled garden" implementation.

The Odeo Podcast Directory and the Odeo Player

Although Odeo's numbers and market penetration remain surprisingly low, this first mover implementation of a social network engine behind Podcast listeners should be examined.

Odeo offers an entirely web-based Podcatching and subscription engine. Users can consume their subscriptions from any Web browser but can also use the feeds from Odeo to sync with the portable media player of your choice (including iPod).

The service includes the ability to view the subscription choices of others in the system providing a user-generation recommendation engine similar to Amazon's "Customers who purchased this product also bought" approach to the upsell.

Odeo also offers a number of (currently free) tools for the Podcaster than include "click here to leave me an audio message" buttons, Web players and more.

Odeo has a very clean, crisp look and feel, entirely free of advertising (at this point) and provides a desktop player for Apple computers but recommends third-party options for the PC.

Even if you never use the software, make sure your Podcast is located in their directory.

Juice Receiver

iPodder Lemon was the software that started it all. The first Podcatching Client was an open-source product called "iPodder." In unique homage to Apple's role in Podcasting, the icon for iPodder was a lemon.

The product is now called the Juice Receiver, remains open source, and has versions for the PC, Apple and Linux platforms. After iTunes, Juice Receiver (and iPodder Lemon) downloads represent the next biggest audience for Marketing Online Live.

With the introduction of Podcasting integration into iTunes (and Apple's cease and desist orders to sites with the iPod name in them), the Juice Receiver product doesn't seem to have the passionate audience it once had. It, does however remain a great product.

Juice Receiver does offer a fascinating (paid) option. Anyone can purchase a version of Juice Receiver preloaded with the feeds of your choice. An example of this, pre-loaded with a number of our Podcasts, can be found in the private member site for this book.

Podshow Plus and the Podshow Plus Player

Podcast pioneer Adam Curry, founded Podshow, Inc. in January of 2005. Nearly 9 million has been invested in the company since then from several high-profile Silicon Valley venture capital firms. Curry's role in the Podcasting industry is undeniable, but the true impact of Podshow is yet to be realized.

Podshow recently launched their Podshow Plus Podcast Directory and Web-based Player. The launch was not without controversy, but seems to have quickly established their position in the "Podosphere."

At this point, the launch is still in "un-beta," still a bit buggy, and its impact is yet to be determined (but we will track in the private member site). Their stated goal is a "social network" site for Podcast consumers similar to MySpace.com.

If Podshow becomes a major player in the industry, the possibilities offered (in both listener metrics and possibilities) are fascinating, and worth monitoring.

Other Podcast Directories of Note

The following Podcast Directories are also worth noting:

Blubrry.com – http://www.Blubrry.com

My Podcast Center – http://www.MyPodcastCenter.com (note: MyPodcastCenter.com is partially owned by the authors of this book)

Podcast Alley – http://www.PodcastAlley.com

The Podcast 411 Directory of Podcast Directories – http://www.podcast411.com/page2.html

The Podcast Directory – http://www.Podcast.net

Podcast Pickle – http://www.PodcastPickle.com

The Podcasting News Podcast Directory - http://www.podcastingnews.com/forum/links.php

Note: In the Private Member Site for this book (see the first appendix for access information), we include a custom developed version of the Juice Podcatching client (both PC and Apple versions) preloaded with recommend Podcasts for those interested in Business Podcasting.

THE BUSINESS **PODCASTING BIBLE**

Our Favorite Podcasts, and Why

Other than ours, of course:

Daily Source Code (http://www.dailysourcecode.com). If it wasn't for Adam Curry's (pretty much) daily Podcast at the beginning, this technology would still be for high-level geeks only. He made it personal, always asked his audience, and is the inspiration for more Podcasts than anything else out there.

Stephen Pierce's Optimization Series (http://www.optimizationseries.com/). "The Optimizer" Stephen Pierce's brilliant Podcast contains great content on business optimization, but also integrates tightly with his other marketing efforts. Study this one for a brilliant example of leveraging Podcasting's strengths in your marketing and communication efforts.

Podcast Brothers (http://www.podcastbrothers.com). Tim and Emile Bourquin leverage their love and passion for the topic with a brilliant (pretty much) weekly infomercial for the Podcast Expo (http://www.podcastexpolive.com). Podcast Expo is the "Detroit Auto Show" for this industry because of this Podcast.

Geekbrief.tv (http://www.geekbrief.tv). Make sure to read the case study for this Podcast in this book (and follow the "What Happened" elements in the Private Member Site). Months before this show launched, the host hadn't a lick of video experience. Now this husband/wife self-produced show is the standard whereby which all other tech/geek video Podcasts are judged. Also note, the show has staying power: It's in our regular rotation, unlike most other video Podcasts that tend to lose their excitement level after a week of consumption.

The Chris Pirillo Show (http://www.thechrispirilloshow.com/). This popular technology show was the first to blend traditional radio elements with a Podcast format and was high enough quality to generate a 6-figure revenue stream at launch. Chris understands, perfectly, the difference between the medium and the channel and leverages both in this very fun, and very profitable Podcast.

Battlestar Galactica (http://www.scifi.com/battlestar/downloads/podcast/). The "director's commentary" for each episode is released as a Podcast the day this popular science fiction is aired. There is no reason to wait for the DVD release. It isn't uncommon for fans of the show to consume the episode multiple times, in a single night, thanks to this new form of communication.

Podcast 411 (http://www.Podcast411.com). Rob Walch interviews the people behind the Podcasts in what has been (aptly) described as the "Inside the Actor's Studio for Podcasters." At time of publication, the interview number exceeded 160. They aren't all Business Podcasters, but they are all fascinating.

This Week in Tech (http://www.twit.tv). Tech pundit Leo Laporte gathers a group of industry insiders in what is best described as the tech insider version of the Sunday morning politics show. TWiT owns the audience it plays to, has amazing download numbers, wields considerable power in the demographic and is downright fun to consume. This show never could have happened anywhere else but as a Podcast. It will be fascinating to see how the history books discuss this one.

Screencasts Online (http://www.screencastsonline.com). This Video Podcast is notable for two reasons: a) The content is first rate (the show is made up of video tutorials about the Macintosh computer platform and b) The monetization strategy is brilliant. Lower quality versions of the screencasts are released to the general public for free. Users who want better detail; and to support the producer, are encouraged to upgrade to the paid (and higher quality) version of the Podcast. Conversion rates are as impressive as the content.

Putting a list like this together is always difficult. We will continue to update our favorite Podcast lists in The Business Podcasting Bible Private Member Site. Please visit the site for our latest picks.

Podcast Creation
Mentors

This is not a book about Podcast creation, it is a book about the Business of Podcasting. If you want mentors in Podcast creation, we recommend the following:

Best Book / Cheapest Entry Point

<u>Podcast Solutions</u> by Michael Geoghegan and Dan Klass tells the whole story on Podcast creation. Although you can pick it up at most Apple stores today, it tells the story of creation in terms the average user can pick up and run with. If you have to buy a book on Podcast creation, this is the one to buy.

Easiest Software Package

<u>Apple Garageband 3.0</u> (or better) is part of the Macintosh iLife Suite, the software package that comes with any new Macintosh computer. Garageband provides a simple and powerful Podcast creation tool (albeit with a definite Apple/iTunes prejudice) that can be quickly learned by any interested party.

Best Home Study Course

123PodcastLaunch.com is the professional Podcast development home study course by author Paul Colligan. He developed it from frustration of not being able to find a course on Podcast production (and launch) for the business user/audience.

Best Package Solutions

The Podcasting Packages at YourPodcastGear.com were assembled by Mike Stewart, the Internet Audio/Video Guy. His packages combine tested gear that works, packages that tell the complete story and a phone number you can call if anything goes wrong.

Best Live Training

Podcast Academy (http://www.PodcastAcademy.com) is a regular production of Gigivox Media. Multiple events are held around the country, every year, and teach Podcasting to anyone interested by the biggest movers and shakers in the industry. Can't attend an event? The content is also available online.

Best Podcast Event

The yearly Podcast Expo (http://www.PodcastExpoLive.com) is the "Detroit Auto Show" for this industry. The best minds, equipment, and training in Podcast creation gather yearly for this event.

As opportunities and mentors arise, we'll track them in the private member site for this book. Please see the first appendix of this book for registration information.

The Podcaster's Reading List

M any of the books we suggest here have nothing to do with the technology behind Podcasting – they deal with the people behind Podcasting, the very audience we suggest you ask and understand before you record your first word. They are listed in alphabetical order.

Art of War, The
Sun-Tzu
Some things never change.

Bible, the
Multiple Authors
The original time and place shifted portable media content that changed the world. Some things never change.

Burn Rate
Michael Wolff
What we should have learned from the first bubble.

Cluetrain Manifesto, the
Christopher Locke, Rick Levine, Doc Searls, and David Weinberger
Markets are conversations.

Ender's Game
Orson Scott Card
The power of the nets in changing public opinion long before we had the nets.

Getting Things Done
David Allen
Stress free productivity is possible.

Global Paradox, the
John Naisbitt
Explained the power of Podcasting in ten years before it had a name.

Good to Great
Jim Collins
Who is on your bus?

8th Habit, the
Stephen Covey
Finding your voice

High Stakes, No Prisoners
Charles Ferguson
A brilliant case study in bubble 1.0. Don't let egos get in the way.

Naked Conversations
Robert Scoble and Shel Israel
Understand the technology, and the power of the technology, that launched Podcasting.

Podcast Solutions
Michael Geoghegan and Dan Klass
The first (and still best) complete guide to Podcasting.

Plato's Apology
Plato
Asking questions.

Promoting Your Podcast
Jason Van Ordern
Soup-to-nuts guerilla Podcast marketing guide.

Public Speaking and Influencing Men in Business
Dale Carnegie
Some things never change

QBQ
John Miller
What is the question behind the question?

Technopoly
Neil Postman
Will we surrender culture to technology?

Tricks of the Podcasting Masters
Rob Walch and Mur Lafferty
The 411 on how Podcasters, of all kinds, are getting the word out.

War of Art, the
Steven Pressfield
Winning the inner creative battle.

Wisdom of Crowds, the
James Surowiecki
Do we trust our audiences?

THE BUSINESS **PODCASTING BIBLE**

The Case Studies

In the book (and at the public Blog), the outline for our case study format is as follows:

What (are you trying to do)?

So What (does it mean)?

Now What (are you doing about it)?

We follow this format because the future is yet to be written on any Podcast we mention as a case study.

There is a 4th element,

What (happened)?

As we get updates from our case study participants, we'll put that information is in the Private Member Site for this book. See the first appendix for more information on access.

We're also actively looking for new Case Studies. We'll place the first three elements in the book's public blog and, as with these printed case studies; we'll track the fourth element in the site. Information about submitting your Podcast can be found in the Private Member Site.

88SLIDE

http://www.88slide.com

Noah Bonnett

88SLIDE: The Daily One Minute Trivia Challenge

What?

88SLIDE is a fast paced, dynamic, daily one-minute trivia challenge format, distributed via the Internet at 88SLIDE.com, and through iTunes as a video Podcast. Cell phone users can also download the 3GP formatted series at 88SLIDE.com.

This micro-game-show releases new episodes Monday through Friday, where viewers are asked to email and text message their answer to the day's multiple choice question. They release the week's outtakes and bloopers on Saturday and Sunday.

88SLIDE's mission is to entertain, interact, and enlighten, daily, in 60 seconds.

So What?

A leader in the interactive Podcast space, 88SLIDE is unique in the sense that it asks its viewers to submit a daily answer to potentially win a prize.

Viewers who submit an answer to 88SLIDE invariably return the next day to a) see the correct answer, and b) see if they've won. As a result, their day-to-day retention is extremely high.

Most recently, 88SLIDE started to attach both daily and weekly sponsors to integrate into the show's content. Dealhack.com sponsored a week's worth of content during their San Francisco road trip in the form of a prize sponsor. This organic approach, sort of a throwback to the golden era of game shows, worked well as an alternative to traditional pre and post roll advertising. In addition, 88SLIDE continued to integrate the brand into daily emails to their growing family, through their blog, and in every episode that week.

Now What?

As 88SLIDE approaches their 100th episode, they're continuing to seek sponsors looking for fun, dynamic and different approaches to incorporating their brand into this growing property. Other clients have recently approached 88SLIDE for either prize sponsorship opportunities, product integration, or the licensing of their content for alternative distribution.

To learn "What Happened" to this Podcast, please visit the Private Member Site for The Business Podcasting Bible. Information can be found in the first appendix of this book.

AFFILIATE GUY PODCAST

http://www.affiliateguypodcast.com

Case Study by Paul Colligan

What?

Affiliate Guy Podcast (http://www.affiliateguypodcast.com) was the first paid (Premium) Podcast ever. It sells for $47 a month and is also provided as a bonus for Paul's Affiliate Rancher Home Study Course (http://www.affiliaterancher.com).

The show uses the PremiumPodcasting.com (http://www.premiumpodcasting.com) Podcast delivery engine and the AutomateSales.com (http://www.automatesales.com) e-commerce engine for payment.

The show also has a "free" version that is usually the first 20 minutes of the paid version. The free version provides a means to market the Podcast through the existing (free) Podcast engines. On occasion, the free channel has been leveraged to market other affiliate related products and services.

So What?

More important than revenue is the fact that Affiliate Guy Podcast proved people were willing to pay for content that is important to them. $47 is a significant price and shatters the perceived model of the one dollar paid Podcast.

The Podcast continues to grow audience share and Paul has been able to leverage the free version as a marketing tool for both the Podcast and other affiliate related products.

The revenue is nice as well!

Now What?

A new cover art and Website for the Podcast are currently under production. Cross promotion elements are starting with other affiliate related properties.

Paul is also examining the possibility of putting the Podcast on the Audible Wordcast Network.

To learn "What Happened" to this Podcast, please visit the Private Member Site for The Business Podcasting Bible. Information can be found in the first appendix of this book.

BEA SYSTEMS INTERNAL PODCAST

Susan M. Siegel

Director, Corporate Communications

BEA Systems

www.bea.com

What?

Radio BEA is a monthly Podcast for BEA employees worldwide. The show provides information on BEA, the industry, the competition, customers, partners, employees or whatever is relevant, controversial or just plain interesting. The format is informal, the three guest speakers vary each month and the show is delivered right to employees' desktops for immediate listening, or they can download it to their iPods and listen as many do, in their cars, their homes, their local Starbucks, the beach, or wherever they happen to be.

So What?

BEA is a $1 billion + software company with over 4000 employees in 35 countries. Employees expressed the need for better communications and dissemination of information so that they had a clearer understanding of company strategy and positioning, and additional insight into our customers and partners. *Radio BEA* is one of the ways we reach a diverse audience in multiple time zones. The conversational format lends itself to easy listening without requiring intense concentration, yet it provides high level information on the company's products, technology, events, partners, customers to give employees an understanding of what's going on. They also get exposure to executives, technologists and industry experts that they wouldn't normally get to hear. And they control where and when they get their information.

Now What?

Radio BEA is less than a year old and interest in it is steadily gaining momentum. While it's still difficult to assess exact numbers, visits to the internal Website on which the file is hosted, plus the number of downloads from iTunes indicated that approximately half the company had attempted to listen to the show in one recent month. This, coupled with anecdotal information from employees and suggestions for topics, indicates that there is growing interest in this as a communication vehicle. The show is promoted via an all-employee email message, on the Radio BEA internal site (along with descriptions and photos), and in a weekly internal newsletter. The plan is to continue to widen the guest list to include customers, partners and industry experts.

To learn "What Happened" to this Podcast, please visit the Private Member Site for The Business Podcasting Bible. Information can be found in the first appendix of this book.

BIG SEMINAR LIVE

http://www.bigseminarlive.com

Case Study by Paul Colligan

What?

Armand Morin's twice yearly "Big Seminar" (http://www.bigseminar now.com) is the world's largest and best attended Internet Marketing Seminar. Tickets are $2,000.00 per person and the event has played to sold-out audiences every time.

The event is marketed through an aggressive affiliate program (commissioned sales), and a very popular pre-event teleseminar series.

It is also marketing through a Podcast produced by one of their top performing affiliates.

Big Seminar Live (http://www.bigseminarlive.com) is a Podcast that highlights the pre-event teleseminar series, selections of content from the event, and additional content from event faculty after each Big Seminar. Revenue is generated from commissioned sales to the event, CD and DVD recordings of the event, and additional post-event sales of product from event faculty.

So What?

The Big Seminar affiliate program pays one thousand dollars per participant and Big Seminar Live has placed dozens of new "butts in seats." The mailing list has never generated less than a dollar per name on any mailing and continues to grow.

Big Seminar Live *is produced almost entirely from already existing content* but has generated a considerable revenue stream through event, recording and faculty product sales. It continues to be one of the top performing Podcasts in the producer's portfolio.

Now What?

A new site was recently launched for BigSeminarLive.com with attention on search engine optimization and affiliate sales of event faculty. At time of publication, Big Seminar 8 is months away and looks to be the most profitable Big Seminar for the Podcast yet.

To learn "What Happened" to this Podcast, please visit the Private Member Site for The Business Podcasting Bible. Information can be found in the first appendix of this book.

CUBICLE DIVAS

Cubicle Divas Podcast
http://www.cubicledivas.com
Leesa Barnes

What?

SaviaLane.com is website dedicated to helping women start a business on a shoestring budget. The founder wanted a way to highlight some of the products on her website without sounding salesy. She also wanted a way to increase traffic to the website without hiring a search engine expert or spending hours analyzing keywords using a free online tool.

So What?

A cute and memorable name was selected to help with branding the Podcast. Cubicle Divas was chosen as most women who use Savia Lane are working full-time in a corporate setting and want to become their own boss.

The Podcast is issues-based and focuses on online strategies women can use to build their expertise and gain clients without spending too much money. Existing content from monthly teleclasses and group coaching sessions is repurposed in the Podcast so that the script for each episode isn't created from scratch.

The repurposed content is about 5-minutes in length. At the end of each episode, listeners are encouraged to purchase the entire recording of the teleclass or group coaching session on CD. They are then directed to the Cubicle Divas website which contains links that lead back to the sales page for the products on the Savia Lane website.

Now What?

After 15 episodes, one of the episodes for Cubicle Divas is ranked #1 on the first page in Google for the keyword phrase "selling mistakes." The audio CD related to that episode is outselling the others 5-to-1 and has become Savia Lane's #1 best seller.

To learn "What Happened" to this Podcast, please visit the Private Member Site for The Business Podcasting Bible. Information can be found in the first appendix of this book.

TIM 'GONZO' GORDON SHOW PODCAST

www.digitalaudioworld.com

On 'air' since April 2005

What?

DigitalAudioWorld.com is a website I'd had for about three years when I first heard of Podcasting. With my radio background of 25+ years on-air, it made sense to create a Podcast that focused on various elements of digital audio: what it takes, what you can do in the studio or 'live on location,' how to record multi-track music, etc..

As a long-time broadcaster, I knew that the importance of creating a persona or using a strong personality was as important as part of the positioning. Since I'd always used the air name of Tim 'Gonzo' Gordon, I named the show The Tim 'Gonzo' Gordon Show.

The Podcast was launched in April of 2005; since Podcasting was so new at that time my goals were modest:

- Drive more traffic to my website: www.digitalaudioworld.com

- Create traction with my name so that I could launch products related to audio and Podcasting

- Increase sign-ups for my newsletter 'Digital Bits'

- See what kind of response I would get from my listenership

So What?

The response to Podcasting surprised me in so many ways! Increased traffic, more clients for my audio production business, the successful launch of a 'how-to-Podcast' product and more:

- Traffic to DigitalAudioWorld.com doubled within the first month of my first Podcast. Within three months, it had tripled.

- A number of listeners contacted me asking for help on Podcasting. This did two things:

  - It brought in a number of paying clients (total revenues approximately $2000 in the past 6 months).

  - It spurred me to develop my first info-product: Podcasting Adventures Online, a comprehensive multi-media 'how-to-Podcast' ebook. (Gross revenues of approximately $5000 in the first six months).

- As a 'Podcast expert' I've been asked to appear on a number of tele-seminars, as well as virtual Podcasting expo.

- I've gone on to create a second Podcast product called 'Podcast Profit Case Studies,' which is now in the launch phase.

- Due to my Podcast experience and 'how-to-Podcast' product, I was involved in a Christmas promotion that added almost 2000 readers to a new newsletter of mine called 'Podcast Info.'

- Listenership response has been interesting, to say the least. I've met people from Toronto, CA; Australia; the USA and England. Some have been on my Podcast; others read my newsletter. In one case I actually recorded a couple of classes at a college in the Midwest who were interested in Podcasting and marketing – they also ended up on a Podcast.

Now What?

Podcasting has opened a lot of doors for me, and I'm just beginning to see where that might eventually lead. I'm engaged in a number of projects with other people, and am discussing more. I have plans to release more new audio and Podcasting related products this year. My Podcast schedule has just been revamped and I'm looking at a heavier schedule, knowing now how important regular Podcasts are to search engine ranking.

Beyond that I'm still networking with Podcasters and prospective Podcasters. Even though I've got 25 years under my belt behind the microphone in radio, I view Podcasting as a related but different beast – and there's always something new to learn.

To learn "What Happened" to this Podcast, please visit the Private Member Site for The Business Podcasting Bible. Information can be found in the first appendix of this book.

THE BUSINESS **PODCASTING BIBLE**

GEEKBRIEF.TV

http://www.Geekbrief.TV

Cali Lewis

What?

GeekBrief.TV is a 3-4 minute video Podcast featuring the latest news about tech tools and toys. The format is fast, fun and flirty. The mission of the Geek Brief is summed up nicely by a viewer who said, "It makes me feel warm and fuzzy about technology. More than anything else, the goal is to give the audience a daily smile break.

The show is produced and written by Neal Campbell and Luria Petrucci (aka, Cali Lewis), a husband and wife team, who started the show following the most common Podcasting advice:

1. Podcast about something you love.

2. Strive for technical quality.

3. Interact with your audience.

We didn't have experience with video production, on camera or off, when we had the idea for GeekBrief.TV, but we were so enamored by the very unique possibilities of Podcasting. The idea that we could independently produce a show and immediately have international distribution was irresistible.

Brief #1 was released December 23, 2005. Within three weeks we had 3000 unique downloads per show, our Web hosting company shut us down, and we appealed to Adam Curry and Ron Bloom at PodShow to help us get back up and running. We were back up a week later and audience growth has been astounding.

So What?

Five months after the first episode of GeekBrief.TV, the producers partnered with PodShow Podcast Network, making it possible for them to quit their day jobs and produce the show full time. Through that partnership, the show has participated in a network wide ad campaign for domain registrar GoDaddy.com and other direct sponsorships are in the queue.

The business goal is to build a brand that has influence and value in the tech space and an audience that is happy with the end result.

Now What?

New media, especially blogging and Podcasting, has an opportunity to think and act different. Old media is primarily one-way communication. They present. We watch, read or listen. New media is a roundtable. Everyone has a voice and every voice has value.

Really our focus hasn't changed since the first episode, we want to continually improve the quality of the show and to continue to make people smile. If we can do that, we believe we'll have a media property advertisers will love.

To learn "What Happened" to this Podcast, please visit the Private Member Site for The Business Podcasting Bible. Information can be found in the first appendix of this book.

GRAND TARGHEE RESORT'S
SKICASTING 2006

CorpCasting & Propel Communications Launch:
Grand Targhee Resort's Industry Groundbreaking Online Initiative:
"Skicasting"

What?

The Ski and Snowboard industry's first (at the time of launch) Resort-centric enhanced Podcast program from Grand Targhee Resort in Alta, Wyoming. (www.grandtarghee.com/winter/mountain/skicasting.html). Nestled at the foot of the Grand Teton in Grand Teton National Park, Grand Targhee Resort is one of the world's hottest ski/snowboard areas for those who love to ski/board light, dry powder with annual depths of up to and beyond 500" of snow. Grand Targhee generates approximately 153,000 skier visits per ski season and roughly 85% of their lodging and event/ski bookings come from their www.grandtarghee.com website. Propel Communications (Grand Targhee Resort's advertising agency in Boise, Idaho) and CorpCasting (Boise, Idaho) established a joint venture to create and deliver Grand Targhee Resort-specific "Skicasts" (mp3 and m4a enhanced Podcasts) episodes via iTunes and other Podcast directories to prospective and current visitors to the resort.

Propel/CorpCasting's goal for this past 2006 winter season was to:

1. Increase unique visits to www.grandtarghee.com by 20%.

2. Increase lodging bookings and conversion rate of inquiry to sale of 2%.

3. Broaden Grand Targhee's brand presence among destination winter travelers who reside in distant, yet larger MSA's with

direct air transportation to Grand Targhee's closest airports (Jackson, WY and Idaho Falls, ID), in addition to those who have the ability to drive to the resort but have not yet visited.

4. Increase repeat visit frequency for lodging and skiing/snow-boarding at the Resort over prior years

5. Develop a new Skicast subscriber base by leveraging email marketing tactics to create and push interest-specific Podcasts to in-house, opt-in email list recipients and promote viral adoption of our Skicasts among passionate skiers and snowboarders.

With over 85% of resort bookings coming from our online activities, this year we created what we believe to be the ski and snowboard industry's first digital "Skicast". Skicasting is, in its most simple definition, vertical industry enhanced audio Podcasting and video blogging for skiers, snowboarders and winter adventure enthusiasts as a means to enhance the visitor experience on-mountain and off by providing skiers and boarders with valuable news, information and fresh perspectives on the winter adventure lifestyle. Skicasting is a way for us to expand Grand Targhee's unique brand experience by taking it mobile in both audio and video formats allowing resort visitors to experience Grand Targhee with as many of their individual senses as possible — audibly, visually and even enabling them to share their memorable Grand Targhee moments with friends and family through Podcast/enhanced Podcast/videocast web distribution. Free of charge, Grand Targhee website visitors can subscribe to (all 11 episodes with a single click) and download a 10 to 12 minute, professionally produced instructional or entertainment MP3 audio file to their PC or Mac computer, iPod or other MP3 player. This frees up visitors to listen to their personal audio/video ski instructor while actually skiing or boarding on the mountain. 2005-2006 Winter season Skicasts covered such topics as 'Riding the Terrain Park,' 'How to Ski Powder with Mark Hansen, Grand Targhee's Ski and Snowboard School Director,' 'Tips for Skiers on New Parabolic and Fat Skis,' 'Telemark Tips,' 'Skiing and Riding for Powder Hounds,' localized content like 'Lost Groomers, Patrol and Instructor Chutes' audio guides, 'Kids Fun Zone' audio guides, etc. Through Skicasting we made available more for guests and listeners than instructional downloads. We gave them direct, no charge access to independent music through our relationship with Adam Curry's Podsafe Music Network (http://music.podshow.com/) allowing users to customize personal playlists along with audio tours of the resort alongside brief audio mentions of on-mountain activities, restaurant specials, scheduled seminars, gear critiques, and event updates. Additionally, we encouraged our guests to create their own Skicasts for distribution through our website to friends and family, all means of extending our brand around the world and capitalizing on the viral capability of Podcasts, email and the Web. Our Skicasts are also formatted for play on such portable media devices as the new Sony PSP platform. The key to Skicasting's subscriber growth lies in our ability to ensure our programs are relevant and fresh and that they maintain the independent spirit of the Podcasting medium. With our initiatives, we are striving to blend corporate brand identity with an honest, independent message.

So What?

The beauty of leveraging Podcasting technology to enhance our online and offline marketing tactics is that it is highly measurable. Bottom Line Results:

- Grand Targhee Resort has identified our Skicasts as the leading driver of their drastic increase in unique website visits by over 60% for the 2005-2006 winter ski season. Our objective was 20%.

- Skicasts contributed substantially to an increase in our lodging bookings conversion rate for the 2005-2006 winter season to a lodging increase in bookings of over 20% versus prior year. Remember, our objective was 2%.

- After the first 10 weeks of Skicasting, Grand Targhee's Skicast generated a combined total of 15,364 Skicast subscribers who listened regularly to the episodes which came out every 2 weeks.

- At launch of the first Skicast in November, 2005, we generated 2,077 subscribers with a sustained weekly average audience of 1,536 over the next 10 weeks.

- These subscriber numbers put the Grand Targhee Skicast in the top 100 Podcasts in the world out of well over 10,000.

- The vast majority of downloads were from people using iTunes 6.0.1 software with a very even split between PC and Mac users.

- The power of our Skicasts are that they engage our audience on a consistent basis and extend our Grand Targhee Resort brand message in addition to building a rapport between our on-mountain resort personalities featured in the Skicasts and our guests and prospective guests.

Now What?

As we begin our comprehensive marketing planning for the upcoming 2006-2007 winter season at Grand Targhee Resort, we are looking, of course, to greatly enhance the Skicast programming and content in addition to encouraging greater audience participation in our programming content. In addition, we strive to make it possible for resort guests to "check out" digital video cameras and iRiver mp3 recorders from our Activity Center on-mountain and record their personal ski/board/snowcat powder adventures of the day and edit and distribute their personal Skicasts to friends and family all over the world, right from our base village edit suite.

To learn "What Happened" to this Podcast, please visit the Private Member Site for The Business Podcasting Bible. Information can be found in the first appendix of this book.

DAVID MAISTER'S BUSINESS MASTERCLASS

http://davidmaister.com/podcasts/

What?

US-based business guru David Maister roke ground as the first top-tier business author to start Podcasting in January 2006. The former Harvard Business School professor, named one of the top 40 business thinkers in the world and widely-hailed as one of the world's leading management authorities, is the author of five best-selling management books including the canonical management textbook, Managing the Professional Services Firm. The weekly 20-minute Podcast episodes on management, marketing, business strategy and client relations draw from Maister's books, as well has his articles, and his observations from over 20 years as a global management consultant. Maister likens each Podcast masterclass series to a full university course in business.

So What?

David Maister writes:

"Podcasting allows me to reorganize and re-present the material written over twenty years and contained in five books and hundreds of articles. I could – and did – extract chapters from all my books, and divide my material into themes – series of Podcasts that connect the dots between things I had written years ago with things I just finished yesterday. It made it all fresh again for me and, I'm told, for old fans.

"Finally, I firmly believe that the best way for an individual or a company to showcase both their expertise and their dedication to client service is to prove they have something to offer by giving

 APPENDIX 9 257

something for free. After a long career, I'm proud to be able to make these resources available."

Now What?

David Maister's Business Masterclass (originally titled: David Maister's Lessons I've Learned) has been featured as a "New and Notable" Podcast in the iTunes Music Store, and after five months has surpassed over 25,000 episodes downloaded. Maister's next Podcast masterclass series on business strategy is under production for release in July 2006.

To learn "What Happened" to this Podcast, please visit the Private Member Site for The Business Podcasting Bible. Information can be found in the first appendix of this book.

MARKETING ONLINE LIVE

http://www.MarketingOnlineLive.com

Case Study by Paul Colligan

What?

Marketing Online Live is a regular Podcast by Internet Marketing experts Alex Mandossian and Paul Colligan. The goal of the show is simple: continue to grow the know/like/trust aspect of our existing audience (as well as grow a new one) through a content-rich regular (free) Podcast on Online Marketing issues.

The format for each episode is simple: 1) A question (usually prompted by something in the news) examined by the two hosts. 2) News about the two hosts and/or the MarketingOnlineLive.com Site. 3) Viewer comments.

Alex and Paul try to keep the show around 20 minutes in length, to match the traditional drive time of a significant percentage of our listeners.

So What?

At time of publication, each episode has been downloaded thousands of times. Viewer comments are regular and we can directly point to a considerable amount of business done as a direct result of the show. As a matter of fact, the original concept of this book came directly from interaction with show subscribers.

The show is respected and consumed in both the Internet Marketing and Podcast Marketing "spheres." The show has a notable popularity rating in iTunes and remains a top reviewed Podcast at Podcasts.Yahoo.com. We also know it is successful because our download and subscriber numbers continue to grow on a weekly basis.

Now What?

The site is undergoing a revision in form that will better direct the conversation with the listeners. Alex and Paul have invested in the equipment to convert the show to a studio quality effort (until this point, Alex usually has been recorded over the telephone). Marketing partnerships are being developed to get the show out to a considerably larger audience. A push to get subscribers to opt-in to an email list will be launched soon.

To learn "What Happened" to this Podcast, please visit the Private Member Site for The Business Podcasting Bible. Information can be found in the first appendix of this book.

MEADOW SPRINGS COMMUNITY CHURCH

http://www.meadowsprings.org

Case Study by Paul Colligan

What?

Meadow Springs, a Community Church in Portland Oregon decided to Podcast their weekly Sunday sermons (http://www.meadowsprings.org). The hope was that the ease of consumption provided would a) enable more people to listen to the sermons and b) lessen the time spent and financial considerations associated with a traditional "tape" distribution model. The weekly Podcast is assembled from a sound board recording by the church secretary on the Monday or Tuesday after each service.

So What?

Consumption of the sermon by Podcast is currently at 17% of the traditional service size. Growth, at this point, is minimal.

Marketing of the Podcast has not been done in any form minus a small informational paragraph in the weekly church bulletin. Church staff is taught to recommend the Podcast if anyone contacts the church for a recording of a previous sermon.

Now What?

Meadow Springs is considering purchasing inexpensive MP3 players for volunteer staff in appreciation for their service. A Podcast demo during a church service is considered for the fall.

The church is also re-examining their Podcast strategy and is going to redo the site based on needs expressed from the audience (easier click to play functionality, simpler directions, etc.). Changes expected Q4 2006.

To learn "What Happened" to this Podcast, please visit the Private Member Site for The Business Podcasting Bible. Information can be found in the first appendix of this book.

MILLIONAIRE MIND VIDEO PODCAST

http://www.themillionairemindvideopodcast.com

Case Study by Paul Colligan

What?

Previously existing (video) content from best selling author T. Harv Eker (The Millionaire Mind) was repurposed into a short 5-10 minute video Podcast series called "The Millionaire Mind Video Podcast." The product contains no advertising, just repurposed video content from this dynamic speaker.

For most of the Podcast, a short Web address is displayed. There is no call to action, simply the Web address. The Web address is only associated with the Podcast (to provide for better tracking opportunities). The goal of the initial Podcast was click-throughs to a site in a very expensive field (personal finance).

So What?

At time of publication, the Podcast was seeing a 3% conversion of downloads to site visits.

Although no money has been spent on advertising, the Podcast enjoys a regular top-twenty ranking in the iTunes Business Category and the show has reached as high as #8, beating out Podcasts standards such at "Time Magazine" and "The Wall Street Journal."

Now What?

The Podcast is a proven success in terms of name recognition, lead generation and viewer interest. Attention to sales conversion is the next focus for this Podcast.

To learn "What Happened" to this Podcast, please visit the Private Member Site for The Business Podcasting Bible. Information can be found in the first appendix of this book.

MORE DONE, LESS TIME

http://www.TheMoreDoneLessTimeShow.com

donna@moredonelesstime.com

What?

Donna Lendzyk, a professional business coach, had an established brand and all that goes with it. The desire to expand and reach many more people generated a difficult decision: whether or not to re-brand her company and herself. Through consultations and feedback, the tough decision was made to rebrand and shift to a new brand name in as little time as possible.

So What?

Undertaking the rebrand was necessary to connect more effectively with her target market and to meet the growing demand in the business market. To aid in the establishment of this new brand it was decided to include Podcasting for a few reasons:

- Exposure: This model will provide a widely consumable forum able to deliver targeted high quality content;

- Subscribers: It will function as a lead generation mechanism that will guide current and future prospects into and through the marketing funnel; and

- Monetization: Donna has discovered that individuals who had listened to a recorded or live teleseminar with her had a much higher probability of purchasing coaching services from her.

Now What?

Donna has decided on a new name that better resonates with her target market. She has now launched http://www.moredonelesstime.com and http://www.themoredonelesstimeshow.com where small business owners can discover proven tips, tools and tactics on how to "Get More Done in Less Time With Greater Ease…So They Can Make More Profits!" She will continue to implement her marketing plan with major objectives targeted by August 31st 2006.

To learn "What Happened" to this Podcast, please visit the Private Member Site for The Business Podcasting Bible. Information can be found in the first appendix of this book.

PODCAST DELA BOLSA

http://www.podcastdelabolsa.com

Jose Espana

What?

PodcastDeLaBolsa.com is a weekly Podcast in Spanish about the American Stock Market. It provides lessons for people that want to learn how to trade successfully in the US markets. Every episode lasts around 20-30 min. and it takes me about 45 min. to produce. I use Sony Soundforge software to and a lapel USB mic to record every episode, so I can record my episodes when I am traveling.

In every episode I ask the listeners to send me feedback by email on the topics they want me to talk about in the future so that I can give my target audience investing tips "a la carte".

So What?

My Podcast is the #1 show in Spanish about the Stock Market.

At one time it was #17 of the highest rated Podcasts in Yahoo.com

Podcasting is soo much fun. I like it a lot. It helps me create a better relationship with my potential customers. When people listen to my Podcast, I am the only person in that moment that has their whole attention.

My shows help me support the sales of my online trading courses. During my Podcasts, I provide exclusive links for people to buy my products so that I can track how effective is this channel to generate sales.

Currently, the Podcast is generating an effective CPM of $156.

Now What?

I am adding special promotions for Podcast listeners only. For example, during the Soccer World Cup in Germany, I asked my listeners to send me what they thought would be the teams to play in the final and also to send me the score. Only one entry per listener is allowed. The winner will get my $597.00 online trading course for free. I have had a great response from the listeners.

I am contacting radio stations, because I want to give them my Podcast content for free in exchange for advertising. This way, the regular radio audience will start to get interested in consuming Podcasts.

To learn "What Happened" to this Podcast, please visit the Private Member Site for The Business Podcasting Bible. Information can be found in the first appendix of this book.

PODCAST TOOLS

http://www.podcasttools.com

Case Study by Paul Colligan

What?

PodcastTools.com is a weekly 5 minute Podcast that highlights a new tool, technique or technology for Podcasters. The goal of the show is to provide a quick explanation of the opportunities at hand and offer insight on their place in the larger Podcasting "picture."

The five-minute format is designed to encourage the Podcaster to implement the technology examined as quickly and as easily as possible. Emphasis is on implementation, not the technologies.

So What?

The Podcaster demographic continues to grow in size and scope and they tend to spend a considerable amount of money on Podcast related technologies and services. There is no better consumer of content via Podcast than Podcast content producers.

The quick format eases production expense and encourages listeners to consume the content and quickly "act" on it. The discussion of product part numbers and website addresses has a better pull to the Podcast's site for "show notes" that can be directed to affiliate sites and services.

Revenue comes from commissioned sales of products introduced during the show and strategically placed at the Podcast Website.

APPENDIX 9 269

Now What?

Several technology companies have approached PodcastTools.com regarding traditional advertising options in the show. At this point, "regular" ad insertion opportunities have been declined but several performance marketing options are being examined.

In Q4 2006, PodcastTools.com will implement several incentive programs to get listeners to subscribe to a targeted email newsletter. Revenue from the newsletter is expected to eventually exceed revenues from the Podcast.

To learn "What Happened" to this Podcast, please visit the Private Member Site for The Business Podcasting Bible. Information can be found in the first appendix of this book.

PROFITABLE PODCASTING

http://www.profitablepodcasting.com

Case Study by Paul Colligan

What?

Tired of the overload of content about Podcast monetization with no facts (or life experience) behind it; the Profitable Podcasting Podcast was launched.

The premise is simple: deep "no holds barred" interviews with Podcasters who are generating a revenue stream from their Podcast. Shows come out when a profitable Podcaster has been identified and has agreed to a probing interview.

At time of publication, 2 episodes have been released. Response is enthusiastic.

So What?

The demographic of Podcasters hoping to see a revenue stream from their Podcast is sought after by many Podcast technology and training companies. Prior to launch, advertising inquiries were made and numbers considerably better than traditional CPM rates were discussed.

Now What?

Currently, the business plan for this Podcast does not include traditional 3rd party ad insertions. After 10 episodes are released, in-Podcast ad revenues are expected from commission sales to the Podcast audience.

The unique nature of the show prevents it from coming out on a regular basis, but other regular communication with the audience is being developed. Items under development include an email newsletter and an active push to audience participation at the Web site. A text RSS feed is also being examined. Commissioned (affiliate) sales revenue is expected from every communication channel.

Also under consideration for this Podcast is a (Premium) paid version.

To learn "What Happened" to this Podcast, please visit the Private Member Site for The Business Podcasting Bible. Information can be found in the first appendix of this book.

SUCCESS UNWRAPPED WITH HEATHER VALE

Website: http://SuccessUnwrappedRadio.com

What?

The show is an online talk show that "unwraps" and reveals the secrets of success through interviews with the world's top experts.

The Podcast is monetized in several different ways:

- Adsense ads

- Affiliate sales

- Archive sales

- Derivative Products

- Donations

- Sponsorship ads

So What?

The Podcast was created in order to attract big-name guests with an immediate promotional outlet, mainly for the creation of derivative products (e-packages with e-book and audios, offline books) but other ideas have grown out of that. Certain guests have products that have proven popular through affiliate sales.

Now What?

I have just started a new Podcasting model I call "Selective Podcasting". My whole talk show is generally 45-60 minutes long, but the Podcast version is just the first 1/3 which works out to 15-20 minutes. Some people are happy with that, which is longer than some Podcasts, but still delivers great content they can use to improve their lives for free.

If they want to "unwrap" the entire interview, they are directed to a sign-up sales page for my membership site, which allows them to choose what level of success they want to "unwrap". For as low as $5 a month they can hear the entire show, plus get extended access to past shows, download-able success articles written by the guests, special deals and more. At the $20 a month level they get full access to the archives of all shows ever pro-duced, and the e-package versions of Success Unwrapped and Today's Success Minute (another Podcast of mine) for free.

> *To learn "What Happened" to this Podcast, please visit the Private Member Site for The Business Podcasting Bible. Information can be found in the first appendix of this book.*

TIMELESS CANDLES PODCAST

http://www.timelesscandles.com/podcast/

What?

The yet to be launched, TimelessCandles.com web store launched, of all things, a Candles Podcast (before the store event went live).

TimelessCandles.com, a new online store selling candles and candle related accessories wanted a new way to connect with their customers. They are banking their long term success on creating more personal ways to connect with their target audience - women who enjoy candles.

So What?

In support of the launch of TimelessCandles.com, an informational and mood setting Podcast specialized for this specific audience was designed. They are trying to create a higher level of marketing intimacy you can only get through a multi-sensory experience.

The Podcast is providing them with an excellent opportunity to really connect with their audience and create that marketing intimacy prior to the launch of their web store. Hopefully, through the Podcast, Timeless Candles becomes a trusted friend and resource - before they became a supplier of great candles and candle accessories.

In addition to the multi-modality connection with their audience, the search engine optimization and relevance factors that happen when utilizing multiple communication methods are a strong potential benefit as well.

Now What?

To help introduce people to who "TimelessCandles.com" is, the Timeless Candles Podcast was launched prior to the web store opening.

Initial episode went out May 2, 2006 with 9 episodes scheduled before the www.TimelessCandles.com goes live on June 30, 2006.

They targeted a relatively aggressive goal for a new Podcast of having 1000 downloads before launch and 25 inbound links (because of their Podcasting efforts) to their website before June 30, 2006.

To learn "What Happened" to this Podcast, please visit the Private Member Site for The Business Podcasting Bible. Information can be found in the first appendix of this book.

WIREDPARISH.COM

Case Study by Jay Kelly

What?

wiredparish.com saw a complete lack of 'talk radio' type content for the 20something christian demographic. we know there is a hunger by this demographic for spiritual content because of significant book purchases and conference attendance, but talk radio content is simply not available let alone electronically accessible. given that 20somethings live in a wired world, it was an absolutely stunning realization that no such content was available—electronically or otherwise. so we assembled a group of 25+ writers and speakers from across the country to provide weekly 15 minute 'casts. most of our hosts are published authors, with many having best-selling titles. all are regular speakers on faith matters across the country. the end result is Podcast network that features profound voices and challenging ideas designed to create dialogue that leads to revolution.

So What?

wiredparish.com created a premium subscription site where subscribers could access all the content for a monthly fee. given that all our hosts have an existing constituency through their writing and speaking schedule, we have built-in marketing targeted directly to people who already buy content from the individual hosts. in addition, we are marketing wiredparish.com through a free Podcast where different hosts are highlighted weekly; as well as through other channels such as blog alliances and group subscriptions through ministry organizations. we generate revenue primarily through paid subscribers.

Now What?

wiredparish.com is in a pre-launch phase until fall 2006, and we are pleased with our pre-launch subscription numbers. the last 9 months have been invested in building our host line up and ironing out the logistics of recording content from hosts from across the country. with those components running smoothly, we are now shifting into an aggressive marketing and pr campaign to grow the wiredparish.com subscriber base.

To learn "What Happened" to this Podcast, please visit the Private Member Site for The Business Podcasting Bible. Information can be found in the first appendix of this book.

WORK AT HOME TALK RADIO

What?

Work at Home Moms Talk Radio http://www.wahmtalkradio.com launched as an Internet Radio Show in November 2003. With no broadcasting experience and a new found love for internet audio, Kelly McCausey set out to provide regular weekly content to the Work at Home Mom Community. With the encouragement and sponsorship of Internet Based Moms owner Alice Seba, the show took off. By interviewing home business and internet marketing experts alongside every day work at home Moms just trying to make a buck to buy groceries, the show is free from hype and dedicated to providing high quality information.

"I started out with a tape recorder and a cheap radio shack part, you can just imagine how awful my sound was then. I've learned a lot by experience and now have a nice array of studio equipment which I really enjoy using. The best thing I ever invested in is my Adobe Audition software, I honestly don't know how I survived without it all this time."

So What?

WAHM Talk Radio enjoys a growing listenership, reaching about 750 moms a week between those who listen on the website and via the Podcast feed. Kelly says "I launched this show at a time when the term 'internet radio' was new to 95% of the people I met online or offline. We have grown steadily and my listenership has been very responsive along the way. I look forward to continued growth as more households get high speed access to the web and more Moms realize that a show like this exists for them. "

Sponsorship from home based business owners cover expenses and pay for an advertising manager but ad income is not a major source of income for the Host. Rather than attempt to over-monetize the show itself, McCausey has been able to build a business around the show that enabled her to quit a full time job this past winter by creating information products and offering coaching services.

Now What?

The niche success of Work at Home Moms Talk Radio inspired McCausey to think bigger and in 2005 she created the Mom's Radio Network http://www.momsradionetwork.com , a casual network of internet radio shows and Podcasts of interest to Moms. She is involved in mentoring other would be mom show hosts, encouraging them as they launch their own shows and then fostering co-promotion between them.

It is a great example of how helping others to succeed ultimately helps you. As more shows launch and reach new groups of Moms, they all benefit from the rising 'water level' of Podcast awareness.

To learn "What Happened" to this Podcast, please visit the Private Member Site for The Business Podcasting Bible. Information can be found in the first appendix of this book.

YOU CAN SELL ONLINE

http://www.youcansellonline.com

Case Study by Paul Colligan

What?

The You Can Sell Online Podcast interviews technology or training providers that enable "anyone" to do e-commerce online. Emphasis on ease of use and immediate implementation are the defining characteristics of the show. Topics include shopping cart systems, merchant account implementation, PayPal use, affiliate marketing, paid membership sites, product (and content) resell opportunities, Google Adsense and more.

So What?

E-commerce is a multi-billion-dollar industry and often offers residual commission payments in affiliate relationships. Sales of shopping cart, merchant account, hosting service or other e-commerce related technologies can result in listeners with a considerable lifetime value.

"Hearing the voice" of the key players in the industry leverages the intimate nature of Podcasting and leads to a better sales conversion than a traditional Web sale could ever provide.

YouCanSellOnline.com offers a unique email newsletter model: Every interviewee in the Podcast is required to offer something of value, for free, to all subscribers to the email newsletter. As each new interview is posted, the value of being a newsletter subscriber increase and conversion rates, to this point, reflect this trend.

The email newsletter is expected to generate significant secondary revenue for e-commerce related opportunities that don't lend themselves to the interview model on the Podcast.

Now What?

Once the Podcast has achieved critical mass, technology providers interviewed on the show will be required to promote the show to their own audiences. This should have the effect of further validating the technology to the interviewer's client base - as well as increasing the You Can Sell Online Podcast audience with every interview.

To learn "What Happened" to this Podcast, please visit the Private Member Site for The Business Podcasting Bible. Information can be found in the first appendix of this book.

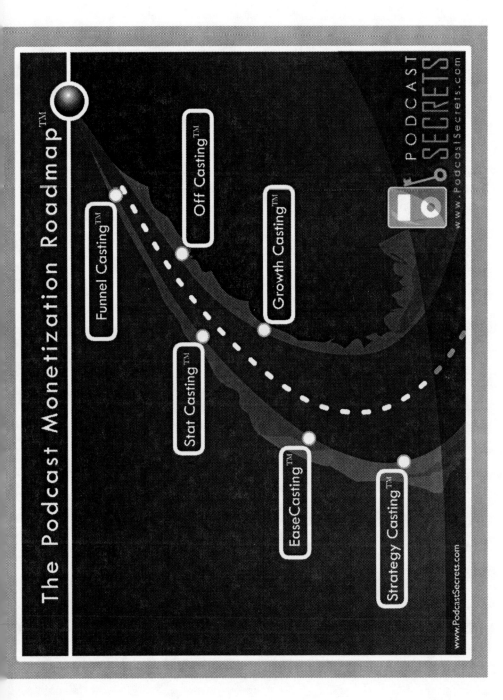

The Podcast Monetization Roadmap™

Funnel Casting™

Off Casting™

Growth Casting™

Start Casting™

EaseCasting™

Strategy Casting™

PODCAST SECRETS
www.PodcastSecrets.com

www.PodcastSecrets.com

APPENDIX 10

THE BUSINESS **PODCASTING BIBLE**

1,000 Gigs of Podcasting Bandwidth For Less Than $10 A Month?

W e recommend that anyone publishing a Podcast follow what we call he "Second Server Delivery Method" where the media files associated with a Podcast are stored on a Web server separate from your corporate site.

Why the double-server approach? Once your Podcast has reached a certain level of success, you could have an onslaught of listeners hoping to download your show in the first hour after release. Without going into detail (this is a business book, not a tech book), a server can handle it, but would slow down considerably – a fine affect for your media server, but not your corporate website.

Don't worry, this is extremely affordable. The nature of hosting and bandwidth required for Podcast delivery is considerably less intensive than what is required for traditional Web applications. There is simply no need to pay for premium services that you don't require.

Let's look at the numbers:

The most recent episode of Marketing Online Live (#37) was 36.5 minutes in length and 23.5 MB in size (the recording quality that we use in the show results in file considerably larger than traditional Podcasts). For the sake of explanation, let's call this a "typical" Podcast.

10,000 listeners consuming the show 4 times a month would require 940,000 MB, or 940 GB of transfer. Let's call this a "typical" schedule.

We currently host our Podcasts on a "Deluxe Hosting Plan" at http://www.1PlaceForEverything.com. We've never had a problem with them and don't foresee any in the future (*full disclosure: 1PlaceforEverything.com is a hosting reseller company owned in part by your authors*). The cost is currently $8.95 a month. Included in the price is 1,000 GB of transfer (more than enough) and 100 GB of hard drive space (enough to hold more than 9 years of shows at our current rate).

The hosting industry is extremely commoditized and there is little reason why you should pay more than $10 for the hosting needs of a "typical" Podcast. Large video or extremely popular audio Podcasts might require additional space – but once you have reached that level of production, you can afford to increase your hosting expenses accordingly.

The downside of the commoditized nature of the hosting industry is that a company can quickly lose quality focus. We will keep an updated list of inexpensive, but reliable hosting options at the private member site and recommend input from our readers on experiences they have had with the providers we discuss.

Printed in the United States
60866LVS00003B/74